WHEN IS A "GANGSTER GOVERNMENT"?
A "GANGSTER GOVERNMENT?"

WHEN IS A "GANGSTER GOVERNMENT" A "GANGSTER GOVERNMENT?"

FREDERICK MONDERSON

SUMON PUBLISHERS

FREDERICK MONDERSON

ISBN - 978-1-61023-063-6
LCCN – 201-992-1072

When is a "Gangster Government" a "Gangster Government?" Photo. At the "Tribute to Professor George Simmonds," Dr. Fred Monderson sat at the feet of his heroes, Professor George Simmonds, Dr. Yosef Ben-Jochannan, Brother X, Michael Carter, Elombe Brathe, Dr. Lewis, Sister Camille Yarbrough, etc.

ABOUT THE AUTHOR

Dr. Frederick Monderson is a retired College Professor and public-school teacher who taught African History in the City University of New York and American History and Government in the New York public schools. He has written more than 1000 articles in the "New York Black Press," *Daily Challenge*, *Afro Times* and *New American* newspapers. In this venture, Monderson lends his expertise as a historian, Egyptologist, journalist and author of several books including *Ladies in the*

WHEN IS A "GANGSTER GOVERNMENT"?
A "GANGSTER GOVERNMENT?"

House; *Michael Jackson: The Last Dance*; *50 on Point*; *Barack Obama: Ready, Fit to Lead*; *Barack Obama: Master of Washington D.C.*; *Obama: Master and Commander and Obama: The Journey Completed*; *Sonny Carson: The Final Triumph (5 Volumes)*; *Black Nationalism: Alive and Well*; *Black Nationalism: Still Alive and Well*; *Guyana: Land of Beauty and Many Waters*; and on **Ancient Egypt**, *Seven Letters to Mike Tyson on Egyptian Temples*; *10 Poems Praising Great Blacks for Mike Tyson*; *Research Essays on Ancient Egypt*; *Temple of Karnak: The Majestic Architecture of Ancient Kemet*; *Where are the Kamite Kings?*; *Abydos and Osiris*; *Temple of Luxor*; *Medinet Habu: Mortuary Temple of Rameses III*; *The Quintessential Book on Ancient Egypt: "Holy Land"* (A Tour Guide Novel on Egypt); *Hatshepsut's Temple at Deir el Bahari*; *Intrigue Through Time*; *An Egyptian Resurrection*, (A Novel on Ancient Egypt); *The Majesty of Egyptian Gods and Temples* (A book of Egyptian Poems); *Egypt Essays on Ancient Kemet*; *The Ramesseum: Mortuary Temple of Rameses II*; *The Colonnade: Then and Now*; *Reflections on Ancient Kemet*; *The Hypostyle Hall*; *Grassroots View of Ancient Egypt*; *Glory of the Ancestors: 19 Letters to O.J. Simpson on Ancient African History*; *Celebrating Dr. Ben-Jochannan*; *Black History Extravaganza: Honoring Dr. Ben Jochannan*; *Let's Liberate the Temple*; *More Woman, More Power*; *Reflections on Ancient Egypt - Book One*; *Reflections on Ancient Egypt - Book Two*; *Black History Everyday - Part One*; *Black History Everyday - Part Two*; and more. A student of the

FREDERICK MONDERSON

esteemed Dr. Yosef ben-Jochannan, Dr. Monderson conducts tours to Egypt. Tour Contact Orleane Brooks-Williams, Nostrand Travel, 730 Nostrand Avenue, Brooklyn, New York 11216. Phone 718-756-5300.

fredsegypt.com@fredsegypt.com
sumonpublishers.com@sumonpublishers.com

During the Obama Presidency Republicans consistently peddled "The country is divided." Then Donald Trump emerged as Republican standard bearer ultimately winning the Presidency. Spouting grandiose promises such as intent to "Drain the Swamp," hire "The Best People," while railing against NAFTA, Climate and PPT agreements, he fell into the egotistical mantra, "Only I can do it!" Next, he unleashed an even more telling mantra, "I'm the Chosen One!" However, Mr. Trump equally revamped a second lane consistent with the "Birther" falsity thereby invoking Mr. Obama's name unceasingly! In this, he unleashed a systematic reversal and overturning of practically every accomplishment and agreement the former President painstakingly achieved, further dividing the country,

However, an additional mantra, "I'm the Chosen One," really pushed the envelope, for in moving the Israeli Embassy to Jerusalem and with Mitch McConnell's assistance in appointing conservative judges, he has gotten the likes of Rick Perry and especially Rudy Giuliani to proclaim or parrot Trump's "I'm the Chosen One" audacity and

WHEN IS A "GANGSTER GOVERNMENT"? A "GANGSTER GOVERNMENT?"

syndrome. Notice, both he and they looked to the heavens; in actuality these folks looked to avoid a possible thunderbolt from the sky for falsely intimating divine acknowledgement that Donald Trump is indeed the chosen one!

The term "Trump fatigue" got more legs when recently the magazine **Christianity Today** founded by evangelist Billy Graham, insisted "Trump be removed from office for being morally lost" through dishonesty and particularly due to the findings of the Impeachment investigation; not to mention his nearly 15,000 lies and misstatements. In this, the New York *Daily News* of December 21, 2019, p. 7 explained: "He has hired and fired a number of people who are now convicted criminals. He himself has admitted to immoral actions in business and his relationship with women, about which he remains proud." Mark Galli, author of the article wrote of Donald Trump: "His Twitter feed alone – with its habitual string of lies, and slanders – is a near perfect example of a human being who is morally lost and confused." Billy Graham's son, Franklin, rather than admit to the glaringly evident observations, even try to soothe or heal, widened the divide by displaying his own disappointing ineptitude, stating: "Yes, my father Billy Graham founded **Christianity Today**, but no, he would not agree with their opinion piece. In fact, he would be very disappointed. For **Christianity Today** to side with the Democratic Party in a totally partisan attack on the President of the United States is

FREDERICK MONDERSON

unfathomable." How sad! Mr. Graham sees Democrats rather than see or smell filth! As Peter Wehmer so eloquently asks pointedly, do people of Franklin Graham's hue, "owe loyalty to the creator of the Ten Commandments or to Donald Trump." In fact, such eloquence can serve as an indictment of Mr. Graham himself in that, "The church is to be the conscience of the state not to cast a blind eye. It must speak truth to power. It must see things through the prism of love, peace, patience, self-control."

Next to creating enormous damage, enormous wreckage to American institutions and to the Presidency, Mr. Trump's "ethics is in conflict with Christian beliefs." There should be "no unholy alliance between church and Mr. Trump." Evangelicals embracing a dangerous person demonstrating a lack of moral compass and at odds with his own identity, as the present author opines is "Selling their souls to the Devil."

Further, the Editor continued, "If we don't reverse course now, will anyone take anything we say about justice and righteousness with any seriousness for decades to come?" Even more, "Can we say with a straight face that abortion is a great evil that cannot be tolerated and, with the same straight face, say that the bent and broken character of our nation's leader doesn't matter in the end?" Remindful, the **General Accounting Office** (GAO) just stated essentially, "President Trump broke the law in withholding aid to Ukraine" which is at core of the Ukraine scandal and **Impeachment** now afoot.

WHEN IS A "GANGSTER GOVERNMENT"? A "GANGSTER GOVERNMENT?"

James Clyburn, (D) South Carolina, also became an item contemporary with **Christianity Today's** call for Evangelicals; currently polled at 72% approval rate; to yet reject Donald Trump because of his moral bankruptcy and confused state of mind. However, Mr. Clyburn's "right wing roast" had to do with Speaker Pelosi's ultimatum to Senate Leader Mitch McConnell stating essentially, "Get your House in order otherwise we're not sending you the Impeachment Articles." There was another issue trending in which 12 Jewish House of Representative members called for the firing of a top White House adviser, Stephen Miller, charging he is a racist and white supremacist and should not be at the center of the nation's leadership and decision making. Thus, Mr. Clyburn, as the House Democratic Whip, who was asked earlier about Ms. Pelosi's statement, responded, "Mitch McConnell wants to," again **IN REVERSE**, (Give him, Trump, a fair trial and then hang him as what was done to Mr. Clyburn's ancestors in slavery and freedom; for example the murder of some 4040 African-Americans the southern legal eagle chronicled in the Lynching states from 1870-1950) "give him [The President] a fair trial then hang him" [in reverse] means the opposite. Thus, use of the term **in reverse**, what Clyburn referred to is an unfair trial, a rigged trial, which many right wingers and the "Little Demagogue," Rudy Giuliani, for propaganda purposes twisted in claim, "Mr. Clyburn wants to hang Donald Trump." What Clyburn actually meant and what McConnell

FREDERICK MONDERSON

and Graham glaringly boasted, **give him a speedy trial and then let him go!** These issues simultaneously fell onto Mr. Clyburn's plate and he responded in the following manner:

1. "These people in the White House and their supporters, including Fox News, are misrepresenting the facts. They are misrepresenting the Congresswoman's views."

2. Calling such miscreants "bullies" for misinterpreting his intent, and referring to "What I have been through" as a citizen of South Carolina, notorious for being the largest slave state, he dismissed threats saying, "I will not be intimidated by anyone in the White House or in the blogger sphere."

Conversely, Senator Roy Blunt held, "A partisan vote in the House results in a partisan vote in the Senate." Senator Dick Durban (D), on the other hand, held "My oath insists on impartial justice, so help me god! Statements of partiality by Mitch McConnell and Lindsey Graham are not what the Constitution implied." He insists, the Senate should "consider not conceal the evidence and render a fair not fake trial." "Taking the case to Court would never finish in a timely manner and so the House had to move forward. The issue of any such vote is a question of conscience. Each member should make their decision based on facts and the Constitution."

"Pelosi is doing everything she can to ensure the process is fair." Senator Cory Booker

**WHEN IS A "GANGSTER GOVERNMENT"?
A "GANGSTER GOVERNMENT?"**

TABLE OF CONTENTS

1. **WHERE THE HECK IS**   12
   MICHELE BACHMANN?
2. **"MYTH OF THE REPUBLICAN**   19
   CAVE"
3. **AN OPEN LETTER TO MAUREEN**
   CALLAHAN – New York Post   27
4. **"BALLS ON THAT WOMAN!"**   38
5. **"A WOMAN OF POWER NOT**   48
   STRAW!
6. **A CONSEQUENTIAL**   57
   ELECTION
7. **ARROGANCE OF THE**   70
   STRONGMAN
8. **BULLY IN THE WHITE HOUSE**   78
9. **KILLING DR. KING, AGAIN**   87
10. **NO TO THAT "NO-BEL" PRIZE!**   92
11. **ABOUT THAT 96 PERCENT**   103
12. **MCCAIN, OBAMA AND TRUMP**   112
13. **ALL THE PRESIDENT'S**   118
    DOMINOES
14. **"WHO LOST AMERICA?"**   124
    Republicans?
15. **THE CHOICE**   135
16. **THE GREAT CAPITULATION**   149
17. **AMERICAN LEADERS**   158

ABROAD
18. SPEAKING FOR GOD!   162
19. NOT 1979   170
20. HERE AS "EYE CANDY"   176
21. OBAMA CARES   180
22. THREE AMIGOS AND HEALTH CARE   184
23. MITCH MCCONNEL "PLOTTER"   186
24. "ONLY I CAN" VERSUS "YES, WE CAN!"   191
25. SELLING ONE'S SOUL   197
26. HOW THE SNAKE LOST ITS TAIL   203
27. COUP VERSUS CONSPIRACY   213
28. STAND STILL ...   222
29. DINKINS AND OBAMA AND RUDY AND DONALD   235
30. OWNING TRUMP   242
31. SOUTH CAROLINA   246
32. STAR SPANGLED BANNER AND BLACK NATIONAL ANTHEM   252
33. LOW IQ   258
34. TRUMP LEAVING OFFICE   267
35. AMERICA AS LAUGHING STOCK   272
36. ANOTHER SNAKE STORY   276

**WHEN IS A "GANGSTER GOVERNMENT"?
A "GANGSTER GOVERNMENT?"**

37.	DEMONIZING WOMEN	279
38.	FLAILING THE MESSENGER	280
39.	"I WANT A TRIAL!"	284
40.	JETTISONING TRUTH TELLERS	287
41.	MINIONS FOR TRUMP'S TYRANNY	291
42.	RIP VAN WINKLE IN RED OUTFIT	294
43.	THE SACRED OATH I TOOK	302
44.	WISHY-WASHY OR ZIG-ZAG SENATOR LINDSEY GRAHAM	307
45.	DECEMBER 7, 2019 – DORIAN MILLER DAY!	310
46.	EMPEROR, MONARCH AND KING	314
47.	SONNY AND RUDY	321
48.	THE CRUX OF THE PROBLEM	329
49.	THE MAN WHO WOULD BE PRESIDENT	331
50.	CONCLUSIONS – Obama and Trump – "What Goes Around Comes Around!"	334

"John Bolton has something to say that will be harmful to Donald Trump." **Kirstin Powers**

FREDERICK MONDERSON

When is a "Gangster Government" a "Gangster Government" Photo? Face on a vessel at the back entrance to the Supreme Court.

"Call a Gangster Government, a Gangster Government!"

"We have done what we set out to do! We have defended the Constitution. We have been fair." **Nancy Pelosi**.

1. WHERE THE HECK IS MICHELE BACHMANN?
BY
DR. FRED MONDERSON

During the 2012 Republican Presidential Primary, Representative Michele Bachmann was famous for; as former Pennsylvania Senator Rick Santorum remarked, after he lost his bid for the Presidency,

WHEN IS A "GANGSTER GOVERNMENT"?
A "GANGSTER GOVERNMENT?"

"Lots of things get said in a campaign;" herself making two particularly pointed false statements. The first is "God told me to run!" Well, if he did, he would have certainly given her practically everything and most important, "Keys to 1600 Pennsylvania Avenue." Most significantly, in 2012 Representative Bachmann accused President Barack Obama of running a "gangster government" in Washington, DC. In this city, the nation's capital, home to nearly two dozen security and intelligence agencies including the FBI, such a claim is preposterous! No less significant, Mr. Obama was re-elected without fanfare in 2012, completed his term of four years, there was no finding of wrongdoing in his administration, especially by the Department of Justice and he is today considered one of the great American presidents of the modern era with some of the highest ratings ever.

Ms. Bachmann, on the other hand, having lost her House seat, has not only dropped out of the political limelight but more important, in doing so, has denied the American public that perspicacious ability to recognize "a gangster government" and given the current administration is mired in behavior that certainly be classed as "gangster" why is Ms. Bachmann silent. Thus, one has to wonder whether those who make pronouncements about "gangster government" do so for their own good or for the benefit of the community or nation at large to identify such behavior; or, as they say, "for an audience of one." Take for instance this new guy, once a Democrat changed parties and in public, pledged

FREDERICK MONDERSON

"undying loyalty" to Donald Trump. Mr. Trump reciprocated in kind. Naturally, thinkers may wonder when did this "light Democrat" get converted to "undying loyalty!" Talk about hypocrisy! Yet, everyone knows, Mr. Trump is famous for either "throwing people under the bus" or responding to a question as to the person, he then says "I hardly know the man!" So, this fellow should be careful.

While many things get said in a campaign, Donald John Trump won his campaign, gone on to become President, but still continues to say many things in "litigating 2016," most of which seems outrageous, even vindictive. One of the things that can be said for Mr. Trump is that he refuses to "move on" and harbors ill-intent.

Today, many people believe the "Birther" *Mea Culpa* Mr. Trump made was a sham or farce, given the way he continues to invoke former President Obama's name with such frequency and the unrelenting and insidious manner in which he tries to demean the man and pursues every legislative or negotiated achievement the former President accomplished. Whether it is race, or whatever, is another matter. Nevertheless, while Mr. Obama may be resting comfortably somewhere, perhaps in a beach hammock drinking "virgin" Pina Coladas or whatever, Donald Trump is busy bailing his leaky boat taking on water at an alarming rate, on a daily basis; he is indeed a troubled man. Perhaps Ms. Bachmann herself is in a place the *News* does not get to; though, like a spiraling uncontrollable object

WHEN IS A "GANGSTER GOVERNMENT"? A "GANGSTER GOVERNMENT?"

reeling in cosmic deep space, she has remained silent in face of Donald Trump's rampant behavior that can certainly be classed as "Gangsterism."

Donald Trump likes to flaunt his "Only I can" mantra. In some respects, he is right. In the history of the 44 Presidents who preceded him, Mr. Trump's administration and his associated campaign personnel who have racked up more dismissals, resignation, indictments, convictions and time in jail than the aforementioned chief executive administrations combined, this certainly fits the bill. Now, add this to the highly unusual batting average of the nearly 15,000 lies or false statements Mr. Trump has committed so far that has been fact-checked, and surprisingly no Republican, not even Ms. Bachmann has had the "balls" to point out "Donald Trump leads a gangster government" in Washington, DC, we can recognize these people as members of the "Liar's Club."

Some say Republicans in Congress are afraid of Mr. Trump's animosity in the ability to weaponize his base to primary his opponents and as such have such voters defeat those who do not toe his line! Thus, these individuals can be equated with "mice in men's clothing" as potentially abrogating their sacred oath to defend the Constitution to the spirit and letter of the law. Such behavior is itself a contradiction to the "Sacred oath they took." More important, ignoring much of Donald Trump's behavior means these individuals have betrayed the moral and ethical tradition regarded as an honor to serve the nation as their constituency empowered them to do. It becomes a difficult task for such lawmakers to go abroad and try to convince others on the efficacy of American Democracy since this form of political institution is under such stress at home, thanks to their abrogation of their inherent responsibility. Can anyone envision an "American fact-finding delegation" going abroad to investigate an issue and the people they hope to critique commenting on events at home! One particular example of note refers to the episode in which Mr. Trump dared to declare "The Constitution is wrong!" The balls on this fellow to think he has "watermelons for nuts" that may actually be balloons.

When is a "Gangster Government" a "Gangster Government" Photo? Front entrance to the Supreme Court that reads overhead – "**Equal Justice Under Law**."

In this and on so many other instances of Constitution trampling, the Republicans who seem as "mice as

WHEN IS A "GANGSTER GOVERNMENT"? A "GANGSTER GOVERNMENT?"

men and women" constantly remain silent. Michele Bachmann, particularly, while no longer in government, her silence in contradiction to her earlier blatant but false pronouncement, signals not simply her own falsity but equally blasphemy having used God's name in vain to pursue a political agenda. Thus, such hypocritical thoughts and deeds using the "God angle" links her with Tommy Faye's husband, Pat Robinson, even Donald Trump and his associate Rudy Giuliani, all who "talk to god" or know what god thinks as they frequently "look to the heavens" to insinuate they are "right with divine prescriptions!" These hypocrites need be careful, not to invoke God's anger for using his name and association in vain. Perhaps, the next time they look to the heavens, they indeed may be stricken by divine vengeance.

When is a "Gangster Government" a "Gangster Government" Photo? Another face on a vessel at the back entrance to the Supreme Court.

FREDERICK MONDERSON

When is a "Gangster Government" a "Gangster Government" Photo? Dr. Martin Luther King in regal splendor as "**A Stone of Hope!**"

"Those who voted for Impeachment, honored their sacred oath." The question then becomes, in reference to Mitch McConnel's statement, "Is it ok for the foreman of the Jury to be in cahoots with the defendant?" **Nancy Pelosi**

"Until we get the witnesses; until we get the documents, those aiding and abetting a cover-up are undermining the process. I'm calling on President Trump to release the documents; release the witnesses. Let them testify. What are you afraid of?" **Senator Chuck Schumer**

**WHEN IS A "GANGSTER GOVERNMENT"?
A "GANGSTER GOVERNMENT?"**

"Every person who does not answer the subpoena is guilty of Contempt of Congress." **Joe Biden**

2. "MYTH OF THE REPUBLICAN CAVE" BY DR. FRED MONDERSON

Plato's "Myth of the Cave" is very applicable to the state of today's Republican Party, who, according to former Speaker John Boehner, "Is off somewhere taking a nap," simply because the "Republican Party is now Donald Trump's Party," and one wonders if this links them in the "Shithole" he so relishes in! That is, with the exception of Representative Amash, who, chose not to retire but left the Republican Party and became an **Independent** Member of Congress, and continues to wage the fight in the **House of Representatives** against the "plague" now engulfing the White House; or, as the New York *Daily News* political cartoon eloquently pointed to: "A cancer has affected the Presidency." This malady essentially is the reason Amash left the Republican Party. Mr. Amash must have been familiar with Edmund Burke's statement in his "Reflections on the Revolution in France" in which he affirmed, "The only thing necessary for evil to triumph is for good men to say or do nothing." Mr. Amash has certainly affirmed his "good man" status by taking a stand against the dark stain that has consumed Washington, the White House as representative of the Executive Branch and the American body-politic landscape with spill-over into the social realm. This action has cost Amash membership in the Republican Party but cleared his conscience, given President Trump's behavior. This whole malady also has implications for practicing "Men of the Cloth," and their congregations.

According to Plato's **Myth**, four prisoners with hands bound behind their backs, were focused on a wall before them. On the wall, images projected showed a variety of movements the prisoners, unable to see behind their backs, attributed to manipulation by the gods. Fortunately, one of the men happened to turn around and glanced at a light at their rear that projected their own images on the wall. This realization revolutionized this individual prisoner's thinking and he removed himself leaving his colleagues in their previous condition. Perhaps in a somewhat analogous situation, Mr. Amash freed himself from the morass and becoming an Independent, can reaffirm the need for a remedy to save this nation.

Bishop T.D. Jakes told the story of a giraffe "feeding at tree-top level" on a clear and sunny day. Along came a tortoise who hailed the ruminant. "Hey, how's it going up there?" he asked. "Great" was the giraffe's response. "Its wonderful up here. The tree shrubs are delicious, the sky is blue and the air is healthfully wonderful. How's it with you?" he responded. "Its terrible down here. All I see is

WHEN IS A "GANGSTER GOVERNMENT"?
A "GANGSTER GOVERNMENT?"

garbage and the air is terribly foul." Both individuals told the truth about their situation, as Dr. Jakes indicated! The giraffe then responded, "You need to come up a notch and enjoy these benefits as well as the awesome view." Unintentionally this was Mr. Amash's invitation to his Republican colleagues to rid themselves of the terrible Trump ball and chain albatross they lug around. These two examples sort of characterizes the act and stance of Rep. Amash who, realized the moral, ethical, political perhaps even legal dilemma of being in association with Donald's Trump's threateningly tyrannical leadership; established himself as a moralist, a patriotic American who believes "no one is above the law;" then particularly applying such to the President and those beneath his boots who remain like chewing gum, even fearful and silent in face of the Trump steam-roller morass.

For long, politicians have been labeled liars and Donald Trump, clocked at approximately 15,000 lies and misstatements so far, "takes the cake." Equally, it's been said, politicians are only concerned with getting elected and then being re-elected. Because Mr. Trump's control of the Republican Party is so all encompassing and punitively uncompromising, despite the avalanche of uncharacteristic American presidential behaviors, Republican lawmakers remain silent as their leader trashes the Constitution and threatens anyone who dares to criticize or prick the numerous "pimples" oozing "streams of pus" on his face full of ill-behavior. Admittedly, Republicans are fearful any such criticism of Mr. Trump will

FREDERICK MONDERSON

generate a primary challenge and threaten their elected seat, and thus reelection to government. These people therefore need to be re-elected, not to serve the Constitution but Donald Trump's insidious interests.

Many view this as not upholding their oath to defend the Constitution, but affirm, unintentionally or not, unchallenged objection to Donald trump. Fortunately, however, the upcoming 2020 national election will be the great equalizer that will empower the American people to accept or reject Donald Trump's presidency and particular Republican members of Congress who, as Abraham Lincoln once affirmed, "Silence in the form of wrongdoing assumes culpability in that wrongdoing."

Today, Marathon Sunday in New York, November 3, 2019, when in both the Men and Women's Marathon, Kenya came in first and second in both races, and appearing on CNN's **State of the Union**, two individuals who represent the two sides of the Donald Trump's coin, presidential Adviser Kellyanne Conway and Representative James Clyburn (D. SC.), the third highest ranking Democrat in the House of Representatives that were interviewed by Dana Bash sitting in for Jake Tapper, in which their answers were right and wrong.

It's 'been known, Kellyanne, Kaylee, Cuccinelli' and several others have ignored facts regarding Mr. Trump, spewing "alternative fact" responses ignoring the reality people listen to the dribble coming from

WHEN IS A "GANGSTER GOVERNMENT"? A "GANGSTER GOVERNMENT?"

their lips. Kellyanne coined the phrase "alternative facts." One has to wonder, do these people listen to themselves in playback? Essentially, four responses Kellyanne gave is a reminder of the tortuous path she has blazed with "alternative facts" and in defense of her boss.

1. "We have no access to transcripts to the Impeachment process."

2. Not a single Republican voted for the Impeachment Resolution.

3. What is your take of Donald Trump calling out Republicans who criticized him in this latest round of fiascos?

4. Adam Schiff lied.

Most people in Congress are lawyers or heavily knowledgeable of the workings of the branch of government they are a part of. To believe Committee Leaders especially would undertake as delicate and important a process as **Impeachment** without sticking to the letter of the law is the sign of poor judgment. Donald Trump does not care about facts or the truth but this is not how the average American functions. The process as followed by today's Democrats is the same as operated in Richard Nixon's case and in Bill Clinton's impeachment. Most important, Republicans essentially have members of their party on all Committees.

FREDERICK MONDERSON

Representatives Jim Jordan and Doug Collins were very vocal in Trump's defense. Therefore, such a claim is false and meaningless.

2. That "Not a single Republican voted for the Impeachment Resolution" and this is actually a reflection of the harsh reality of the Trump boot on the necks of any Republican who would criticize him. This is totalitarianism and certainly not the American way. When Barack Obama was attacked, he simply shrugged it off claiming "Politics is a contact sport." Trump, on the other hand, would "shoot someone on Fifth Avenue." The interesting thing about the vote is despite the avalanche of evidence, not that Republicans did not want to vote for it, they could not because of Trump's vice grip on their re-election chances. Fact is, they were looking at the alternative facts and so could not see or vote on the real facts.

3. That Donald Trump determined, any Republican who challenged him or pointed out wrongdoing in his behavior is considered "Scum" or "rat;" yet, hugely contradictory, Ms. Conway said something to the effect, "I respect people's rights." Her boss certainly does not respect all people's rights! The Justice Department determined Hillary Clinton broke no laws, yet Donald Trump pounds her at his rallies to the "Gullible Base!"

4. Adam Schiff lied! The same thing was said about Barack Obama that he lied about the Affordable Care Act. Well, the "Trump moralists can't count" and are blind to 15,000 lies by their man!

WHEN IS A "GANGSTER GOVERNMENT"?
A "GANGSTER GOVERNMENT?"

Representative James Clyburn, following up on Speaker Nancy Pelosi's comment that "Donald Trump is not worth it," states in regard to the need for an impeachment investigation, "certainly," giving there is rising support for the legal action. Stating that Republican support is not exclusively a necessity, and that Independents are split, but Democrats are overwhelmingly in support of the measure, she proceeded upon credible circumstances. Given that Impeachment is a political act, there needs to be some calculation of the issue. In as much as, there is "lots of smoke in Donald Trump's behavior," Democrats "must seek the source of the fire in order to extinguish that fire." The President's behavior has been inappropriate, involving bribery and obstruction where such behavior reflects "High Crimes and Misbehaviors."

As Democrats released the transcripts, public hearings were designed for a viewing audience to see and hear witnesses' testimony. In this way, the public is able to determine what constitutes "bribery," even "obstruction" and whether such crimes were committed. "This country is worth saving. This country's democracy is worth saving." "Sunshine patriots" have been challenging the process but ignoring the facts. Soon we will begin "exposing the sunshine patriots" for the fraud they truly are.

FREDERICK MONDERSON

When is a "Gangster Government" a "Gangster Government" Photo? Emblem of the **Big Red One** with back entrance to the **Executive Office** building at its rear.

"It is a disgrace what the President is doing tonight in Michigan." **Gloria Borgia**

"The President has been making deeply personal, deeply strident remarks at the rally in Michigan, to both Representative Debbie Dingell and her departed husband who served in the House of Representatives for nearly 50 years." **Jim Acosta**.

WHEN IS A "GANGSTER GOVERNMENT"? A "GANGSTER GOVERNMENT?"

When is a "Gangster Government" a "Gangster Government" Photo? Sharpton's **Keepers of the Dream Conference Logo** in 2019.

3. AN OPEN LETTER TO MAUREEN CALLAHAN – New York Post
BY
DR. FRED MONDERSON

Ms. Callahan, I read with great interest your shameful vilification "Dems bow down to a Clown – Disgrace selves by wooing Vile Rev Al's favor," *New York Post*, April 4, 2019, p. 7. This hatchet job you so eloquently blundered betrays a pathological malignancy long associated with the *New York Post's* maladjustment which earned the appropriate epithet, "Bird-Cage Dropping mat." This description was so

FREDERICK MONDERSON

expertly applied when *The Post* characterized the newly elected African-American President Barack Obama as an ape lying prone, after being shot by a New York City cop. Naturally, this characterization so inflamed people of goodwill and especially the African-American Community, untold numbers took to the streets to show disgust with your rag newspaper where the descriptive epithet was respondingly exclaimed in protest across the nation.

The interesting thing about your piece, overwhelmingly full of animus on a day sacred to the African-American Community, as if Biblically prophetic asks, "Where were you when they crucified our Lord?" That is, April 4, 1968, the day the world and America suffered the indignant assassination of Dr. King. There you were sadly, April 4, 2019, savaging Rev. Al Sharpton, a tremendously effective activist, marching proudly upholding high the banner praising Dr. King, continuing his efforts to bring about true justice and a voice for the voiceless. We know Dr. King was a constant victim of attacks and therefore the attack on Sharpton was simply a continuation of the hateful movement in which you employed some 24 disturbing and pejoratively vile terms in your savage front page and page 7 By-line.

On the day your paper ranted the intended malicious missive, a thousand people filled the Conference's main audience room of the Midtown Sheraton Hotel to heap praise and support for Rev. Al Sharpton's efforts "Keeping the Dream Alive" at **National Action Network's 2019 National**

WHEN IS A "GANGSTER GOVERNMENT"? A "GANGSTER GOVERNMENT?"

Convention. One "better Angel" of the American psyche is the blessedness of forgiveness. But your malicious sketch of the tortuous path Rev. Sharpton traveled to the ascent of becoming a presidential candidate for the highest office of the land, is not properly recounted and lost in the vicious attack your hatchet job demonstrates.

When Robin Hood rescued "Lady Marion" he was praised as a hero. When Sharpton stood up for Tawana Brawley, he was and continues to be villainized for his courageous stance. You people never forgive nor forget good or bad actions by Black men and trot out this disapproval every so often. Say what you will, here was a young Black woman, found in a miserable state, claiming she was raped by a gang of white men upstate, however high their social and political standing in the community. What then is a courageous champion of one oppressed to do but stand with the victim, unquestioned? The world knows the story of how "the powers that be" crushed Brawley and her champions to arrive at an orchestrated and faulty verdict. Naturally, neither you, nor Brawley's opponents, especially your newspaper, the *New York Post*, have given a credible account or even mentioned in your article why one of the accused men committed suicide. Thus, the evil intent of your intended character assassination missed the mark given the Convention Audience and so many others keep pushing Sharpton higher and higher. You mention his briefcase, but Terence Howard described the briefcase as "ready for business," and Sharpton's change from a jump suit to one tailor-made represents evolution of consciousness, courageousness and audacity of a Black man who pointedly speaks truth to power. Along the way, this fighter for justice established some 100 chapters of the National Action Network across the American political landscape giving political and organizational voice to millions. This is what the politicians realize and you people don't. Sadly, not only are you not able to comprehend you're not dealing with a "Private" but a "General" whose tactical and bold effort as a civil rights activist, has given voice to untold numbers but time and time again your caustic efforts fall short. Perhaps some examples expressed by those who understand and support Sharpton's movement may help to underscore his and the National Action Network's significance.

1. **Charter Communications**, in acknowledging their being proud to be a part of **NAN's** "Annual Grassroots Convention" affirmed, they are "proud to join the ground breakers. The obstacle-tacklers. The paradigm shifters."

2. **AFSME**, "Who make America Happen," offered "Congratulations on behalf of the 1.6 million members."

3. **AIRBNB** has affirmed: "Put people first and the entire community prospers."

WHEN IS A "GANGSTER GOVERNMENT"? A "GANGSTER GOVERNMENT?"

4. **COMCAST-NBCUniversal** admitted: "Diversity and inclusion is our foundation for motivating and drives our business forward."

5. **WBLS** – 1207.5 FM offered "Congratulations to Rev. Al Sharpton and the **National Action Network's** 2019 **Keepers of the Dream** Awards Gala."

6. **OVATION TV.COM** was "Proud to support **NAN** – No Justice, No Peace. Inclusion, Impact. Inspiration."

7. **COMBS ENTERPRISE** supplied Congratulations to the 2019 Honorees: "In their unapologetic pursuit as Keepers of the Dream."

8. While **FACEBOOK** is "Proud to Support the National Action Network," 1199 SEIU United Health Care Workers East that provide "Quality care and good jobs for all," boldly let it be known: "We applaud the National Action Network for keeping the spirit and social justice tradition of Dr. Martin Luther King Jr., alive – Congratulations to all of tonight's Honorees. Thank you for your steadfast commitment to civil rights, social justice and equality for all."

9. While **McDonald** proudly supports **National Action Network** who believe "Diversity is Inclusion" and **The RAI Group**

FREDERICK MONDERSON

salutes **National Action Network**, recognizing the role of "Passionate Principled People" in "transformation" and "Innovation," **VERIZON** "thanks the National Action Network for its leadership in advancing civil rights."

10. **Healthy Housing Foundation.Net** is a "Proud supporter of National Action Network" for they:

PREVENT - gentrification and homelessness by keeping rents under control and discouraging evictions.

PRESERVE – communities by supporting progressive, sustainable land-use policies that maintain neighborhood integrity." Ms. Callahan, such resounding praise and support counters the false message you intend.

PRODUCE - Affordable housing through adaptive reuse and cost-effective new construction.

Further, elaborations on such praiseworthy statements, the National Action Network, in the **President's Welcome**, Al Sharpton states its intent "to renew our resolve and commitment to the fight for equality, fairness and justice." More specifically, the Convention sought: "Over the course of the next few days, we will have the opportunity to hear from Presidential candidates and other notable

WHEN IS A "GANGSTER GOVERNMENT"?
A "GANGSTER GOVERNMENT?"

elected officials, civil rights activists, legal experts, important media voices, business executives, youth leaders and many more. We will listen, share ideas and information, and of course organize and strategize for the next steps forward on this great road towards freedom." Callahan, you can't touch this!

Even more, "This year holds special significance as it marks the 400-year anniversary of when the first documented slaves were forcefully brought to what would become the state of Virginia. Four centuries later, African Americans have broken barriers across the board and made immense strides everywhere, but institutional racism and systemic barriers still persist throughout society. While there has been tremendous obvious achievement from the election of the first Black President to the most diverse Congress, to advances in every industry, there is much work that remains before us."

For over 25 years, **National Action Network** has been on the forefront of key civil rights issues such as police brutality and criminal justice reform, voting rights, jobs and justice, affordable housing, equality in education, pay equality, a livable wage, eliminating discrimination in all its forms and so much more. During the 2019 annual convention we commit to continuing that dedication until there is equality and justice for all."

Equally too, Dr. W. Franklyn Richardson, in the **Chairman's Message of Welcome** was equally instructive for he pointed out: "Our journey has taken us through slavery, a failed reconstruction, Jim Crow, lynching periods, discrimination and segregation. Yet, in the face of it all, we have accomplished so much. However, while it is true that we have come a long way in our fight for justice, we must not be paralyzed by the nostalgia of past achievements and minimal rewards."

"Racism is embedded in this current climate and hate is on the rise. Even as we gather here, forces are being marshalled to take away the hard-fought gains that we have made. Nevertheless, our capacity to resist this onslaught of maliciousness designed to set us back can only be defeated by our endless resolve to use every weapon in our arsenal. Our armaments are many – our economic strength, the education of our youth, and moreover our VOTE! In each area, we must be resilient – when we are knocked down, we must get back up."

WHEN IS A "GANGSTER GOVERNMENT"? A "GANGSTER GOVERNMENT?"

When is a "Gangster Government" a "Gangster Government" Photo? The Bransfield "Knowledge Wheel" in the Jefferson Branch of the Library of Congress depicting references to nation states from Egypt to America, as shown in an upside-down position, though here it is in the reverse.

Therefore, and sadly, Ms. Callahan, you missed the objective of the shining light. Even further and underscoring the Reverend's significance; some years ago, when undercover cops fired untold numbers of bullets into Sean Bell at the height of the Christmas season, Rev. Sharpton called for and led a

FREDERICK MONDERSON

"March to Shop for Justice" in Mid-Manhattan. Tens of thousands responded out of respect and in appreciative support for Rev. Sharpton as a man, an activist, a fighter, civil rights icon. Those supporters recognized no matter how the ilks of you try to cut Rev. Sharpton, he does not bleed, doing the Lord's work, as he does.

Receiving the "Lighthouse Award" at the culminating **Fashion Show** on Saturday April, 6, 2019, Rev. Devon Patrick praised Rev. Sharpton for, "He uplifts and inspires the world." In Prayer, he asked, "Never let those around us direct our story, only god can do that. Light has to shine into darkness not into light." This is what our hero does! In response, Reverend Al Sharpton instructed his audience, "Each of us has been called for a purpose. Your coming light is great." There he implored the audience, "Pray for us. Pray for an end to violence. In place of evil, place love. There must be love, power, protection. Not even death can keep god's love away."

Finally, even though you may not recognize this admonition and its significance; Rev. Sharpton, in a futuristic call to action, implored all people to put in your work right now, "Do not wait for pie in the sky when you die, what you do on the ground while you stick around, is what is most important." Such profound philosophic symbolism is what Sharpton means to so many. Ms. Callaghan, I know it's hard for you, but do not let history view your actions only through clouded, prejudiced and negative lens. Come

WHEN IS A "GANGSTER GOVERNMENT"?
A "GANGSTER GOVERNMENT?"

aboard for the great victory Sharpton's efforts seeks to bring about. All are welcome!

Sincerely

Dr. Fred Monderson

When is a "Gangster Government" a "Gangster Government" Photo? A majestic view of the Washington Monument.

"Republicans have asked for Democrats to go to Court. Now Nancy Pelosi can go to Court with Impeachment in hand." **Paul Begala**

FREDERICK MONDERSON

Remembering Elijah Cummings, **Nancy Pelosi** repeated his refrain, "When the history books are written, let it be said, I stood up to lawlessness and for humanity."

4. "BALLS ON THAT WOMAN!" BY DR. FRED MONDERSON

House Speaker Nancy Pelosi cautioned on Impeaching President Donald J. Trump; still she wants him in Jail! The Constitution's prescription for "High Crimes and Misdemeanors" is an effective tool but the Republican controlled Senate comprises "sunshine loyalists" who worship "mammoth before morals" and would not convict an impeached President Trump who practices "Isfit before Ma'at." Therefore, Speaker Pelosi, an experienced hand, who steers her caucus through challenging times, expresses caution in face of many young Democratic (nearly 60) lawmaker colleagues chomping at the bit for **Impeachment** without seeming to realize the full ramification of this step. **Impeachment means an Inquiry, Impeachment vote in the House and trial in the Senate**. It may also provide for removal from office

Article 1 of the Constitution lays it out on the method of removing an official, be it President, Governor or Mayor from office for "Treason, Bribery, and High

WHEN IS A "GANGSTER GOVERNMENT"? A "GANGSTER GOVERNMENT?"

Crimes and Misdemeanors." According to Jack C. Plano and Milton Greenberg in *The American Political Dictionary* (eighth Edition, New York: Holt, Rinehart and Winston, Inc., 1962) who define **Impeachment**, states such an action is: "A formal accusation, rendered by the lower house of a legislative body, that commits an accused civil official for trial in the upper house. Impeachment is, therefore, merely the first step in a two-stage process. In the national government, constitutional authority to impeach is vested in the House [of Representatives] and the power to try **Impeachment** cases rests with the Senate (Art. 1, sec. 2 and 3; Art II, sec. 4; and Art III, sect. 2). All civil officers of the United states are subject to impeachment, including military officers and members of Congress. The **Impeachment** process begins with preferring of charges by a representative, followed by referral to either the Judiciary Committee or to a special investigating committee. A simple majority vote of the House is sufficient to impeach. 'Articles of Impeachment' are drawn up, setting forth the basis for removal. The House appoints managers who prosecute the case in a trial before the Senate. If a President is on trial, the Chief Justice of the United States presides. The procedure during the trial closely resembles that of a court of law. A two-thirds vote of the Senators present is necessary for conviction. The only punishments that may be meted out are removal from office and disqualification from holding any office in the future. Once removed, however, the individual may be tried in a regular court of law if he or she has committed a criminal act. The President's pardoning power does not apply to impeachment conviction."

Given such, the significance of these proceedings, according to Plano and Greenberg (1989:132) is stated as follows. "In the course of American history, the House has instituted impeachment proceeding against fifty individuals, but only fourteen have been impeached, the most recent in 1986. Twelve have come to trial before the Senate, and only five - all judges – have been convicted. Charges have included bribery, incompetence, immorality, treason, sedition, insanity, tyranny, and advocacy of secession. In one notable case, President Andrew Johnson was acquitted by the margin of a single vote in 1868 of the charge of violating the **Tenure of Office Act** by removing an appointed official without congressional consent (the Act was later declared unconstitutional by the Supreme Court); in another case, Justice Samuel Chase was acquitted in 1805 of alleged political conduct on the Supreme Court. Few state officials have been convicted and removed by state legislatures. Occasionally, partisan politics may influence the exercise of the power, as was true in the Johnson case, and in the removal of several state officials by their legislatures. The process is always political in nature, but open partisanship can weaken public support. In 1974, President Richard M. Nixon resigned in the face of House preparation to begin impeachment proceedings. The threat of impeachment is often effective in securing the resignation of the official. However, in 1986 the

WHEN IS A "GANGSTER GOVERNMENT"?
A "GANGSTER GOVERNMENT?"

Senate convicted and removed federal judge Harry E. Claiborne of Nevada when he refused to vacate the judgeship even though serving a two-year prison sentence for tax evasion.

The interesting thing about the Trump Administration is indeed remarkable, for, during the Republican Primary and Presidential Campaign, Mr. Trump consistently and effectively played, "I will hire only the best people!" In fact, as events unfolded, Senator Bernie Sanders called him "a pathological liar!" How sad, the man is a damn liar! At last count he had parlayed some 15,000 lies or misstatements. Rather than "Drain the Swamp," the Trump team appears to have been "Swamp things" embroiled in behaviors resulting in nearly three dozen removals, voluntary or involuntary, from office. Some believe the "fish is rotten from the head" down to the tail.

With the release of the Muller Report, the evidence seemed to point increasingly towards Impeachment of the President of the United States of America, particularly for "Obstruction of Justice." Accumulation of his behaviors, antics and tactics, many assess to be of a "High crimes and misdemeanors" nature. Despite what has been said, "If a tree falls in the forest and no one is nearby to hear it, does it make a sound?" The fact and answer are, "It does make a sound," whether a human is there or not. The animals do hear sounds. They are startled and oftentimes run away. The thump of the sound oftentimes makes a depression in the ground. More especially given Senator Bernie Sanders reminded,

FREDERICK MONDERSON

"Donald Trump is a pathological liar," when he the President touts: "No Collusion, No Obstruction" he lies according to the Muller Report given Muller said, "Charging the president was not an option we considered" from day one. Equally too, "If we did not find the President did not commit a crime we would have said so."

Now, analyzing Counsel Muller's published **Report**, he contradicts Attorney General William Barr's denial of "Obstruction" uttered in order to protect the President through a misleading false narrative. Compounding this sad situation and given the House of Representatives, as a separate and equal branch of government, that has requested the President's taxes and Treasury Secretary Steve Mnuchin's refusal of this request along with Bill Barr's actions, both are considered on the verge of being in contempt; thus, both are subjects of possible impeachment. Talk about the best people and we now come to the "Swamp King" himself who, according to Speaker Nancy Pelosi, "The President is goading us to impeach him." This is Mr. Trump's calculating strategy using the impeachment of Bill Clinton in 1998 that ultimately backfired as his approval ratings rose significantly. This is because the economy was in a positive upturn with employment figures on the rise, and so significant in Bill Clinton's Impeachment raised his approval ratings.

That Mr. Trump's future will upturn is still questionable; yet, Speaker Pelosi insists on caution

WHEN IS A "GANGSTER GOVERNMENT"? A "GANGSTER GOVERNMENT?"

about impeachment talk. Nevertheless, and fact is, whether the Clinton and Trump Impeachment are comparable, it is as a "Mountain toa Mole Hill."

One of the good things of the American system is, experts are encouraged and allowed to express their considered views on burning contemporary issues. For example, despite Bill Barr's false narrative of the **Muller Report**, according to Speaker Pelosi, "more than 1000-former Attorney Generals," from both parties across the nation, signed a letter saying the President committed a crime and had it not been for the Justice Department's policy, "a sitting President cannot be indicted," any other individual would have been charged. This is why Speaker Pelosi has encouraged the work of multiple committees continue to conduct multiple investigations to unmask Trump in totality. The two recent court rulings against Mr. Trump has also been helpful to Ms. Pelosi's position.

In similar analysis manner and appearing on CNN News Program, a practicing defense attorney has sketched a political strategy to Impeach Mr. Trump that could be bad for him, given "the impossible is happening all the time." As such, here is the scenario he proffers to impeach Mr. Trump. It needs be pointed out, the House of Representatives can bring charges against the President but the Senate has to conduct the trial that renders a verdict which requires two-thirds or 67 votes to convict. Presently there are 52 Republicans, 1 Independent and 47 Democrats.

FREDERICK MONDERSON

The Democrats need a significant number of Republicans to vote to impeach and given their "fear of Trump," Speaker Pelosi's methods may be the most viable.

Now, according to the expert, the House of Representatives can open pandora's box by televising an inquiry into Mr. Trump's taxes, Real Estate and bank relationships. The following week they would expose to the American people the issues with the "models," and Michael Cohen. The next week they would expose the issues of collusion in which the Russian activities and Trump campaign personnel's expectation of resulting therefrom, despite Muller not charging collusion on their part. Then in the fourth week, they would expose to the American people the Mr. Trump obstruction efforts. This comprehensive exposure of Trump's totality could not in the true sense benefit Mr. Trump for it would be an extensive and systematic airing of his "dirty linen." Coupled with high-lighting his extraordinary history of lying then perhaps the "Ogre" is not as invulnerable as many, particularly his misguided followers, himself and fearful Republicans believe. Still, the largely loyal base must therefore own the entire "kith and caboose" of the Trump mechanism.

Another of these experts voicing analysis of unfolding events, Harry Littman, a former U.S. Attorney General has expressed his take on Mr. Muller's brief statement underscoring his Report.

WHEN IS A "GANGSTER GOVERNMENT"? A "GANGSTER GOVERNMENT?"

1. Special Counsel Robert Muller has essentially affirmed President Trump has crossed the criminal line.

2. Mr. Muller and his team conducted a methodological and professional criminal investigation.

3. The Report clearly indicates obstruction of justice did occur.

4. Despite the general findings of wrong-doing and criminal behavior, Department of Justice standing policy dictates "A sitting President cannot be indicted." Otherwise, the President would be prohibited from completely fulfilling his responsibilities of running the country as he prepares to defend himself in an ongoing capacity.

5. After two years of silence as his investigation unfolded, Mr. Muller painted a riveting picture as he gave voice to the Report.

6. This new reality that vocally and graphically highlights the Muller Report, now makes it different for the House of Representatives to stand silent given, as the Constitution dictates, this body has a "responsibility to check the President." Therefore, Impeachment is a credible option as some in Congress have advocated, though they may not be there yet! Speaker Pelosi, on the other hand, "Playing the long game," has insisted "the multiple

committees conducting investigations are the right way to go," for now.

7. Unfolding events and strategies will have a tremendous impact on the 2020 national elections. While Mr. Trump and his allies may want to rush and close the case, the opposition on the other hand, wants to play it slow, mobilize opinion as more and more information is revealed about Donald Trump's operations exposing wrong doing.

8. Seeming unclear concessions on Impeachment insist they shy away or go for it. Then again, a compromise could be to censure Mr. Trump and save the nation from the trauma of such a final act. It must be remembered, Mr. Muller reminded, "The Russians" engaged in "multiple, systematic efforts of interference in our election and this must be a concern for every American" and "deserves every American attention."

9. A number of change agents working in consort will certainly get to the bottom of the issue facing Mr. Trump. Equally, even after his tenure of office, Mr. Trump still has several legal issues to deal with, particularly those in New York State.

10. Ms. Pelosi is, in many ways, "a strict constructionist" and realized the Constitution, the spirit and integrity of the nation has been tremendously affected and there has been criminal behavior on part of the President, and so Mr. Trump may still find himself in jail.

WHEN IS A "GANGSTER GOVERNMENT"?
A "GANGSTER GOVERNMENT?"

When is a "Gangster Government" a "Gangster Government" Photo? Dr. Martin Luther King stands proudly, looking across the tidal Basin, from his Memorial.

"We have never had a trial without witnesses. Schumer wants four witnesses! Bolton, Mulvaney ...." **Paul Begala**

When is a "Gangster Government" a "Gangster Government" Photo? Wonderful fountain with the Capitol Building in the background.

"Speaker Pelosi has the option to withhold the **Instruments of Impeachment**. This is a clash of titans – Mitch McConnell and Nancy Pelosi. The Founding Fathers laid out a way to deal with an uncontrolled President." **Kerri Cordero**

5. "A WOMAN OF POWER NOT STRAW!" BY DR. FRED MONDERSON

How strange that Donald Trump, whom many believe is a misogynist, fears one person in America, a woman, Nancy Pelosi. This woman, a consummate political practitioner, wields the art of politics with the extraordinary skill of a well-experienced surgeon. In this case, her arena of political combat, exercising a full repertoire of skillful tools in the art of the possible, Ms. Pelosi gives further meaning to the phrase and title of this work, "More Woman, More Power." Equally significant, the 2018 Mid-Term Election saw a great many women run for national and state office and particularly in the House of Representatives, many such women were successful in enlarging and advancing woman power in

WHEN IS A "GANGSTER GOVERNMENT"?
A "GANGSTER GOVERNMENT?"

Congress. If only we could clone Ms. Pelosi then we may increase the already significant number serving in both bodies of the nation's legislature, and therefore, many active and impending social problems may appear solvable.

Scientists have posited the view, negativity towards women reaches back to childhood evolving behavior patterns and the earliest such encounters begins with one's mother, the first nurturer, and this may be the genesis of the malady.

Next to Donald Trump's foolish "Birther" escapade, some say dislike even hatred for women ranks high on his scale. Whether his attack on Megyn Kelly, even Rosie O'Donnell, Mr. Trump first signaled his contempt for women. Then the "Hollywood Access" tape happened with the man expressing disrespect for women in an era when "Me-Too" proponents began exposing and fighting back against how they were treated by men in powerful positions. Fortunately, however, in recent times, many of these men were either fired, brought to trial or thrown in jail. On the other hand, unfortunately though his behavior turned disgusting, to his base Mr. Trump's actions did not affect him very much.

As candidate Trump had said earlier in the campaign, "If I shoot someone on 5th Avenue, I would not lose a single vote." Cocky! In response, he developed a base who either didn't care and with other revelations yet falsely painted him a victim. Then demonstrating arrogance in style and disrespect in disposition, Mr.

FREDERICK MONDERSON

Trump, upon being elected, turned his back on the media that had given him unprecedented coverage at minimal cost, as they began to focus on his eye-brow raising behavior. Like a spoiled brat, Trump coined the phrase, "Fake news" and began labeling the media "Enemy of the people." In retrospect and given what we know to be Mr. Trump's seeming ties to the Russians or certainly his acquiescence to Vladimir Putin, his pronouncements seem to come right out of the Russian playbook. After that he resumed the assault on women, targeting and disrespecting Senator Elizabeth Warren calling her "Pocahontas." After the **Special Operations** soldier was killed in Niger, the President insensitively addressed the grieving and expectant widow in a manner many persons thought was not only disrespectful but even racist. Congresswoman Maxine Walters, a constant critic of Mr. Trump labeling him "unfit for office," came in for her share of attacks; and so, observers began to understand the true nature of the man occupying the sacred office of President of the United States of America. Amidst that unfolding crisis, Mr. Trump attacked the female Mayor of Puerto Rico who criticized his response to the hurricane that devastated the island, killing many, though some figures claim upwards of four thousand fatalities.

Colin Kaepernick, the **NFL** quarterback who was waging a campaign against police brutality by "taking a knee," so enraged the President, he implored team owners to "Get that SOB off the field." Many interpreted this as an attack on

WHEN IS A "GANGSTER GOVERNMENT"?
A "GANGSTER GOVERNMENT?"

Kaepernick's mother. In response, though many fellow **NFL** players supported Kaepernick, even **NBA** players of the year's winning title refused to attend the customary White House reception after such an event. Stephen Curry, the basketball superstar, dissented and when the President took on Lebron James, the star ball-player, Lebron responded by Tweeting "You bum. Going to the White House was fun until you got there!"

When is a "Gangster Government" a "Gangster Government" Photo? Arches fronting Union Station in Washington, DC.

FREDERICK MONDERSON

When is a "Gangster Government" a "Gangster Government" Photo? One of two judicial wisdom figures in the Plaza fronting the Supreme Court building.

This and more Nancy Pelosi and the world watched in astonishment as the Republicans, Mr. Trump's "Base" cheered, rationalized and encouraged their man onwards. Meanwhile Republicans in both the House and Senate ignored the antics. In both the

WHEN IS A "GANGSTER GOVERNMENT"?
A "GANGSTER GOVERNMENT?"

Cohen hearing and with John Dean, Congressman Jordan not only became a "yes man for Trump," in fact, he became "a yes attack dog." If only he would view his own presentation. He is, nevertheless, dancing and singing in chorus to the White House Pied Piper as he tottered and assembled his followers near the cliff's edge. All this "Nancy" observed then the people exercised the sacred ballot at the 2018 Mid-Term Election giving Democrats control of the House of Representatives; a co-equal branch of government with the power and authority to check Mr. Trump's excesses! While the Senate remained in Republican hands as these lawmakers turned a blind eye or ear to Mr. Trump's ridiculous behavior, all this underscored a total disrespect of the sacred nature of the Office of the President. This is what Speaker Pelosi paid strict observance to, and returned as Speaker of the House, un-knowing to the "Outside world," Ms. Pelosi was taking score, while standing as the last obstacle to the swamp behemoth!

Through all his antics, Mr. Trump's base, his enablers and the many who encouraged his actions in and through the Media, enabled him to believe he was "essentially above the law." Then the **Muller Report** dropped. As required, yet Attorney General William Barr unfortunately gave a false assessment of the document. Unfortunately, running interference for Donald Trump, his refusal to accord the House its equal branch of government status and responsibilities as a check on the Executive Branch was poor judgment, perhaps illegal. Many thought

FREDERICK MONDERSON

Mr. Barr's credibility sank into the gutter after these displays. So, Mr. Trump, feeling larger than life, began the process of ignoring legitimate subpoenas and instructing many underlings so similarly ignore such requests. In fact, he ordered individuals who could truthfully testify under oath not to respond to legally binding House of Representatives' subpoenas. He next attacked a number of America's allies, while "Kissing up" to the nation's enemies as Russian Vladimir Putin; North Korea's Kim Jung Un; Venezuela's Madura; and others, actions all below the dignity of the Office of the President of the United states. No man dared question the Ogre! No man dared stand up against Mr. Trump. In fact, one man did stand up to Mr. Trump and that man was a woman, Speaker Nancy Pelosi!

Undeterred, Mr. Trump, whose vocabulary, despite his threats or bluffs, seem limited in addition to his hallmark "You1re fired;" To "We'll see," and oh, the use of the "Nasty" as well as "Witch Hunt," words among his continuous derogatory name calling. In all of this, Speaker Nancy Pelosi has come to realize, since no one wants to stand up to Donald Trump, then "it's up to me. It is my responsibility to the Constitution and to my constituency which, essentially, is the entire country and that I should work to ensure the president sticks to his oath of office." She was careful to point out, her stance is not political but essentially in defense of this **Constitution** Mr. Trump continued to trample, ignoring his oath to defend and preserve the **sacred**

WHEN IS A "GANGSTER GOVERNMENT"?
A "GANGSTER GOVERNMENT?"

document and all it stands for. Therefore, while initially nearly one quarter of her caucus keep pressing for Impeachment, Nancy played the long game. Her strategy included allowing the Oversight, Justice, Intelligence and Ways and Means Committees conduct their inquiries into Mr. Trump and his business. Having won two court decisions against Mr. Trump, Ms. Pelosi hopes to cap all and given the Muller Report and appearance on public TV to explain the full ramifications of his work was not too compelling though it did provide a roadmap to obstruction by the president, she still believes the key to Mr. Trump lies in the courts.

Nonetheless, as a woman, Speaker Pelosi is committed to empowering women and so is in step with Senator Kirstin Gillibrand who wants to preserve *Roe v. Wade*; Repeal the Hyde Act; she insists Abortion Services must be preserved; shows support for a woman's reproduction freedom; demand equal pay for equal work; and will not compromise on equal rights for women. Nancy Pelosi is a classic case of what Senator Gillibrand believes, "When women lead, we get things done!" The Senator insisted there should be working mothers in Congress and in the White House. "They should be at the table and at the head of the table." As a mother, the Speaker certainly became incensed over separation of children from their mothers at the border with Mexico over the issue of immigration. More important, when Mr. Trump reverted to his disgusting habit of name calling such as classing persons as "Nasty," this became the last straw. And, while Mr. Trump seems to be goading Democrats to impeach him, he does not realize fully the Speaker is the last barrier between the horde of Impeachers and himself. Finally, Speaker Pelosi, perhaps in an exasperated moment is quoted as saying, "I don't want Trump impeached, I want him in jail" and believes there is good reason for such a view.

In that tumultuous sea of legislative push to "Get at Trump," on her part, at the Democratic Debate Senator Marianne Williamson insisted, "A big truth defeats a big lie" and "Hope and love touch people's hearts" she insisted, "Republicans don't walk their talk." She pointed to "how deeply divided our country has become," insisting "Mr. Trump is not held accountable for his lies." We know he has told more than 15,000 such falsities to date.

"Democrats rejected Impeachment three times in 2017, 2018 and in July of 2019 before the phone call. President Trump's appointees confirmed the basis of the Articles of Impeachment. They laid out a compelling case in full. Democrats provided every opportunity for the President to clear his name and he refused!" Majority Leader Hoyer.

"Majority Leader Hoyer's **Summation** was substantive while Minority McCarty's was chaff of the wheat." **Fred Monderson**

WHEN IS A "GANGSTER GOVERNMENT"? A "GANGSTER GOVERNMENT?"

6. A CONSEQUENTIAL ELECTION BY DR. FRED MONDERSON

The African-American "Shining Prince" Malcolm X, often held, "History is a good teacher." Today, as we seek to determine what is meant by a "Consequential Election," there are a number of landmark instances along the historical continuum that serve as good examples of this important occurrence. The time periods in which these elections occur, the resulting social, civic even economic consequences that result, always serve as barometers of future political and election action. As such, and to further help understand elections, we look to the U.S. Census which happens every 10 years and is the basis upon which "redistricting" of Election Districts is done. Generally, the party in government, more often than not, redraw district lines that favor them in the next and hopefully subsequent elections. Oftentimes they go too far and such actions are termed "Gerrymandering." When challenged in the courts, their actions are oftentimes deemed illegal since their skewing of the political landscape is generally designed to suppress the voting strength of a particular group who may vote against the interest of the party in power.

FREDERICK MONDERSON

Because elections are a state responsibility, that party with a legislative majority generally seeks to legislate any number of measures that "cleanse the voting rolls" which in fact is disfranchisement. Recently pushed by Republicans, this action has been in the form of requiring state issued identification which slowed the registration process when offices are closed, sparse or placed at a distance making it a challenge to get there, especially for the elderly. Some voter registration offices are oftentimes closed, reducing the number of such places in which voter services are facilitated, thereby reducing the number of registered voters. Felony prisoners are often stripped of their right to vote, generally even after they have paid their debt to society. When calamities such as hurricanes, floods, even fires destroy record keeping centers, this sets back the identification process and hinders registration and therefore meaningfully affects the right to express the ballot vote. Registrars sometimes make demands for identification of Seniors and the poor which is often difficult to provide. As such, if persons are not vigilant, upgrade and frequently maintain their voting record, they can be easily purged from the voting rolls. Then there are the natural, run-of-the-mill errors, which happens at the Board of Election, whether human or mechanical. These can include mis-filing of names of persons registered, broken machines, otherwise missing or defective registration, and let's not forget, more negative campaigning directed against opponents and all other possible means hopefuls can concoct to get elected. Very often, caught up on the throes of being elected

WHEN IS A "GANGSTER GOVERNMENT"?
A "GANGSTER GOVERNMENT?"

or getting re-elected, politicians or representatives "low key" addressing citizens' concerns and together with election day shenanigans which impacts turnout, these go a long-way in determining the consequential nature of an election and final vote tally. Thus, the end result of not being active and vigilantly involved results in what former President Barack Obama expressed regarding the 2016 election, "What if we are wrong," about the projected outcome.

The Constitution requires federal officers face the voters every two years. That is to say; first, they are 435 Representative Districts across the country creating that number of House of Representative members. This number is calculated and demarcated based on population size occupying each district. These House of Representative members essentially serve for a two-year period and in this category are, therefore, up for re-election. The Senate is representative of the 50 states with two Senators each who serve for a period of 6 years per term. Because of the great responsibility of this deliberative body; more so than the House of Representative which is essentially a "money" or "finance" institution as part of its legislative function; only one third of the Senate faces the electorate every two years. For example, in case of the recent 2018 Mid-Term Election, even the upcoming 2020 general election all 435 House of Representative members are up for re-election but only 33 Senators of a regular term for the full six-year duration are on the ballot. However, because of

FREDERICK MONDERSON

contemporary and prevailing societal conditions in the "Age of Trump," this mid-term becomes Consequential; and in 2 years, 2020, the same situation applies but with even more dramatic impact. The Office of the President, however, is the principal office up for reelection in 2020 and every four years. Oftentimes persons run on the President's "Slate" and this creates a "coat-tail effect." Given the current situation, the 2020 election takes on more meaning.

Back in time, Adam Clayton Powell gave a remarkable speech in Harlem, New York, in which he asked, as entitled, "What's in your hand?" There he highlighted Jesus' "two nails on the cross" and the significance of the 1965 Voting Rights Act, which in fact reinforced the 1868 - 15th Amendment to the Constitution giving the vote, essentially, to males born in the U.S. Significantly, these two legislative accomplishments empowered African-Americans through the right to vote. However, nefarious individuals especially, often choose to nullify that entitlement or are generally happy when Blacks refuse to exercise the inherent power such political gains represent. Malcolm X, on the other hand, insightfully recognized how evenly divided or politically balanced Republicans and Democrats are, and so emphasized the importance of the Black vote which could help determine, "Who goes to the White House and who goes to the dog house." A modern example of this phenomenon was the "Judge Roy Moore for Senate" fiasco in which the race was "close" until; unexpectedly, Blacks threw their

WHEN IS A "GANGSTER GOVERNMENT"?
A "GANGSTER GOVERNMENT?"

weight, their vote, behind the Judge's opponent, and this force of will determined the result.

Even more significant, given African-Americans have fought unending for America's defense and traveled a long and arduous road to win the vote, register to vote, and struggled to exercise the privilege of the vote; we must, therefore, never lose sight of the importance of the vote. In South Africa, people spent hours and hours standing in line to cast the ballot for the first time in the most consequential election of their time brought about by global pressures against Apartheid and Nelson Mandela's 26-years in prison standing on the principle of the sanctity of one man, one vote.

Perhaps elements of the population in these United States do not understand the inherent power of the vote; how the vote influences the nation's economic, political and moral-social landscape, and thereby the true meaning of a consequential election. On the other hand, people with a true sense of history and an understanding of the African-American experience and how difficult it has been to ascend to the "mountain-top" Barack Obama represented, are involved to the political hilt. Sadly, however, within a mere 18-months, gains Mr. Obama struggled to achieve as the nation's first twice-elected African-American President, much have been revoked by Donald Trump; others that "still stand" are threatened and strictures are being put in place that will impact, control and determine the nation's path for the "next 40-years." "While the cat is away, the mouse will play" to win! Nevertheless, traps and glue sticks can keep that mouse in check. The House of Representatives, after the democratic surge in the 2018-Mid-Term election, has come to represent one example of a check on the awesome power of the President.

As an example, of the "inherent hatred of the Blackman;" what else, since he "footballs" Mr. Obama every day, the following are some significant Obama accomplishments Donald Trump has reversed.

1. DACA – Deferred Action for Childhood Arrivals - 2012

2. Transfer of surplus Military equipment to local police – 2015

3. Normalizing Relations with Cuba – 2014

4. The Paris Climate Agreement

5. Offshore and Artic Oil Drilling – 2016

6. Net-Neutrality – 2015

7. The Clean Water Rule

8. Caps on Greenhouse Gas Emissions at Power

WHEN IS A "GANGSTER GOVERNMENT"? A "GANGSTER GOVERNMENT?"

Plants

9. Scope of National Monuments

10. Bathroom Protections for Transgender Students

11. NAFTA North America Free Trade Agreement

12. Trans-Pacific Partnership.

Given Donald Trump's unending invoking of the "Cool Ruler's" name, one has to wonder whether it is, "P, Q, R. S, or T" envy.

Nevertheless, torrential outpouring of voting strength can send a clear and convincing message not simply to Mr. Trump but to Republicans and Democrats as well. "Respect the Black vote!" This way, Black respected input can help shape the future direction of the nation. Again, we must never relinquish the significance of the vote.

In January of 2016, Rep. James Clyburn (D. SC) pointed to the consequential nature of the upcoming presidential election. Throughout that year, President Obama strenuously and vigorously expressed such in campaigning for Hillary Clinton. With all her "imperfections" Blacks would have had influence with Hillary! Instead, many followed Sean Combs, "Puff Daddy," "Puffy," "P. Diddy," "Diddy," a confused young man, who insisted Blacks "Hold the Vote." Instead we get Paris Dennard, Mark Burns, Kanye West, Ben Carson, the Heritage Foundation poster image, all of whom earned their "30 pieces of chitlins," Malcolm X called it "guts." To these we also recognize Black guards for Mr. Trump, Black waiters, Black men with mops, Black golf caddies, but no Black millionaires, but significant roll backs of Criminal Justice reforms, designed to be more equitable in sentencing, time served and re-entry efforts designed to reduce recidivism from a place Blacks seem to be purposely placed. Noticeable is the private prison industry undergoing a tremendous resurgence and Black and Brown people overwhelmingly their tenants behind this profit motive surge.

Nonetheless and much more significant, many still do not realize, the transformation of America Donald Trump is effectuating can practically be viewed especially from the judicial appointments he has put in place. The Internet is reporting, "as of July 10, 2018, the United States Senate has confirmed 43 Article III judges nominated by President Trump, including 2 Associate Justice of the Supreme Court of the United States, 22 Judges for the United States Courts of Appeals, 20 Judges for the United States District Courts, and 0 Judges for the United States Court of International Trade.[2] There are currently 91 nominations to Article III courts awaiting Senate action, 12 for the Courts of Appeals, 76 for the

WHEN IS A "GANGSTER GOVERNMENT"? A "GANGSTER GOVERNMENT?"

District Courts, and 2 for the Court of International Trade.[3] There are currently [0 vacancy] on the Supreme Court, 14 vacancies on the U.S. Courts of Appeals, 129 vacancies on the U.S. District Courts, 2 vacancies on the U.S. Court of International Trade, [3] and 31 announced federal judicial vacancies that will occur before the end of Trump's first term (0 for the Supreme Court, 7 for the Courts of Appeals, and 22 for District Courts). Trump has not made any recess appointments to the federal courts."

When is a "Gangster Government" a "Gangster Government" Photo? From the front Plaza of the Capitol Building, view of the Jefferson Building of the Library of Congress.

FREDERICK MONDERSON

When is a "Gangster Government" a "Gangster Government" Photo? The other of two judicial wisdom figures in the Plaza fronting the Supreme Court building.

WHEN IS A "GANGSTER GOVERNMENT"? A "GANGSTER GOVERNMENT?"

As we look to the future, African-Americans must never forget African people's blood, sacrifice and tears that soaked and fertilized this American land; and they must also realize, "there are no permanent enemies only permanent interests." Our ancestors were oftentimes worked to death, unpaid and penniless under cruel and inhumane conditions; our men, women and children were brutalized, disrespected, killed and abused, as we faced racism, discrimination and terrorism responsible for nearly 4000 lynchings from 1870-1950 alone. The FBI reported more than "100 unsolved civil rights murders" on its books. There's been no accounting for this tragedy and none held accountable as the government turned a blind eye toward our plight. Still, like the Mother Emanuel Saints, we forgive the "dirty, Rotten Scoundrels."

While African-Americans have fought in every war America has been a part of, from Crispus Attucks to World Wars One and Two with Dorian Miller "our Hero," then "Pork Chop Hill" in Korea, Vietnam and even Afghanistan and Iraq, it must never be forgotten, particularly on this date, December 7, 2019, Black have served in America's military with great distinction. Now the theater is Africa to extinguish the "bogey man" threatening America; yet, the most potent and viable weapon we have is the vote. While Malcolm X pointed to the "Ballot or Bullet" option, we recognize across the political landscape today the former is more potently effective if we use it wisely and consistently. Without question, we must hold both Democrats and Republican accountable. However, in this we must force Republicans to respect and contend with the Black vote while keeping Democrats' feet to the fire. Clearly, as Republicans continue to ignore Mr. Trump's nearly 15,000 lies, falsity and other pernicious shortcomings, ignore the supposed illegitimacy of his election caused by Russian meddling in this sacred American institution practice and as they process and band together to protect him in the Ukraine falsity as they have in the Muller investigation, Black issues are not even on the "back burner." Thus, we must take a stand for our children and grand-children, against the oppressor and to save this great Republic which voted Barack Obama the Greatest American President of our lifetime. We must not let Obama's gains in interest of the American people be erased by Donald Trump and his party of enablers and disbelievers.

Therefore, we must play a more active role in unfolding circumstances and not be passive bystanders. As such then, if the Black vote turns out enmasse to Spearhead an effective coalition with the #Metoo Movement, Black Lives Matter, disrespected Latino voters, women across the spectrum, youth affected by gun violence and good and decent people, this combined effort can upset the upcoming 2020 election to send Donald Trump packing to his possible new residence in Moscow.

WHEN IS A "GANGSTER GOVERNMENT"?
A "GANGSTER GOVERNMENT?"

When is a "Gangster Government" a "Gangster Government" Photo? "Equal Justice Under Law," reads the **Cornice** at the front entrance to the Supreme Court of the United States.

When is a "Gangster Government" a "Gangster Government" Photo? "Justice – The Guardian of Liberty" reads the **Cornice** at the rear of the Supreme Court of the United States, Washington, DC.

FREDERICK MONDERSON

"He stonewalled and choose not to defend himself but sent a six-page letter, a rant, to be his response."
Tim Naftali

"President Trump used the power of his office to the detriment of the United States. He is a President who subverts the Constitution and puts himself above the law. In this case, the Constitutional Order is at risk. The rule of law is at risk. A President must not be allowed to become a dictator." **Jerry Nadler**

7. ARROGANCE OF THE STRONGMAN
BY
DR. FRED MONDERSON

Goliath was big and arrogant but David took him down! Achilles faced his giant opponent and quickly dispatched him. Important, however, in more recent times, Benito Mussolini, Adolf Hitler and Joseph Stalin, were strongmen but they created much distress and destruction in lives and property. Now, Donald Trump is a horse with another name, current, and "wickedly brilliant." In actuality, Mr. Trump is the clearest manifestation of the arrogance of power having affirmed, "as President, I can do anything" and as in the campaign rhetoric, "If I shoot someone on 5th Avenue, I won't lose any votes!"

In Bruce Willis' movie **Die Hard**, the arch-villain said to his associate trying to crack the Safe's Code of the Nakatone Towers, "You ask for a miracle and

WHEN IS A "GANGSTER GOVERNMENT"?
A "GANGSTER GOVERNMENT?"

I give you the FBI." The scuttlebutt is that Republican voters are disenchanted with the "Republican establishment" and even though they had essentially won the 2010 and 2014 mid-term elections resulting in control of first the House, and then control of both House and Senate; yet these Republican voters rated the Republican controlled Congress at less than 35 percent. Thus, they remain dissatisfied with its performance and "looked to the heavens" for relief. In the movie **High Plains Drifter**, the young woman asked for a miracle and Clint Eastwood the "Preacher" appeared! Now, to Republicans' heavenly gaze, Donald Trump materialized, coming down the escalator, even borne in his air-mobile **Trump** and to many the "Messiah" had arrived. Thus, this "great white hope" burst on the scene making outlandish promises. With great fanfare and relatively speaking he began attracting numbers of attendees at his rallies including blue collar workers, many of the 43 percent who voted against Obama and some of the disaffected Republicans, Independents and even Democrats. However, starved for "strong man speak;" such followers in their wide tumultuous support began overlooking elements of speech not considered "Presidential" but more "street." All of a sudden, in the late innings of the 2016 Republican Presidential campaign game, as the star-burst exploded, opponents of Mr. Trump, such as high echelon Republicans in and out of government, his competitors, even potential Democratic rivals as well as commentators far and wide across the global spectrum began to sound an alarm, enquiring: "What manner of man is this!" Yet, Mr. Trump's supporters continued to voice, no matter what, "Trump is the man;" "he is saying what we believe and want to hear." As such, as put to President Obama at a recent press conference in question and answer period: "Are you surprised at the rise of Trump?" to his followers Mr. Obama asked, "What if we are wrong?"

In "ancient times" when intellectual and academic racists of the 1970s William Shockley and Christopher Jenks, even Morgan Worthy types, presented their complex missives articulating their racial theories, "folks" needed the Harvard University Psychologist Alvin Puissant to decode the camouflaged racist rants. While such professional help can prove useful in deconstructing Mr. Trump's mentality, seeking to fully understand the nature of the man, average persons could admit, even "Stevie Wonder and Ray Charles could see through" the Republican front-runner as he thundered towards the cliff playing that wonderfully-melodic Pied Piper tunes with his supporters following in full gallop.

Well, to begin. Mr. Obama pointedly stated in answer to the question, "I'm not surprised!" In this he referred to the sinister intent with which Mr. Trump pursued his "Birther charade." His demands for President Obama's college transcripts and more. Even today, now having confessed the foolishness of his misguided ways, yet secretly harboring the false notion Mr. Obama is not a citizen and that he is a Muslim, Mr. Trump and his followers are today tap-

WHEN IS A "GANGSTER GOVERNMENT"?
A "GANGSTER GOVERNMENT?"

dancing to wonderfully melodic orchestral renditions of the Pied Piper aboard the American Titanic. How desperate his supporters must be!

Searching for the human spirit of God which is resident in all of us can be contrasted between Bill Gates and Donald Trump. While Bill Gates personifies that graciousness of God and humility of the hermit that manifests in and distinguishes us from the 4-foot animals, this extraordinary human quality is not a character trait of Donald Trump. Mr. Trump's recent characterization of Hillary Clinton barking like a dog is a good example of "as a man thinketh, so is he" stinketh!

In the American tradition, history has shown, Presidential contenders generally carry their home-state because of the pride and success a "favorite son" brings. Equally, hometown newspapers generally get into the act praising and pitching for "homeboy." Not so for the New York City newspapers that either lambast Mr. Trump or feed him with a "long, long spoon."

The New York **Daily News** has referred to Mr. Trump as "clown," "circus performer," "Just-Ass," and many other juicy descriptions but new comers have still wondered how we got to this fork in the road, where Republican leadership faced with the inevitability of Mr. Trump becoming their party's standard-bearer were appearing and appealing with

FREDERICK MONDERSON

hat in hand to the wizard to yet "tone it down" but, "can a leopard change its spots?"

A general consensus is Mr. Trump still believes Mr. Obama is not a citizen. Either he is a fool or a very sinister individual. Conversely, he tried the "Birther" tune on Ted Cruz but that "pig did not fly." I recognized Mr. Cruz was born in Canada but his mother is an American citizen. So, Mr. Trump toned down this element of his strategy. John McCain was born on an army base in Panama, yet no one questioned his citizenship. Bernie Sanders put it right; his parents were from Poland but no one asked him about his citizenship. That is, "don't ask white folks about their citizenship" but ask the Black man Obama whose mother was an American citizen from Kansas, USA.

Significantly, in a recent pronouncement President Obama exclaimed "Donald Trump will not become President." With all we know about President Obama, Columbia and Harvard Graduate, President of the **Harvard Law Review**, twice elected President, enlightened through eight years of Intelligence Daily Briefings, he must know something. When George W. Bush unveiled his image in the White House, he gleefully admonished, when President Obama is faced with a difficult decision he should turn to the portrait and ask, "What would George say or do?" So, perhaps Mr. Obama called on the former President and asked, "George, do you think Trump will be president?" to which Mr. Bush equally and probably responded, "Nah!"

WHEN IS A "GANGSTER GOVERNMENT"? A "GANGSTER GOVERNMENT?"

Perhaps the same could be applied to Ted Cruz, "the fraud" as Republican Representative King of New York called him. Imagine because Mr. Obama did not attend Nancy Reagan's funeral, having sent his high-level delegation probably including "Mighty Michelle," Mr. Cruz labeled him "Lawless." A man who stole Ben Carson's people in a shady announcement, as Donald Trump pointed out.

But Trump is a special case, perhaps a "Basket Case," arrogantly drunk with the billions he possesses; in no way possessing the wealth, humility or mannerism of Bill Gates, a philanthropist and humanitarian with a global outreach. So, it is important, to recount some of what is being said of Donald Trump.

Governor Kasich – I'm "Deeply disturbed by the toxic and atrocious atmosphere Donald Trump has created in his campaign."

Tara Sethmayer- "He is duping people." "Mr. Trump is brilliantly frightening." "He never admits he is wrong." "The media gave him a pass." "He was never vetted."

President Obama - "My belief is that some Republicans will have to re-examine their position on Mr. Trump."

Kayleigh McEnamy – A Trump supporter and commentator said, he has "changed his rhetoric." But

FREDERICK MONDERSON

can a zebra really change his stripes? He still worships at the "Birther altar."

Dan Rather offered, "I hope Donald Trump would reassess himself."

Senator Lindsey Graham (R. SC.) initially remarked, Donald Trump spews "xenophobia, race bating, and religious bigotry." Today, Graham "Kisses Trump's ring!"

Equally too **Mitt Romney** feels "repulsed" by Donald Trump. Thus, he asserted, "Trumpism," is associated with "racism, misogyny, bigotry, xenophobia, vulgarity, threats and violence."

In the movie **Collateral Damage**, after the trial, the lead attorney said to the Department of State official who had withheld crucial evidence, "Do you know how it feels like to have a pissed-off Marine on your case?" Well, Mr. Trump will have two men of substance with "axes to grind."

Carl Bernstein offered, "Donald Trump is about Donald Trump."

William Vogel, in deep reflection, reminded, "If you unite behind a man you don't believe in, it's a lie." And even more, "I can't sort one statement from another."

WHEN IS A "GANGSTER GOVERNMENT"?
A "GANGSTER GOVERNMENT?"

Sure, he will be pitted against Hillary Clinton, experienced in political battles, but her husband Bill Clinton is another matter. He will step up because Trump insulted his wife in having her "barking like a dog," or is that the polite word. Mr. Obama, in words of the Mighty Sparrow, "In his own words I paid him back" will take to the road to close the "Birther Door." However, there is much at stake since Republicans and especially Mr. Trump has threatened to eviscerate many of Mr. Obama's signature accomplishments such as the Affordable Care Act, the Iran Nuclear Deal, his opening to Cuba and other Executive Actions he introduced. Let us not equally forget the many negative things Donald Trump has said about women that a current Ad is pointing out, that "This is what he is saying about our wives, sisters, mothers, aunts, etc." What a waste!

When is a "Gangster Government" a "Gangster Government" Photo? Another view of the entrance to the Supreme Court with its magnificent two rows of columns and "Old Glory!"

"The Republican narrative is false. It ignores the truth." **John Kasich**

FREDERICK MONDERSON

"The President of the United States has been Impeached! Will the Senate allow a fair trial, one that is fair to the President but also fair to the American people? He has not provided the documents and the people required to testify. Do the Senators want a fair trial? The remedy is incomplete as long as the President continues to flaunt the rule of law." **Adam Schiff**

8. BULLY IN THE WHITE HOUSE
BY
DR. FRED MONDERSON

We have heard of the "School Yard Bully;" "Bully on the Block;" "Bully on the Court;" even the "Bully Pulpit," but this is the first time we have recognized a "Bully in the White House." However, since a "Bully in the White House" is an oxymoron, the current occupant is therefore, not really a bully. For, like all true bullies, when seriously challenged, they cower. Interesting how this contradiction, in reality, appropriately applies to President Donald Trump. That is to say, a line of argument holds, throughout the 2016 Presidential Campaign because Mr. Trump manifested the "New Penny Phenomenon" the Media was fascinated by his brashness and lavished extensive coverage all over him. As a result of the high cost of TV, radio and newspaper coverage in advertising, candidates expend a great deal of their "war chest" in the overall cost of getting out their messaging. However, having parlayed his largess,

WHEN IS A "GANGSTER GOVERNMENT"?
A "GANGSTER GOVERNMENT?"

Mr. Trump often boasted how fortunate he had been, how skillfully he waged his campaign and how little he expended in advertising, due to the tremendous media coverage he received! Like the bully he was purported to be, "once over the river," he did not at first cower, but disdainfully began labeling as "fake news" critical media who covered him."

The success of his victory encouraged Mr. Trump to speak unending and abashedly about everything and everyone in the most unflattering manner. In no time, the lofty accomplishment of becoming President of the United States soon descended into the lowness of name calling, criticism of men, women, allies, adversaries, the disabled, the media and anyone who did not and does not pledge loyalty to him or genuflect in his presence to "Kiss his ring!". At his first State of the Union address, he charged "Treason" because everyone, particularly Democrats did not applaud. He sorts of wants everyone to kiss his anatomy and Republicans seem to do a good job at it! Mr. Trump's perennial outrageousness became so ridiculous in one episode, Senator Flake remarked. "The good news is, we have hit the bottom." Some have wondered and questioned whether that place was Mr. Trump's "shithole."

As Mr. Trump basked in his new glory, he appeared at the United Nations annual summit representing the United States. Stepping up to the Podium, in cold, calculated, merciless bully fashion, Mr. Trump shocked the world leaders gathered for the summit in arrogantly proclaiming, after his many taunts leading to that crescendo, "I will destroy North Korea!" He meant nuclear obliteration. After the awe had subsided; no one, particularly Republicans, certainly not the wider world, dared upbraid this man of power whose trump suit is arrogance. And so, many wondered what's next. Sadly, a Biblical verse, Micah 6: 8 can instruct wonderfully well for it admonishes, "Love Mercy, Love Justice, Walk Humbly." Sadly, however, no such admonition applies to President Trump as leader of the Western Alliance and the "free world," though he chastises those who criticize him as "fake news."

The coat of arrogance Mr. Trump wears so disdainfully-well is rooted in his character as a business man, real estate mogul, but specially in his persona as a political animal and opportunist who probably made harsh and unethical decisions in his climb to success, that painfully victimized many.

Bob Baer, the CIA's "Man in Russia" revealed the Agency was "looking at Donald Trump" as early as 1987 when he began uttering "Russian talking points." Much of this was covered in the *Washington Post*, *The New York Times* and *Boston Globe*. The book *House of Trump, House of Putin* indicates Russians were funneling money to Trump as early as 1984. Perhaps this is why from his position of power he consistently labeled all relating expose as "fake news;" even describing 4th estate institutions "enemies of the people." Mr. Baer spoke of Trump seeking investments for his Real Estate ventures in Bedrock, Toronto and "Russians carried the note on

WHEN IS A "GANGSTER GOVERNMENT"?
A "GANGSTER GOVERNMENT?"

Trump." He may have been "compromised" from back then and this is why probably "Putin wanted him to win" the 2016 Election and so as the great body of American intelligence agencies reported, "Putin helped him to win." However, and significantly, despite his millions, some give him perhaps one or two billion, Mr. trump possessed a personality defect that blocked his full and eloquent optimization as statesman, diplomat and a fully adjusted social and humane member of society. It's been said, "God moves in mysterious ways," but sometimes God's sons are just as pervasive in generating the wherewithal to propel bad actors toward a pinnacle but contradictorily expose that quintessential germinating seed in challenge to the aspiring personality. In that quintessential psychological journey at the fork, the "right turn" can prove and was certainly wrong. Unaided, the genie pops out of the bottle. The bad seed germinates and the true nature of the animal appears despite the decades-long circus cover-up of cerebral maladjustment despite truly "fake news" sugar-coating his personality while suppressing exposure to his defects.

In an interesting accident of history, citizen Trump found his nemesis in Senator, later President, Barack Hussein Obama and the vehicle that tied the two at the hip, unintentionally, was the "Birther falsity." This is America. In this day and age, "When a White man takes after a Black man" with the ferocity and vindictiveness Mr. Trump visited upon Mr. Obama, invariably the motivating principle is about race. As Malcolm X explained, such is to be expected "no matter what's your professional standing" and that "You are not victimized because you are a Mason or an Elk, but because you are Black. The sad thing about the social and political climb and the unfolding caustic experiences of the sojourn to the celebrity plateau; during the campaign and subsequently, regarding Mr. Trump's behavior, the number of people who faced the cameras on TV, and those who wrote on print media to defend him, even those in political and official positions who rationalized his actions; they themselves are afraid to criticize but worship Trump in a cultist manner and genuflect before him. Sadly, these apologists who rationalize Mr. Trump in the public eye never really and fully assess the indefensible positions they articulate on his behalf. More important, these apologists never truly listened to themselves as we, part of the listening audience, do. If they did, in deconstructing such thoughts, these people, even Mr. Trump, should realize how vindictive, silly and stupid his pronouncements and their rationalizing really sound, but they hardly do.

Nevertheless, the unchanging ferociousness with which Mr. Trump perpetuated the "Birther falsity;" the overturning and dismantling of Mr. Obama's hard fought for signature accomplishments legislative and globally, in the interest of the American people, and especially the Affordable Care Act betrays and lays bare Mr. Trump's insidious racial animosity. You know, the Cretan says "All Cretans are liars," and though one of Mr. Trump's popular refrains has been, "I am the least racist of all persons," his insidiousness

WHEN IS A "GANGSTER GOVERNMENT"? A "GANGSTER GOVERNMENT?"

toward Mr. Obama and Blacks in general is nothing but bitter, blue, racial animus. The man in the picture cannot see the picture but we see him clear as day. "You are what you are" and given the opportunity to write upon the pages of history, and having done so, the ink of such actions cannot be erased. Mr. Trump has telegraphed to the world the true animal beneath the mask he wears in his effort to deceive through misstatements and lies.

Sill, with all the goings on particularly on the world stage, a general "go to" refrain of Mr. Trump has been "Played like a fiddle." He has been particularly a victim of this refrain, or perhaps a milder word is "sucker" to this "con." Sadly, it is quite an achievement to "con a con man." However, Mike Bloomberg did warn of this mindset. Before he left for China, Thomas Friedman opined, "The Chinese believe Trump is a chump" and will treat him as such. In his Summit with the Korean Head of State to whom he gave much and achieved little, Kim Jung Un "played him" in explaining the difference of interpretation of what is meant by "denuclearization and the rapidity with which it will be achieved if at all." In Helsinki, "full of it" in his deal-making and believed intellectual invincibility, "his Boy Putin" mesmerized him in a "two-hour private meeting" in which all of Russia knows what happened in the room and "all of America does not know what happened;" for certain this nation's "intelligence community" is still in the dark. As such, while Aaron David Miller called the Helsinki demonstration "A disaster and betrayal of American interests," given that Trump

FREDERICK MONDERSON

attacked Obama, Macron, Theresa May, Angela Merkel, Presidents Xi and Kim Jung Un, but cowered to the Russian in Helsinki, Mike turner rightfully believes, "Trump is being manipulated by Putin," and he expressed "grave concern about what may be next." A look at both men as they entered the room to conduct the Press Conference, Putin was all smiles and Trump all glum!

Seeking to shamefacedly correct his mistakes, in view of the backlash he cowered and "got lost in the woulds." Pretty soon, however, he resorted to his own, "Leopards never lose their stripes," set of lies and name calling obfuscation.

Summing it all up, whereas President Obama's biggest blunder for which he received the highest criticism, in which he wore a "light colored suit," Chris Cillizza on CNN listed "5 take aways" for the week that began with the Trump/Putin Summit and Republicans are missing their testicular fortitude in fearfully, failing to call out trump the bully.

1. Putin's interview about what transpired in the 2-hour long private meeting, while Americans have no clue in not being honestly represented by the President.

2. Director of National Intelligence Dan Coats was clueless as to what happened at the meeting.

3. While Senators John McCain and Jeff Flake voiced opposition, Majority Leader Mitch

WHEN IS A "GANGSTER GOVERNMENT"?
A "GANGSTER GOVERNMENT?"

McConnell and Speaker Ryan lost their voice, and so Congressional Republicans in fear, cowered and did nothing to hold Trump accountable.

4. Donald Trump proposed to invite Vladimir Putin to the White House in the Fall and DNI Dan Coats heard of it on Twitter.

5. Tapes seized from Michael Cohen by the FBI were released in which Trump's lawyer and he are heard discussing payment to the Playboy Bunny McDougal who claimed she had a 9-month affair with Trump cheating on his wife but which he denied.

Calling the last a distraction, Chris Cuomo on CNN's **Cuomo Prime Time** opined regarding the tape's release, President Trump would prefer, regarding the American people, "Having the Playmate peccadillo in the air than Putin in your ear."

The poetic irony in all of this, while President Trump beats up on former President Obama, Obama laughs his head off as Trump makes a fool of himself on a scale of global proportions. No less significant, while Donald Trump may seem to postulate the strongman bully image, as he cowered while beside Putin in Helsinki; at home, when the citizenry push back enmasse on any policy or action, he reverses himself, then resumes his original intent. Through it all, this guy is not "Vaseline slick;" he is "axle grease slick."

FREDERICK MONDERSON

"Lindsey is about to go down in a way I think he will regret his whole life." **Joe Biden**

When is a "Gangster Government" a "Gangster Government" Photo? Female beauty in majestic form, rests atop Iconic Columns so characteristic of Washington, DC "Colonnades" as the authors sought to replicate Rome in America.

"The measure of a man is not where he stands in times of comfort and convenience but where he stands in time of conflict and controversy." **Dr. Martin Luther King**, Jr.

**WHEN IS A "GANGSTER GOVERNMENT"?
A "GANGSTER GOVERNMENT?"**

9. KILLING DR. KING, AGAIN
BY
DR. FRED MONDERSON

On April 4, 1968, Dr. Martin Luther King, Jr., a "drum major for justice," was assassinated as backlash to his involvement in the Civil Rights Movement then underway. However, on April 4, 2019, pens of perniciousness in the *New York Post*, in an **Editorial** and Front-page article, attacked to vilify the Rev. Al Sharpton as he hosted this year's "Keepers of the Dream Convention" honoring the work and vision of Dr. King. Despite all the platitudes of peace, equality and progress in this nation, where profit, privilege and power run rampant, the day this saintly man was murdered should be a day of commemoration and penance simply because Dr. King sought to help mold and propagate the best in "The better angels of America." Instead, we get the gall of the *New York Post*, rather than calling upon the United States' President to help elevate the high moral ideals Dr. King sought to cultivate in the American character, *The Post* attacked to vilify the "last man standing" who hoists aloft standards of equality and justice so righteousness can indeed roll down like a mighty stream in order to realize America's true identity, purportedly "the last hope for humanity." Sadly, in today's environment we see more "last" than "hope."

FREDERICK MONDERSON

What makes *The Post* mischaracterization of Rev. Sharpton on this holy day of reflection through civil, political and social activism, is unquestionably a reminder of how American elements can be unforgiving, vindictive and destructive. After all, that killing and silencing through vilification of Black leadership has been centuries in the making. From the beginning, Denmark Vesey, Gabriel Prosser, Nat Turner, Henry Highland Garner, Frederick Douglass, Booker T. Washington, Marcus Garvey, Patrice Lumumba, Stephen Beko, Malcolm X, Toussaint L'Ouverture, Maurice Bishop, Odinga, Chokwe Lumumba, Richard Green, Harold Washington, Medgar Evers, have all been victimized by "Pen, Pressure and Projectiles." Thus, in killing Black leaders and visiting a new form of slavery on Black citizens evident in the practices of civil and institutional racial discrimination, police brutality, Incarcerated Criminal Justice vindictiveness, poor housing, inadequate and poor education, poor health care, negative stereotyping and desecration of Black places of worship in burning, bombing and killing, one wonders, "Is the nation progressing or regressing?" Without question, Dr. King had been a constant victim of personal attacks and in the Press as well. Therefore, the attack on Sharpton is simply a continuation of the same sick maliciousness because he is continuing the work of the great martyr. Yet and significantly, despite those atrocities, Blacks in general refuse to be burdened by the albatross of hate and racial animus so readily perpetrated by the oppressor class particularly among those they influence even incite, especially in today's climate

WHEN IS A "GANGSTER GOVERNMENT"? A "GANGSTER GOVERNMENT?"

seeking to "Make America Great Again." All this transpires amidst a materialist culture of lies, hate, racism, vindictiveness and untrustworthiness.

Notwithstanding, while oppressive forces kill or persecute Black leaders, we celebrate and commemorate these martyrs, commending their courage and steadfastness in commitment to principled behavior in challenge to orchestrated and ongoing oppression and injustice.

As such, the 2019 **National Action Network Convention** – "400 years since the first Enslaved Africans were Brought to America," individuals who attended and participated, held Sharpton in high esteem as he in turn beamed in the brightness of his brain child represented in the "Keepers of the Dream" memorial, the past's vile mischaracterization, notwithstanding.

Thus, we recognize, the politicians who came to present at NAN's annual convention, do so for a number of reasons. Chief of which, despite the vilification, *The Post* **Editorial** sought to visit on Al Sharpton and in this case, even lumping Jesse Jackson and Barack Obama, the established sponsors and supporters unqualifiedly recognize, Reverend Sharpton is significantly a national leader with demonstrated credentials. The reality here is, though politicians may make pronouncements for public consumption, after the cameras depart, only Sharpton remains standing alongside the victims visited by the many injustices. This is especially so regarding the broad spectrum of people Dr. King sought to help in his efforts to transform America.

Therefore, the attack on Sharpton is understood and welcome. Such a display is thus a modern example of the 2019 Convention theme, paralleling the 1619-2019, 400-years of oppressive onslaught against African people on these shores.

Second, owing to his lengthy travels beginning as an 8-year old preacher and the travails along the dusty road of civil and social rights activism; wise politicians, Democrats, sadly not Republicans, realize, "When Sharpton speaks people listen;" but more important Sharpton's people, enlightened, listen and can and do mobilize for action. That is not simply his supporters, but more important the oppressor and those who feign support as well for they realize how formidable a champion of the people Sharpton really is. More to the point, as the people's representative, Sharpton can and does hold the decision makers' feet to the fire. Holding them accountable, they come not simply for his endorsement since he seldom publicly takes such a stand, but they are permitted a platform to pitch their programs of promised legislative action or to indicate what enacted legislation will benefit Sharpton's constituency, the American people, irrespective. Also, those returning come to report to the people what stated goals they have accomplished since the last time of their appearance at such a Convention.

WHEN IS A "GANGSTER GOVERNMENT"?
A "GANGSTER GOVERNMENT?"

Again, rather than castigate Sharpton, The *New York Post* should vigorously investigate the nearly 15,000 lies or misstatements President Trump has uttered thus far, which many Republicans purposely ignore and the impact the administration's behavior is having on the nation, the view from abroad, and most important on the minds of the young living through these turbulent times. In fact, rather than vilify Al Sharpton whose ancestor was a slave owned by an ancestor of a great segregationist Strom Thurmond; Barack Obama whose wife Michelle Obama is a descendant of slaves; Jesse Jackson, whose heritage is equally of the slave experience; and the question as to why and how these great men emerged to play significant roles in the Reconstruction of the nation, truly investigative reporting should champion the work of such great Black leaders, whose efforts have certainly benefitted America and Americans. Instead, the little people at the *New York Post*, an institution bristling in "fake News" vindictive reporting and racial mischaracterization, should come to realize, on April 4, 2019, as they vilified Rev. Al Sharpton, the thousands in attendance did not buy *The Post* that day. Therefore, mobilizing and getting out the vote and wise and targeted spending of Black dollars should be the effective projectiles that pressure poison pen proponents.

"Republicans put effort over courage and avarice over Constitution." **Bill Pascrell**

FREDERICK MONDERSON

When is a "Gangster Government" a "Gangster Government" Photo? A side view of the Capitol Building against the beautifully manicured green lawn.

"Donald Trump now has a tin can tied to his feet that will rattle throughout history for all time." **Patrick Mahoney**.

10. NO TO THAT "NO-BEL" PRIZE!
BY
DR. FRED MONDERSON

In times past the "Noble Prize" meant something! Sure, it meant a recognition of exceptional performance or successful function in a particular area of expertise. Concomitantly, the behavior exhibited must represent high moral standards of conduct befitting a "Noble" recipient. The great Blacks who received the Noble Peace and other Prize, Albert John Luthuli, Ralph Bunche, Martin Luther King, Anwar el Sadat, and Barack Obama, Sir

WHEN IS A "GANGSTER GOVERNMENT"?
A "GANGSTER GOVERNMENT?"

William Arthur Lewis, Archbishop Desmond Tutu, Wole Soyinka, Derek Walcott, Toni Morrison, Nelson Mandela, Kofi Annan, Wangari Maathai, Ellen Johnson Sirleaf, Leymah Gbowee, and Tawakel Karman were awarded the prestigious award for peace, in science, literature, whatever, but all were "civilized." That is, they demonstrated and functioned at the highest level of social behavior and acceptance, intellectual fortitude and possessed elegance of mind and nobility of spirit. Such behaviors undergird the prestigious nature of the achievement, as expected by the global community who views such behavior. Conversely, the Warlords, Winston Churchill, Joseph Stalin, Delano Roosevelt and Dwight Eisenhower, who saw the great war to its end, possessed noble character and equally demonstrated exceptional work habits; still, these individuals never received the Noble Peace Prize for ending that great conflict. That is because "Noble means Noble" which is despite the work one puts in it's also contingent upon the behavior a recipient exhibits before and after the recognition. Lying is not a positive trait nor is egotistical behavior that betrays moral bankruptcy. Trampling on the rule of law in exercising high elected office designed to represent all and not some individuals of a community or nation, is in the same category expecting and demonstrating high moral behavior.

Today, questionable characters vigorously seek a prestigious Noble award that praises exceptional accomplishment for Mr. Trump. However, this globally respected achievement comes with the expectation its awardees are people of high moral character and ethical behavior in their actions. Banter now being propagated insists, Donald J. Trump should be awarded the "Noble Prize for Peace" along the Korean Peninsula. In objection, one may argue, his "baggage," is "greater than Kareem in **Coming to America** which not only disqualifies this insidious individual but sullies global perception as to awarding this "high hanging fruit" bringing it to the base of the tree's trunk. Equally, Mr. Trump's overall thoughts, actions, behaviors also color global perception of America for the world is watching and wondering, what's really going on in these United States of America.

Sure, the current debate regarding nuclear weaponry on the Korean Peninsula is significant yet raises profound questions as to who should get a Noble Prize for any breakthrough. In this respect, what must be considered is the character of the individuals who are to receive such an award; whether any of the parties are actually pushing the award for personal reasons; and how, truly significant this breakthrough will really be, how much time it will take to accomplish stated goals all of which depend on a number of factors beyond potential cessation of hostilities. President Jimmy Carter was awarded the Peace Prize for bringing Anwar Sadat and Menachem Begin to Camp David where they hammered out a Peace Treaty between Israel and Egypt. This agreement has held for more than 40 years because the parties vowed to make the agreement work. Naturally and sadly, Sadat paid with his life for

WHEN IS A "GANGSTER GOVERNMENT"?
A "GANGSTER GOVERNMENT?"

taking the bold step in breaking with Arab intransigence towards Israel.

Now, after Donald Trump's supporters have given him "a Mulligan," should there be "additional Mulligans?" Clearly, the question is, "How many Mulligans will it take to erase the stains and odious offense of this hypocritical behavior emanating from deep in a questionable mentality?" According to the award-willing journalist Carl Bernstein, we are forced to admit "Trump is president of his base and not all Americans." Bernstein calls this relationship, "a cult of his base." Equally significant, not only does Mr. Trump not apologize for any intransigence when he makes mistakes or lies, he never accepts correction and so many have placed him, as hugely egotistical, in an alternative universe. Realistically, the man's behavior and personality disqualify him from being a Noble recipient!

To affirm that view, if we assess how Trump has dealt with former President Barack Obama, we can begin with the "5-year Birther charade" of falsity that elevated Trump politically. The man is seen as uncomfortable with his victory, and his administration's hostile propaganda tirade and actions that are designed to effectively undo every constructive accomplishment Mr. Obama achieved on behalf of the American people; and such behavior is appalling, to say the least. In his anti-Obama vendetta, Mr. Trump has "Nit Picked" NAFTA, the IRAN-Nuclear Deal, the PARIS Climate Change

FREDERICK MONDERSON

Agreement, the Pacific Partnership, the Cuba Agreement and especially the long overdue reforms the Obama Administration instituted in Criminal Justice practices. Adding to his disdain for and efforts to dismantle these significant Obama accomplishments, we could include Mr. Trump's unending insistence that "Barack Obama wire-tapped Trump Tower" during the 2016 election; and more recently, again, seeming falsely claiming the "Obama Administration planted an FBI spy in the Trump campaign." These claims have been debunked through **FACT-CHECK**, especially by Mr. Trump's personally appointed heads of the FBI, CIA and NIS. The recently released Inspector General Report dismissed these two. His unending conspiracy theories span the "deep-state" and "spy-gate" claims, insertion into the NFL unfolding practices and accusations against *ABC News*, the *Washington Post*, even *Amazon* are not only personal but represents the works of a sinister ubiquitous mind. NFL, ABC, CNN, NBC, Amazon, "deep-state," and "spy-gate," and more; where does it end? Now Trey Gowdy, a high-ranking Republican representative who led the Benghazi Investigation against Hillary Clinton has publicly debunked the "spy-gate" falsity similarly as heads of intelligence agencies have done. Now House Speaker Paul Ryan and the Senate Republican Chairman of the Intelligence Committee have expressed essentially, "The FBI acted appropriately."

The Cretans have long held, "All Cretans are liars." Whether Mr. Trump is a Cretan is debatable but he is certainly a LIAR, with 15,000 lies to his credit and

WHEN IS A "GANGSTER GOVERNMENT"? A "GANGSTER GOVERNMENT?"

counting. Beside him dictating a description of his health to his doctor and more especially wants to be privy to the investigation about himself, helps shed some light into the mind of "the man who wants to be Noble" but miserably falls short. His lawyers' letter now links him to the falsity he dictated in his son Don Jr.'s claim as to the given "adoption" reason for the "Russian meeting" in Trump Tower. Let us not forget, Mr. Trump and his propagandists are doing everything to discredit the Muller Probe into Russian interference in the 2016 Election and so his actions are designed to trample upon the rule of law. As General Michael Hayden, former CIA and NSA Chief earlier explained, alluding to Donald Trump's seeming hatred for former President Obama, Trump "sees himself not as his predecessor" is putting it mildly diplomatic. Later and regarding Trump's "Memorial Day Tweet," the General continued, "Presidents often put people behind them such as EMS, Fire, Police, the Clergy, etc. In this case, the President placed the FALLEN behind him." This meant Memorial Day was not about those who served and gave their lives for this country, but for an egotistical Commander-in-Chief businessman who, as a young man sought and got five (5) military deferrals for such ridiculous ailments as "Bone spurs." Americans cannot forget, Trump evaded serving in the military; neither his sons or son-in-law served but today they are "riding in military style." What's with the Veterans who unquestionably support Mr. Trump? John McCain served and bled, yet the President disrespected him. Vice-President Joe Biden's son, Bo Biden served and died. Even

FREDERICK MONDERSON

Trump's Chief-of-Staff General John Kelly's son served and died in military action. Today the evaders are setting military policy and calling out persons. Trump disrespected the wife of the soldier who died in Niger, during his watch as Commander-In-Chief.

Trump never served, he never showed any evidence of patriotism, other than evasive actions and crafty words, as he "tunnel-vision wise" built his real estate empire. Yet, if memory serves correctly, the Supreme Court ruled "flag-burning" was "constitutionally protected speech." However, in Trump's sordid world, "taking a knee" by footballers protesting social injustice in police brutality is "unpatriotic" and he has referred to those who do so as "Sons of Bitches." Inserting his personal views into the sports arena is part of his disregard for people's feelings, refusal to acknowledge the purpose of such protests expresses a "first amendment right," and his "unrelenting assault on the rule of law" is not "Noble behavior." After all, "If you put lipstick on a pig, it is still a pig!" No less significant, the undermining of law enforcement and intelligence institutions such as the FBI, DOJ, NSA, the Muller Probe, etc., all create the belief Trump thinks he is above the law. Even Mr. Trump's "second pea in the pod" lawyer Giuliani ("**Brutaliani**") has lost the moral high ground. When we assess such behaviors, it is equally fair to assume, the "King of Lies and Bankruptcy" must have trampled upon many in his rise to becoming a real estate mogul for evident in the Republican Campaign Jeb Bush pointedly noted, "Donald Trump is insulting his way to the Presidency." Now he is

WHEN IS A "GANGSTER GOVERNMENT"?
A "GANGSTER GOVERNMENT?"

lying to hold on to the position. Let's not forget Obama's profound question in retrospect, "What if we are wrong" in electing Donald J. Trump President? Highlighting that same vein, Trump's mantra to "Make America Great Again" has, as some have pointed out, in fact resulted in "Make America Hate Again." Pundits have also opined, putting "America first" in trade and other global issues really results in placing "America alone" in some respects Evidence therefore seems to show, the climate emanating from the Trump White House encouraged and manifested in behaviors such as "Roseanne's;" "Charlottesville;" calling NFL players who "take a knee" "sons of bitches;" his unrelenting "birther falsity;" demeaning Mexicans, women, judges, the disabled, and a whole lot more, are certainly not "Noble behaviors." Mr. Trump has so far been silent on 4000 Puerto Rican deaths from Hurricane Maria, even though these are American citizens. Regarding the second hurricane to hit the island, he has not said anything publicly. Call it character flaw or what, this intractable individual even demeans those who work for him such as Jeff Sessions and Rosenberg. Assessing all such behaviors, Max Boot believes, "Trump is normalizing racism," but more important, "he disagrees and demeans the opposition." Imagine him saying, "Nancy Pelosi loves MS-13" and one of his staunches Congressional defenders Doug Collins, unabashedly stated, "Democrats love terrorists!"

In analogy, after former President Obama came upon the American economy badly wounded by the roadside, he stemmed the bleeding, bind the wounds and began treatment as a corrective measure. Along came Donald Trump. He removed the bandages, lacerated or opened the wounds, rolled back much and took undue credit for the economic foundation Obama constructed. In all this, President Trump created and encouraged, all while consistently fueling a climate of racism, hatred and disrespect towards his predecessor Barack Obama and this evil intent has never let up. In furthering his shameful and destructive character flaw, as Frank Bruni of *The New York Times* put it, "Trump changed from borderline to full racist." In pedaling and promoting racism and bigotry from his high office, the end result as Republican strategist Ana Navarro put it, "Bigots now proclaim: 'Yea, I'm a bigot,' the President does it." A good question for Republican supporters and apologists, what if your 6, 7, or 8-year old child tells you, 'I what to be a liar like President Trump,' how would you respond?

Michael D'Antonio who wrote the book on Trump feels, "he lacks the intelligence and creativity to be president. He does not take the responsibility of the office seriously. He is more interested in his own economic and egotistical aggrandizement. He has opened the door to the worse in us. Such behaviors demean and lowers our standards." That means American standards and standings are lowered in the global mindset of nations and people who will judge the current Noble award issuance and recipient, as they stand in amazing wonder how, "the White House has fallen down." According to Jeff Flake, "The good

WHEN IS A "GANGSTER GOVERNMENT"?
A "GANGSTER GOVERNMENT?"

news is we have reached rock-bottom." The million-dollar question is whether it is in "the Shithole!"

Therefore, in the broad sweep of his behavior, many have argued, Mr. Trump has surrendered the moral high ground. But, perhaps, he never stood on such high ground. Philosophically speaking, a man's life in his later years is a clear indication of the challenging, perhaps objective, even destructive climb demonstrated in his rise to the top. While an old adage holds, "Cream rises to the top," so too does "garbage after the flood."

Still, we are left to believe the Noble Committee can and will be able to smell the "stink of garbage," human and moral, and respect and prize their award more than anyone who receives it.

"Many have sacrificed for this unique land. The idea of America is the rule of law. The idea of America is in peril." Denny Heck

FREDERICK MONDERSON

When is a "Gangster Government" a Gangster Government" Photo? Back of the Capital Building with stairs and columns, on the "Marble Terrace" with a view of the "Great Lawn" accessing the "Washington Monument," "Reflecting Pool" and "Lincoln Memorial" further on.

In 2020, "For instance, there are at least five major Supreme Court decisions that will arrive by June. According to *The New York Times's* Adam Liptak, they involve weighty question that could completely change the conversation, and, I would submit, cause a cultural crisis. They are cases that will decide whether the court will restrict abortion rights and possibly revisit *Row v. Wade*, whether Trump can strip protections from Dreamers and whether civil rights laws extend to the protection of L.G.B.T. people." **Charles M. Blow**

WHEN IS A "GANGSTER GOVERNMENT"?
A "GANGSTER GOVERNMENT?"

11. ABOUT THAT "96 PERCENT" BY DR. FRED MONDERSON

During the time Donald Trump was waging his campaign in the 2016 Presidential Election, even after he had exposed his racist underbelly in the "Birther falsity;" expressed his "proclivity for grabbing women by the genitals;" accused Mexicans of being rapists; mocked a disabled reporter; accused an American born federal judge of Mexican heritage of potential bias in a case he was presiding in; had unflattering things to say about Megyn Kelly and Rosie O'Donnell; Mr. Trump had the unmitigated gall and temerity to proclaim, by the next, 2020, election 96 percent of African-Americans would vote for him. Evidence seems to indicate Donald Trump is so contaminated from his disgusting description of African nations, here he relishes in a false sense of clarity and fragrance, others see odiousness and disgust.

While President Trump may boast of having the greatest memory, he yet has lapses in remembering things such as the "Stormy Daniels" debacle despite being smacked on the bottom with her **TIME** magazine copy. Naturally Mr. Trump forgot "in ancient times," he and his dad were sued by the Federal Government for racist practices in their real estate dealings. When the "Central Park Jogger's" unfortunate incident broke, Donald Trump

FREDERICK MONDERSON

practically "lynched" the "Central Park Five" by taking out a full-page AD in *The New York Times* newspaper. Strange, at that time and for convenience, The Times was not "fake news." There he insisted on all manner of horrible resolutions such as "They should be executed" and "Bring Back the Death Penalty, Bring Back Our police." Yet, after their lengthy years in prison and being declared innocent, New York City offered a settlement for wrongful imprisonment. Mr. Trump objected to the payment in compensation.

Not only is Donald Trump labeled a bigot, liar and racist, an "idiot," "professional liar," but those in his camp, 99 percent of Republicans, including Kelly-Ann Conway, Sarah Huckabee Sanders, and the untold numbers who "enable him," rationalize his behavior, defend his actions in words and deeds, even believe his untruths are not really what they actually are. Given he has told his supporters, "Don't believe what you see. Don't believe what you hear. Don't believe what you read. This is not what is happening." Yes Sir, **Impeachment** is happening! Does this mean Trump's supporters are blind, deaf and dumb who "See no evil, hear no evil, speak no evil" against him? Can they be painted with the same filthy and disgusting brush he deserves? Strange that many have criticized Sarah Huckabee Sanders for enabling, even lying, for President Trump and while her father, Rev. Huckabee criticizes so many but won't say a word regarding his daughter's daily misleading at the White House

WHEN IS A "GANGSTER GOVERNMENT"?
A "GANGSTER GOVERNMENT?"

briefing. They both are included in Hillary's "basket of deplorables."

While people of goodwill strive to correct the nation's misdirection, the President continues to move the nation off the page. This pseudo-leader; clocked at 15,000 lies and misstatements in 36 months in office, some half-a-dozen and now at more than 20 per day; has no remorse about his truthlessness because he never apologizes and if he ever does as with "Birther," it is generally not genuine. Sadly, the "moral majority" and others who supports and enables the Trump aberration have not only lost the moral high ground in religious, political and ethical discussions, but as history will acknowledge, they are mired yet and falsely, relishing in the cesspool that has infested the White House. With the exception of Fox News, all commentators are agreed the behemothic Trump administration is a "culture of corruption." Unfortunately, that misogynous leader, having been "played like a fiddle" by North Korea's Kim Jung Un; considered a "chump" by China; laughed at by Vladimir Putin as Ohio governor John Kasich has demonstrated in a tweet, and because he is supported by a few blacks, viz., Carson, Dennard, West, Darrell Scott, and, oh yes, that "Blacks for Trump" individual who acts clownish and is probably very underpaid for his antics. Notwithstanding, Mr. Trump foolishly stated and still believes, "96 percent of African-Americans" are ill-informed enough and don't care about his record but will flock to the polls to vote for an "equal opportunity abuser." Oh well, time will tell.

FREDERICK MONDERSON

Now, gauging the ante-bellum mentality of many in the Trump's base whose ancestors helped encourage the reality of the 3/5 Compromise; cultivated and managed slave farms in an institution of degradation, destitution and death; that gave support and strength to the reality of the Dred Scott Decision; relished in Jim Crow practices and benefitted from the "Grandfather Clause" helped perpetuate share crop peonage that essentially created economic enslavement; participated in KKK and Knights of the White Camelia intimidation, terrorism and death that resulted in some 3,973 lynchings from 1870 to 1950 in Southern states; many of those benefitted from the "White Primary" and Southern disfranchisement of Blacks aided through literacy tests, poll taxes and denial of the secret ballot. These and similar machinations as that of the "Bull Connors" and his cohorts unrestricted functioning brutality in an age of more than 100-unsolved Civil Rights murders; thinking individuals expect Mr. Trump will be proven wrong in his expectation of Black support.

The putative record indicates there have been 43 white men as President and once Barack Obama, an African-American, secured the democratic nomination then elected to the Office, Donald Trump and associated ilks unfolded and perennially perpetuated their "Birther" falsity seeking to delegitimize the man and his presidency. Thus, there resulted many fronts of assault on the integrity of Mr. Obama and his administration; yet he persevered because people of goodwill, black and white, prayed

WHEN IS A "GANGSTER GOVERNMENT"?
A "GANGSTER GOVERNMENT?"

for him and showered good vibes on his efforts. This tremendous spiritual support strengthened his resolve and helped bring about his divine mission of rescuing a ship of state adrift, yet many fails to acknowledge this effort particularly because a Black President brought it about.

Miscreant behaviors represented in the person of "Joe the Plumber;" "Tea party" gatherings displaying signs and sounds portraying Mr. Obama as a "witch doctor" and chanting "kill the Nigger;" putrid dribbles of the Sarah Palins, Joe Wilsons, Jim DeMints, Allen West, "Black Protester with Guns" and his "Pastor praying for Obama's death;" the "White House Protester" in shorts and with "middle finger in the air" helped perpetuate a climate of systemic racism, hatred and disrespect toward President Obama. Let us not forget Mitch McConnell's racist and failed diatribe "I intend to make Barack Obama a one-term resident;" all aided by the obstructionist Republican "Party of No's" chokehold on the federal legislature. Much of this Donald Trump inherited and actively exploited in pursuing his agenda. What a conglomeration of persons acting negatively against an individual, a black man; extraordinary in many ways, still his superior intellect best them time and time again. Obama learned tremendously form his time I office. Trump's lies and reprehensible behavior grew tremendously. And so, one has to wonder about the conspiratorial nature of Mr. Trump and is enablers' intent. That aside, Obama persevered in rescuing the nation from a debilitating recession and its devastating economic impact, a besmirched nation's image abroad, and having to contend with two wars raging in Iraq and Afghanistan. Notwithstanding, the perverted state of mind disguised in racist machinations became manifest when, after the 2012 Presidential Election witnessed during October 2013, *The New York Times* newspaper published an article entitled "A strategy long in planning" that involved Mitch McConnell, Ed Meese and top Republican operatives aided by some 20-CEOs of Republican NGOs particularly targeting the Affordable Care Act, maliciously misnomered "Obamacare."

Countering the treasonous behavior and intent and unleashing religious and ethical soul-force with spiritual power because of its sincerity, resoundingly enabled grand-mothers to consistently undergird Obama and strengthen his faith in face of the many challenges and doubt. Persevering, he is today considered and has been Polled the greatest American President in modern times.

Many saw the conspiracy as early as 2008 but the 2012 actions involving the same actors was documented proof of a crime against the Presidency. These were conspirators who clearly failed in their primary effort of restricting Obama's election and re-election.

Fast forward to 2018 and in preparation for the gubernatorial mid-term election in Florida, surprises emerged in the Primary contest. Just before, President Trump appeared before Republican

WHEN IS A "GANGSTER GOVERNMENT"?
A "GANGSTER GOVERNMENT?"

preachers seeking their support to counter the "coming Democratic wave" expected at the mid-term November election by saying, "If Democrats win control of Congress there will be violence." He probably referred to those anti-Obama forces who support him and will be toppled from their questionable perch to this end. This master manipulator invoked fear in the minds of these pastoral leaders creating a religious, political and ethical dilemma for them and their followers tethered to a man with such terribly negatively impeccable credentials, given instilling fear is one of the malevolent tools Donald Trump loves to use.

Today, the nation currently has 50 governors, one for each state. All of a sudden one African-American, Andrew Gillum, the Democratic contender emerged victorious in the Florida primary. He was instantly attacked by both Mr. Trump and the Republican standard bearer for governor, Ron DeSantis. The sad thing is, practically before the final voter count was in, Mr. Trump's attack on Gillum emboldened Mr. DeSantis who referred to Mr. Gillum as "articulate." White men are never addressed as "articulate." More significant, he also used the term "monkey" in referring to the results of a potential vote for Mr. Gillum.

For years, decades and more, ill-intentioned individuals have used the term "monkey" to refer to African-Americans. Monkeys have hair on their chests and while a few African-Americans do have hair on their chests, most whites do have this monkey distinguishing physical characteristic. Early in his first tenure, the *New York Post* published a political cartoon showing two New York policemen "shooting Mr. Obama" characterized as a monkey or ape. Even more recent, Roseann Barr lost her TV show by referring to Valerie Jarrett, an Obama aide, as a "monkey." The disturbing reality, like the dog running after its master, this Trump clone DeSantis seemed well-trained in "lowness." However, and significantly, as Michelle Obama laid it down, "When they go low, we go high." Gillum did just that and stuck to the issues of Health Care, Joblessness, infrastructure repairs, climate change, clean air, Women's Rights', etc. Amidst all this and unquestionably, Barack Obama can be considered an aristocrat, political, ethical and intellectual, because of his elegance of mind and nobility of spirit, as well as being "frighteningly prepared" to execute his extraordinary work ethic as his oath of office dictates. This is a somewhat similar "presidential timber" that characterized Senator John McCain. Donald Trump, on the other hand, is a low class, billionaire with white supremacist tendencies and, as he struggles to "hold back the dawn," his world is coming apart based on the possibility of criminality linking him and his associates. That is why he will forever be a subject of historical discussion but as villain not hero.

Sadly, African-Americans who have struggled across this nation for equality in human and civil rights; consistently profiled "while Black;" been victimized through poor education, joblessness, lack of quality health care and efforts of consistent political

WHEN IS A "GANGSTER GOVERNMENT"? A "GANGSTER GOVERNMENT?"

disfranchisement; and as Ayana Pressly a new personality on the scene who spoke against the Trump "firehose of insult and assault" we must insist all persons "fight, organize and mobilize." All this, despite being misrepresented by a few Blacks who "see the world differently" and support Donald Trump unquestionably. The question then becomes, "Will these thinking Black-Americans rush to vote, 96 percent of them, for a man described as a crook, bigot and racist?" Such is hardly the case for as John Anthony West indicated, "the snowball goes down the hill only until its momentum is expended."

When is a "Gangster Government" a Gangster Government" Photo? Another view of the Capitol Building with stairs and columns, as the flag flies majestically for all to see.

"What we see here is corruption without consequences."

FREDERICK MONDERSON

When is a "Gangster Government" a "Gangster Government" Photo? "In the beginning ...."

"It is a sad day that not one Republican has crossed over. We're so divided. Not at a great place in America. Too many people hate other people." **John Kasich**.

12. MCCAIN, OBAMA AND TRUMP BY DR. FRED MONDERSON

John McCain has gone on to American glory; Barack Obama, having asked, "What if we were wrong?" has appeared on the world stage assuring many "Things will be alright;" yet still, he laughs his head off especially since being voted the "greatest American President in modern times," and this is especially worthwhile, particularly coming in ahead of Ronald Reagan. On the other hand, Donald Trump in

WHEN IS A "GANGSTER GOVERNMENT"? A "GANGSTER GOVERNMENT?"

employing "fear" presides over "Crazy town." Such is a stunning conclusion stemming from recent developments regarding the former and literary revelations of the latter in a number of penetrating titles as: *The Truth About Donald Trump* – Michael Di Antonio; Michael Wolff's *Fear and Fury*; *House of Trump, House of Putin* - Craig Unger; Amoroso's *Unhinged*; and now *Fear* by Bob Woodward and added to this "body of Work" the anonymously written *New York Times* Op-Ed helps to cumulatively paint a tremendously disturbing and dangerous state of American Presidential politics particularly in its current administration. This is certainly a far-cry from the McCain thoughts and aspirations as expressed at his funeral and the relatively stable yet progressive Administration of the former President. After all, Barack Obama ended his tenure unscathed and triumphantly polled as "The Greatest American President in modern times." He polled ahead of Ronald Reagan, George Bush and Bill Clinton. Given today's "Crazy town," the Obama administration can be considered as belonging to the "Good Old Days."

Now, the 63-million people who voted for Donald Trump should realize he has "potty mouth" and all "foot and mouth diseases" that came with the malady. Giving such persons' credit, one has to assume, even believe, they expected Mr. Trump would rise to the practical, philosophical, ethical and moral high standards presiding over "Mount Olympus" requires. Sadly, this base continues to wallow aimlessly in non-belief even as expose' after expose' paint Mr.

FREDERICK MONDERSON

Trump as an irresponsible leader with myriads of faults and problems.

For a man who has spent a lifetime parlaying a million-dollar loan from his father into purported billions particularly in real estate, employing all forms of chicanery, ruthless business practices, declaring numerous bankruptcies, securing five military deferrals, created a sham university, slammed by the Feds for housing discrimination and undeniable manifested racist exhortations, viz., "The Central Park Five," unquestionably buttressed by an egotistical mentality that held, "Only I can do it," seems to signal something's wrong with this person. Unfortunately, only Republicans see Mr. Trump as invincible; yet, they go to great lengths to shield and protect him. If this was so, Why? As such, despite mountains of evidence painting the real picture of the man, his loyal supporters encourage and enable Donald Trump to descend to unimaginable depths of incivility, untruthfulness and amorality. They argue instead, the economy's booming, he appoints judges, the nation got a big tax cut, etc.

Jumping ahead, but in his response to *The New York Times* Op-Ed in his usual diatribe, Mr. Trump insisted: "Nobody has done what I have done." He was certainly right; but, in more ways than one, especially his 14,440 lies.

First, he began reading off accomplishments such as nearly 4 percent growth in the economy; the

WHEN IS A "GANGSTER GOVERNMENT"?
A "GANGSTER GOVERNMENT?"

unemployment rate is down to 4 percent; appointment of federal judges and two Supreme Court appointments; not to discount rejection of NAFTA, PTP, the Paris Climate Agreement, the Iran Deal, and more. A special effort was made to rescind many of Obama's hard won legislative and other negotiated accomplishments. He did emphasize the low unemployment numbers among African-Americans as he spoke to more than three dozen Sheriffs of which only one was African-American. Sure, Blacks are visibly seen in jobs, but mostly with brooms and mops, as guards and as waiters.

Nonetheless and second, "Nobody has certainly done what Mr. Trump has done" as evidenced in the following litany:

He spoke more than 15,000 lies and misstatements in 18 months and now in three years, these are approaching 15,000; his national poll numbers hover around 36-42 percent and his un-favorability is high in many respects; there are four recent books that revealed the inner working of the Trump White House and paint a sordid picture of Mr. Trump's mentality. Then there are the problematic challenges of Michael Cohen, Paul Manafort, Dekker and David Wexelberg. Let's not forget Karen McDougal as well as Stormy Daniels and her attorney who were paid off. Now Cohen wants his money back. There has been an extraordinary turnover of personnel in 36 months, more so than any administration ever. After revoking Mr. Brennan's Security Clearance, Admiral

FREDERICK MONDERSON

McGreevy said to the President, "Revoke my Clearance so I can stand beside Brennan." Then Mr. Trump published a list of 10 names, a sort of "enemies list" of persons he is considering revoking their Security Clearance. Responding in solidarity, 15 intelligence personnel signed their names to a letter supporting Mr. Brennan's stance. Then another 60 did the same while a further 175 expressed the same sentiments. The Trump White House is therefore under siege from events he essentially manufactured. Sadly, in contrast with Mr. Trump's, the Obama Administration's turnover of personnel has been, mini, miniscule in comparison.

Thus, contrasting John McCain's "Duty, Honor, Country" service mantra and in comparison, John Dean referencing Donald Trump's leadership, insisted he has "no knowledge, experience, background and now he is denigrating the office." To wit, and amplifying his woes, the following have been applied among other things in describing Mr. Trump's demeanor and personality. He is said to be paranoid, unstable, managed, consumed, does not forgive, does not forget, uses government agencies to punish opponents, off the rails, rants, very impulsive, deranged, insanity, deep, extreme narcissism, megalomaniac, can't handle the truth, crook, bigot and racist. He is sympathetic to Neo-Nazis, White Supremacists, Alt-Rights and other fringe "nuts." In sum, these depictions and associations certainly question the President's "fitness for office."

WHEN IS A "GANGSTER GOVERNMENT"?
A "GANGSTER GOVERNMENT?"

In comparing the three men, McCain, Obama and Trump, the moral compasses of the first two were steady and functional while Mr. Trump's has gone in the opposite direction. Whereas Mr. McCain fought to encourage and cultivate the better side of America, seeking higher priorities and aspirations while at times working across the aisle in compromise; Mr. Obama has been described as possessing elegance of mind and nobility of spirit with a terrific work ethic. In a stark contrast, Donald Trump, who publicly demeaned women, Mexicans, the disabled, not to forget the "Birther Charade," denigrated and defamed 16 women who accused him of sexual misconduct, disrespected the wife of the soldier, Johnson, killed in Niger, maligned Maxine Walters, Nancy Pelosi, criticized the Judge of Mexican heritage presiding over a case relating to his interests, though born American, insulted NFL players, a great many of whom are Black, as they protested against Police brutality by "taking a knee" during playing of the anthem. Let us not forget, during the Vietnam Conflict, the Supreme Court ruled it was constitutionally protected to "Burn the American flag." Mr. Trump even abused and labeled CBS, CNN, ABC, NBC, as "fake news" while extolling Fox News many consider a joke, manned by crackpots. In his take, David Fromm labeled the White House "a snake pit" and it is simply because "the President raises snakes."

"What is our obligation to those who follow us?"
Denny Heck

FREDERICK MONDERSON

When is a "Gangster Government" a "Gangster Government Photo? What a wonderful miniature replica of five of Washington's most memorable structures – The Capital Building in the forefront, Washington Monument (behind), and the Lincoln Memorial (further on), with the Thomas Jefferson Memorial (left) and the White House (right). Don't miss the Great Eagle (front) and people "Caucusing" (right).

"The call was inappropriate. People do not do it all the time as Mulvaney has asserted. To say nothing happened is a travesty." **John Kasich**.

13. ALL THE PRESIDENT'S DOMINOES BY DR. FRED MONDERSON

Never in the history of American politics has the rain thundered on such sunny days as we now see during the Trump Administration. Events surrounding this

WHEN IS A "GANGSTER GOVERNMENT"?
A "GANGSTER GOVERNMENT?"

development are akin to the classical scholar Diogenes' statement as he was observed toting a lit lantern at noontime. When asked why, he responded, "I'm looking for an honest man!" He meant, there was not sufficient light at high-noon with the sun in its magnificent brilliance to locate an honest person and hopefully the lit lantern may possibly aid the cause. A number of people have defended President Trump on Television and across the media spectrum. However, many in the viewing audience often wonder, "Is this person who is making the statement hearing what he or she is saying?" One such person is Jason Miller, a former Donald Trump campaign and transition team aide who often appeared on CNN to provide analysis on issues of the day connected to the President. Like so many others of similar disposition, Mr. Miller often either "cuts the feet to fit the shoes" or "cuts the slipper to fit the foot." Whatever, he has never acceded to wrongdoing on the part of Mr. Trump, whether the evidence was overwhelming or not. Like so many others, he simply chose to rationally explain away Mr. Trump's position even if it seemed to make sense only to him.

Reflecting on the age we have passed and the age we have now entered, a number of individuals have stood up to educate the public but it turns out many of these people have sometimes camouflaged skeletons of themselves and the person they defend. In another context but still relevant, Bill Cosby is one such individual who, from his position of prominence commented on behaviors of Blackmen in social conditions across the nation. A sitting judge ruled

FREDERICK MONDERSON

Cosby is a public figure and his "closet" must be opened to public scrutiny. The rest is history.

In the case of Mr. Miller, a TV analyst, on the public airwaves, the New York *Daily News* of September 24, 2018, p. 6, quotes him as saying on Twitter: "I have decided to step away from my role as a political commentator at CNN to focus on clearing my name and fighting the false and defamatory accusations being made against me. To be clear, none of this is in anyway true." This is somewhat reminiscence of what O.J. Simpson said regarding finding Nicole Simpson's killer and more especially what the young prisoner in the movie **Shawshank Redemption** said and did in which the elders fell in love with him immediately. However, when he tried to enquire what some of his fellows "were in for" the principal protagonist responded, to a hearty laugh by all, "Don't you know everyone in here is innocent." Nevertheless, whatever is being said, Mr. Miller did not "fall on his sword," "his sword fell on him." A thousand men in similar manner and situations, more likely responds in similar fashion, but once the focus has been removed from them, they fade from memory and perhaps only one person is "cleared." Nonetheless, Mr. Miller is not the first domino to fall and will certainly not be the last in the evolving Trump circus.

In fact, the first domino to fall was General Michael Flynn, Chief National Security Adviser to President Trump and a prominent figure in his campaign. Brother Walter Brown always advised, "Don't get on

WHEN IS A "GANGSTER GOVERNMENT"?
A "GANGSTER GOVERNMENT?"

the road" and unfortunately General Flynn who often echoed "Lock her up," was "on the road" and "in bed with Russians" and others without registering as a foreign agent. Perhaps inebriated by being in the drumbeat of the Trump campaign circus, Mr. Flynn made a false statement to the FBI and ended up being fired by the President. News reports seem to indicate his son was also implicated in his father's dealings and when Robert Muller leaned on him, to save his son, the Flynn domino fell.

A number of high-level Trump administration officials took advantage of their good graces with the President and misused that relationship. These dominoes fell with the weight of their own doing and as such were fired for betraying the public trust.

No less significant, even as the "party revelers" were in full enjoyment mode, the dominoes Papadopoulos, Cohen and Manafort fell, but the extent of their impact remained obscured at the time. Meanwhile, legal minds on both sides jockeyed and "talking heads" offered their take, and Muller, for his part, kept walking silently while carrying his big stick. As he began parsing the cases against various actors, a number of Trump loyalist were retired from the field as their dominoes fell.

In the first inning, George Paralogous struck out and sought a deal with Mr. Muller. Even more significant, Michael Cohen, who for the longest, has held, "I will do everything in my legal skills to protect Mr. Trump," his turn was next. The totality of such boastful machinations earned Mr. Cohen the title, "Mr. Trump's fixer." But, with Special Counsel possessing the mother lode of Mr. Cohen's body of work in the form of documents, tapes, computers, phones and more in raiding his home, office and hotel room, Mr. Cohen represented a cork pulled by a big fish swimming away with the bait and hook in its mouth. So, "the fixer" pleaded guilty to two counts of election law violations and simultaneously implicated his client in breaking the law. Significantly, one piece of data, a recorded conversation between Mr. Trump and Mr. Cohen not only admitted to the realty of Mr. Trump's knowledge and participation in the Stormy Daniels' situation but equally implicated two other "big fish" operating in the Trump orbit. These, Decker and Weisenbaum were ultimately granted immunity for their testimony and supplying documents that may potentially and seriously impact and aid the investigation into Mr. Trump's conduct before and after becoming President.

As all this transpired, Paul Manafort served as President Trump's campaign manager during the most critical period of his rise to greatness. Thus, he was privy to key developments relating to the campaign. Like the strongman Mr. Manafort was projected to be, he stood defiantly in court while showing no remorse and was convicted on 8 counts. President Trump applauded this "last man standing." In this, some have argued Mr. Trump "dangled a pardon" for Mr. Manafort's "steadfast loyalty." Meanwhile, Mr. Muller keenly eyed these

WHEN IS A "GANGSTER GOVERNMENT"? A "GANGSTER GOVERNMENT?"

developments as potential "witness tampering and obstruction of justice." However, as reality sank in and a second trial loomed large, Mr. Manafort rather than stand, sat, and his domino fell. He agreed to cooperate with the Muller investigation and we can only guess as to what he knows and is willing to divulge. And so, what appears to be the entire pack of Mr. Trump's dominoes have either fallen or will fall imminently.

In all this, if it was possible to feel the seat of Mr. Trump's pants it should or would be wet despite his bravado and that of Rudy Giuliani and all his apologists, Mr. Trump is in trouble.

"The moment of gravity is so because Republicans did not choose to see the evidence as it truly is. Despite the egregious nature of his offense, Republicans fall in line without any evidence of his innocence. We're in a dangerous place. He has been lying and has not defended the Constitution." Carl Bernstein.

"I don't want to be involved in a 'drug deal' Sondland and Mulvaney are cooking up. Rudy is a 'hand grenade' that will blow up everyone." **John Bolton**

FREDERICK MONDERSON

"What has been astounding to me. I did see a partisan divide." **John Kasich**.

14. "WHO LOST AMERICA?"
Republicans?
By
Dr. Fred Monderson

"While the Constitution burns, Republican fiddle!"

On the train some weeks ago, a gentleman railed loudly, "America is going down!" Recently, the internet reported a Republican group, in their fund-raising outreach labeled Representative Alexandria Ocasio Cortez "a terrorist." She herself decried Republicans "weaponizing" Rep. Omar's recent comments. "AOC" herself vehemently responded; however, such statements equally exposes her to harmful behavior posing a threat to her own life. Interesting, on **CNN's AC-360** the **Gold Star Father** member, a now recognized national figure, Mr. Khan reminded, "threatening a Congress person is a federal crime, punishable by imprisonment and a fine." Given the caustic and disturbingly enabling language President Donald Trump uses, one wonders if such actions are not foreshadowing and preaching to even paving the way for "The fall of America."

In his 2005 **Inaugural Address**, President George Bush II, decried racism in the American

WHEN IS A "GANGSTER GOVERNMENT"?
A "GANGSTER GOVERNMENT?"

cultural and social systems, even its body-politic. Then in 2008, Barack Hussein Obama was elected as the first African-American President, enabling former Newark, New Jersey, Mayor and now Senator Cory Booker to respond, "We have entered a Post-racial America." Of course, that success was paid for through nearly 400 years of vicious American slavery forcefully exacting associated free labor, significantly important developmental foundations in building this nation. In response, and now evident, not the "better angels" in America but we see the "worst devils" who tried to "lynch" President Barack Obama.

First, Michel Bachmann claimed, "God told me to run" but unfortunately did not give her the wherewithal to win; yet, she accused President Obama of "running a gangster government" in Washington, D.C. Despite more than two dozen turnovers for the Trump Administrations, particularly for questionable, conflicting behaviors, as well as perceived conflicts of interest, the likes of Ms. Bachmann do not possess the testicular fortitude to describe Mr. Trump's as leading a "gangster government" in Washington, D.C. During Michael Cohen's testimony to the House of Representative's Oversight Committee, no Republican member, particularly Jim Jordan asked a question seeking the truth regarding Mr. Trump's actions. All, particularly the Republican "bull dog Jordan," sought to negate Cohen! Falsely claiming themselves defenders of America, not a peep was heard when Mr. Trump himself falsely proclaimed, "No Collusion, No

FREDERICK MONDERSON

Obstruction" in response to Attorney General William Barr's false summary of the Mueller Report. Now, after the famous "Press Conference" before release of the Muller Report, one commentator remarked, "Bill Barr's credibility is now in the gutter."

Strange, over the years, encouraging "The rise of Birtherism," Mr. Trump Presidential campaign, and the years of his Presidency, himself and his defenders, enablers from Conway to Sanders; bad as they are, there a need to include Fox News especially after the airing of the Video-collage aired on **CNN's Tonight with Don Lemon** and astonishingly before final revelation every thought, the subject of the "purportedly truthful" comments, viz., lying, etc., though they appeared applicable to President Trump, President Obama was actually the malicious target. Purportedly in 2 terms Barack Obama told "18 lies." Donald Trump, on the other hand, in a space of 3 years told approximately 15,000 lies or false statements and not a peep is heard by Republicans. Today, after completion of two terms of service President Obama's respect and admiration has soared while Mr. Trump's wallows in that disgusting "Hole" he coined. Neither Mr. Trump nor his defenders see nor smell the rank odiousness of Mr. Trump's behavior. During his tenure, so far, moral and ethical standards associated with the Office of the Presidency have plummeted. The man has certainly sullen the near mythical stature of the Office of the Presidency, yet Republicans are silent. That is to say, such silence begs the question, "If there is one, two

WHEN IS A "GANGSTER GOVERNMENT"?
A "GANGSTER GOVERNMENT?"

or three flies in the milk," does one have to wait until there's two dozen flies in the milk to publicly affirm, "There are flies in the milk." Perhaps only Rep Amash, understands the Muller Report, and who has now rejected the Republican Party himself becoming an Independent, has really voiced dissent.

Astonishingly, not a Republican has voiced an opinion consistent with the findings of former Speaker Boehner, himself a hypocrite, who remarked, the "Republicans are taking a nap" now that its "Trump's party." In response to this morass, even the practicing Christian evangelicals have not uttered a word against the unethical behavior, morally reprehensible conduct, in which 17 women accused Trump of sexual misconduct and not a word has been uttered in moral indignation. He denies it all and "the base is satisfied" with his answer! Let's remember, "The Cretan is a liar!"

However, the reality is, instead of focusing on the "beam" of Trump, they focus on the "mole" of Obama. For example, in the chamber of the august House of Representatives, during a State of the Union Address, Joe Wilson called President Obama a "liar." The next day he received more than one million dollars in donations. In shameful Mea-culpa Wilson asked to meet Mr. Obama to apologize, to which the President responded, "Put it in the mail." If one lie is worth a million dollars, for 15,000 lies Trump must have racked up a billion dollars! Along the way, in interacting with President Obama, not only did "Joe the Plumber," accuse Mr. Obama of introducing

FREDERICK MONDERSON

"socialism," while "Lipstick on a pig" Sarah Palin accused Mr. Obama of "Palling around with terrorists;" then South Carolina Senator Jim DeMint, proclaimed "If we stop Obama on Obamacare, it will be his Waterloo" to which Billy Krystal encouraged, "Go for the jugular." To crown it all, Ted Nugent, addressed President Obama as "The Nigger in the White House." There caustic irony manifested; where, at a Trump White House Gala, Nugent and Sarah Palin posed for the camera under George Washington's portrait. "Birds…." Nonetheless, a good question is, "Where are some of these folks, false patriots, today," as Donald Trump tramples upon and trashes the Constitution. Trump even had the gall to say "The Constitution is wrong!" If so, the Republicans and Mr. Trump are all illegal. The above false or "sunshine patriots" are probably in some "Old folks' home," while Obama's ratings are in the sky! That is, while Obama may be off somewhere drinking virgin Pina Coladas, Trump is wondering whether the men in white jackets or the FBI will be waiting for him after noon on January 20, 2021.

The record is replete with examples; where despite the "Birth of the Tea Party," somewhat reminiscence of the "Birth of the KKK" as a Reconstruction backlash; incessant militia mobilization while threateningly showcasing their "readiness" against Mr. Obama. Yet standing down on Trump; Mitch McConnell publicly pronounced, "I intend to make Barack Obama a one-term President" and blocking Merrick Garland's selection; yet, he stands ready to "appoint" the next Supreme Court Justice himself!

WHEN IS A "GANGSTER GOVERNMENT"?
A "GANGSTER GOVERNMENT?"

One must again ask, where are the pseudo or "Sunshine Patriots" today as Rep. Clyburn calls them, as the nation swelters under moral, racial and ethical threats? Significantly, investigative revelations in 2013 revealed a potentially shrouded 2008 gathering, but a more pronounced 2012 re-gathering of high-ranking Republican operatives featuring Ed Meese and others who conspired to undermine the administration and legitimate legislative agenda of Mr. Obama. They, however, failed to derail his re-election as they did his election! *The New York Times* did the revealing report in 2013 and the graphic labeled Mitch McConnel's involvement, calling him "a plotter." Yet, despite the troublesome political thunderstorm, with Republicans in full-overdrive to block every legislative effort of the President earning them the "Party of No" label, Mr. Obama's administration bailed out Wall Street; made loans to banks; poured money into the auto industry; instituted economic and financial legislative reform; halted the hemorrhaging housing industry; paid Black farmers; passed the Lilly Ledbetter equal pay for equal work legislation; gave a boost to community colleges; and pursued clean air legislation, renewable energy, while expressing far-reaching concerns about climate change; and even encouraging mothers to return to college. Again, Mr. Obama rescued the American economy, improved the American persona and image abroad, all while under serious Republican assault as they wallowed in profound disrespect and racial animus simply because he is a Black-American. The reality is, Mr. Obama rescued his beloved America, and so as Maya Angela wrote, "Still I rise," he continues to be a positive force in America, perhaps the last hope. Astonishingly, as Obama rises, Trump plummets and though Republicans refuse to accept such, they're tied at Trump's ankle with lead weights. Objective observers believe "There should be an Obama Day, August 4th, his birthday." Such a recognition would remind the nation the meaning of dignity and truthfulness in and respect for the Office, that is seriously lacking in the Age of Trump.

Lo and behold, we stumbled into the 2016 Presidential election in which Donald John Trump, was elected to lead the nation as Number 45. From his inception, his behavior was rancid, to say the least. Yet, supporters even opponents bellowed, "The President is new, he's a businessman, not a politician. So, give him time." That was soon after he told his first lie! Now he has nearly 15,000 and expeditiously manufacturing more. However, very early Michael Bloomberg made all aware, "I know a con when I see one." Nevertheless, as his outrageous behavior unfolded in full gear, in characterizing the new reality, in inviting the winning NBA championship, amidst the Kaepernick Protest, Donald Trump felt slighted and so lashed out. He spoke disparagingly about LeBron James. Lebron responded after President Trump's tweet, "You bum, visiting the White House was fun before you got there!"

This and more essentially began the unhinging of Donald Trump. Sure, he demolished more than a

WHEN IS A "GANGSTER GOVERNMENT"?
A "GANGSTER GOVERNMENT?"

dozen Republican competitors to win his party's nomination and ultimately became President despite not being the favorite to win. However, contrary to theories the high office transforms the individual into, at least, an ethically, morally superior person whose thoughts, actions and writings emanate from behind the revered Oval Office desk. Such was lost in Donald Trump! First and foremost, President Trump, fresh from his disgusting "Birther" falsity, began systematically reversing or overturning practically every important Obama legislative and diplomatic accomplishment he could get his hands on. Many saw this and the intense manner in which it was pursued as racial and disrespectful animus in action. Along the road, it became evident, not only did Mr. Trump behave as a hyper-pathological liar committing some 15,000 lies or misstatements, he encouraged and enabled untold numbers of Americans to behave in a threatening manner contrary to the world's view of a compassionate American persona and behavior.

The so-called "Base" Mr. Trump panders to, falling hook, line and sinker for the roll-backs he has instituted, the conservative judges he has appointed, and the fact he has uttered unquestioned promises from the time of his campaign through the nearly three years of his tenure remain silent on his behavior, proving they are not really true patriots. This conundrum is akin to two significant contradictions historians have had to grapple with.

FREDERICK MONDERSON

We remain mindful in the movie **Olympus has Fallen**, one of the anti-heroes confessed, "I lost my way." In his stern rebuke to the Republicans who called for Representative Adam Schiff's resignation, his scathing and enumerated response siting the morally threatening clouds centered around Trump's behaviors and thus, those making pronouncements should, equally ask the question, "Have we lost our way?"

There is a concept called conscionable leadership, a behavior Mr. Trump seems sorely lacking. However, even though the American system separates church from state, religious elements have nonetheless played an important role in the political process. Case in point, Evangelicals, particularly those who profess to be Republicans, in fact, whatever their political persuasion, these individuals have not taken a moral stance against the many actions the President has displayed because, as the rationale holds, he appoints conservative judges and the Stock market is booming while unemployment numbers are down. Vice-President Mike Pence flaunts his Christian beliefs but he stands firmly behind, not objecting to Donald Trump's behavior, name calling, incitement, contradiction to known facts; in fact, offering alternative facts, lies, etc. We know 4 and 4 equals 8. What then is the "alternative fact" of 4 plus 4?" At such a price, many Bible believing Christian Evangelicals further give President Trump "a Mulligan" despite his questionable moral behaviors, among which can be enumerated his "Hollywood Access" behavior and payment to "Porn and Playboy

WHEN IS A "GANGSTER GOVERNMENT"?
A "GANGSTER GOVERNMENT?"

stars." But, most important, his enabling, influencing, even inciting racial animosity directed against a broad swath of minority elements is unbecoming of the President of the United States. As such, and for long, many have assessed the man and expressed, "Donald Trump is unfit to be President!"

Interestingly enough, an underlying aspiration of Evangelicals, with the Vice-President's Holy Bible faith as a guide, is the approach to enter and dwell within the "Pearly Gates" for eternity. The principal gate-keeper, St Peter generally conducts inquiries of potential entrants. One has to wonder what will be the answer to, "Why were you generally silent on the actions of Donald Trump?" "How many Mulligans have you given him?" "Why, after the first One?" "Why was there no Pushback?" "Why was he not rebuked?" Can we envision V.P. Pence, "Up there," being stumped by these questions!

Without question, Mr. Trump attacked long-standing and viable American institutions, and disparaged the nation's principal allies, yet Republicans are silent. His "love affair" with Kim Jung Un and that terrific cartoon illustration of him riding horseback and embracing the shirtless Vladimir Putin, says much, regardless. Praise for foreign dictators but condemning American citizens, patriots, raises serious questions about the occupant of the White House. The best examples are his dismissing the intelligence officers' evidence but believing Putin's and other dictators' words. In such behaviors, calling the press, "Enemies of the people," and even referring to democratic opponents as enemies, certainly messages, "We have lost our way." Thus, in actuality such a pronouncement refers to Republicans who refuses to acknowledge, among the raging storms, "The ship of state is Sinking!" Therefore, patriotic action is needed to correct the impending and unfolding challenge to the perception of and respect for the nation's institutions and time-tested traditions. As such, true Americans must reinforce the rule of law and restore integrity to the Presidency.

"Clearly President Trump is troubled. He is not used to be told what to do. Someone called and put a mark on his name. We do not tolerate this type of behavior in this country." John Dean.

When is a "Gangster Government" a "Gangster Government" Photo? It is what we are about!

WHEN IS A "GANGSTER GOVERNMENT"? A "GANGSTER GOVERNMENT?"

"Rudy's role is playing out in public as he is playing into Russia's hands repeating their false narrative of hacking the American 2016 election so as to deflect from their involvement as the American Intelligence Community has concluded."

15. THE CHOICE BY DR. FRED MONDERSON

The old adage about "An educated consumer," most appropriately also applies to an "educated voter." A current dissatisfied view correctly expressed on television is that "Democrats take the Black vote for granted." Ironically, this view may be both correct and incorrect. It is mostly incorrect, however, and "educated voters" more fully understand the dynamics at play in the political process of what can be achieved within and between political parties. Still, before we examine events in the history of the vote, let us explain what is first the "Choice for Black voters." We either:

1.   Vote Democrat

2.   Vote Republican

3.   Don't Vote

4.   Don't count or matter

FREDERICK MONDERSON

In order to exist, all organism must struggle! America is a nation of laws and no matter how some persons seem to bend the law, stretch the law, even break the law, the law is flexible and ultimately springs back to its unbiased legality. This is underscored in Dr. Martin Luther King's exhortation: "The Arc of the Moral Universe is long but it bends towards justice."

The **Congressional Black Caucus** is an entity operating at the federal level of government in Washington, D.C. The effectiveness of such a body has encouraged state law makers to form similar groups, even forming coalitions to increase and strengthen the effectiveness of their representation. One such group is the **Black and Puerto Rican Caucus** functioning in the New York State Assembly. Such groupings also form on the city and county levels, again establishing coalitions to leverage political strength.

The late Congressman Major Owens, himself a member of the federal **Congressional Black Caucus**, at a past forum organized in Brooklyn, New York, posed and answered his own question, "Why are we, as members of the Congressional Black Caucus, in Congress?" To this he replied, "It is not so much the legislation that we propose or author, but the legislation we block because so much frivolous legislation is proposed on the floor of the House and Senate. It is only through the coalitions we form with liberals, progressives and like-minded persons that

WHEN IS A "GANGSTER GOVERNMENT"? A "GANGSTER GOVERNMENT?"

are able to effectively block such proposals particularly aimed at Blacks, Browns and the poor.

Now, this brings us to the Vote and Why we vote Democrat. But first.

There are 435 Congressional Districts across the country each with a representative seated in the House. The 50 states each elects 2 Senators for a total of 100. The **House of Representatives** is the principal legislation and finance-driven body that originates most legislation, particularly "money bills." The **House** can also bring Impeachment charges against the President but he must be tried in the **Senate** which determines guilt or innocence. Once **Impeached** in the **House** he is then tried in the **Senate**, the Chief Justice of the Supreme Court presides at this stage. In the House of Representatives large states have greater representation based on population size more so than small states. In ratifying the **Constitution of 1787**, the "**Connecticut Compromise**" addressed this disparity of large against small states. So, a "Two House Chamber" was formed, giving each state equal representation in the Senate with two votes or Senators. This brings up the issue of "**D.C. Statehood**" which would essentially create "2 Black Senators" given the predominant and permanent Black population of the District of Columbia.

FREDERICK MONDERSON

Still, before we answer the question as to why we vote Democrat, we must also have some understanding of the struggle to achieve the vote, before and after the Civil War from 1860 to 1865. But first, before and after "Declaration" and "War for Independence" (1776-1783) the vote belonged to the wealthy, essentially land owners or merchants. A few Blacks enjoyed this privilege, even owning slaves themselves. The Civil War Amendments, the 13th abolished slavery; the 14th gave citizenship to persons born in the United States regardless of prior status or skin color; the 15th Amendment bestowed the right to vote on all able-bodied men over the age of 21. This for the most part, covered the African Freedman, emancipated in the 13th Amendment. That being so, with passage of the 15th Amendment nearly two million Blacks registered and were eligible to vote, particularly in the Southern States. They elected state and federal representatives to both the House and Senate. This was part of the Reconstruction movement which lasted, essentially from 1865 to 1877.

WHEN IS A "GANGSTER GOVERNMENT"?
A "GANGSTER GOVERNMENT?"

When is a "Gangster Government" a "Gangster Government" Photo? View of the front entrance to the Capitol Building from the "Senate side."

In the election of 1876, the "Southern Candidate," Rutherford B. Hayes succeeded Ulysses S. Grant to the Presidency in what many termed a "Union betrayal." This often-criticized development opened the floodwaters of Southern backlash that enabled the reemergence of "Southern supremacy" that equally gave rise to terrorist groups and activities that ultimately changed the new status of the Freedman. The Ku Klux Klan was formed by General Forester and the Knights of the White Camellia was instituted as one of several terrorists, racist, organs to oppress Blacks as part of a disfranchisement and subjugation movement. The harsh reactionary climate that developed sought to short-change the newly freed men economically with property ownership, as well as jobs and wages that emboldened the sharecropping fiasco, creating economic peonage. This new reality meant, anytime a Black was observed and not "toeing the line" any action was possible even by the "lowest white man." Throughout, the federal government ignored the ongoing terrorism meted out to its Black citizens. So much so, nearly 4000 lynchings occurred in the South from approximately 1870 to 1950. This has been documented!

Meanwhile, a more sinister and practical societal move was afoot to reinstitute "Southern Supremacy" and regain the political and economic clout the South had enjoyed before the Civil War which they lost. In the process, a systematic disfranchisement movement reduced Black voting strength from something like three million to less than ten thousand in a matter of decades. A good reason for this is because Blacks had, in appreciation of "Lincoln freeing the slaves," voted "the Party of Lincoln" spearheaded by its "Radical Republicans." As a good example, in

WHEN IS A "GANGSTER GOVERNMENT"?
A "GANGSTER GOVERNMENT?"

discussing "constitutional disfranchisement of the Negroes," Joanne Grant in *Black Protest* (New York: Fawcett Books, 1968: 111) wrote: "In Louisiana in 1896 there were 164,088 whites registered and 130,344 Negroes. In 1900, the first registration year after a new constitution had been adopted, there were 125,437 white and 5,340 Negroes registered. By 1904 Negro registration had declined to 1,718, and white registration was 106,360. This represented a 96 percent decrease in Negro registration, and a four percent decrease in white."

"In Alabama, Mississippi and South Carolina disfranchisement began earlier. In 1883 in Alabama there were only 3,742 registered Negroes out of the 140,000 formerly registered. In South Carolina Negro registration decreased from 92,081 in 1876 to 2,823 in 1898. In Mississippi the decrease was from 52,705 in 1876 to 3,573 in 1898. Systematic exclusion continued up to through the present time [1968]. Between 1920 and 1930 about 10,000 Negroes voted in Georgia out of a potential Negro electorate of 369,511, and in Virginia the Negro vote at any time in that decade was 12,000 to 18,000 out of a voting-age-or-over and literate Negro population of 248,347."

All of a sudden, in this unfolding injustice, voter registration officials insisted Blacks take "literacy tests," show proof of payment of property taxes, pay poll taxes, and in the post-Civil War backlash seeking "Southern Supremacy" the dreaded "Grandfather Clause" was invoked insisting only persons whose grandfather had voted previously could vote. This essentially covered almost 99 percent of Black voters. In addition, on the labor front, an unequal system called "share-cropping" became the principal form of wage earning for Blacks but this amounted to "economic peonage" for it trapped Blacks into working unending on white owned, but leased farms, and "never coming out ahead." Though Blacks had technical skills from slavery days, they were paid pittances as employers robbed them blind. Meanwhile terrorism became the order of the day while practices of "Jim Crow" segregation became enshrined into law and practice aided by the legally culminating *Plessy V. Ferguson* Supreme Court ruling of 1896. These two, "Jim Crow" and the Supreme Court ruling on *Plessy* were both significant, influenced by a prior ruling in the *Dred Scott Decision of 1857* in which Scott sued for his freedom after being taken to a "Free State" then returned to the "Slave State" Missouri. In this historic ruling, the Supreme Court declared, as a slave, like the millions of other Africans then held in perpetual bondage, "Scott was not a citizen and could not bring suit in an American Court." More important and significant, the ruling made it clear "a black man had no rights which a white man was bound to respect!" Here then, despite all that would later transpire, the Black man was stamped with the negatively pernicious visibility that would shape nefarious white views of him allowing all forms of prejudged behaviors, legal and otherwise.

WHEN IS A "GANGSTER GOVERNMENT"? A "GANGSTER GOVERNMENT?"

Fortunately, the "Grandfather Clause" was outlawed by the Supreme Court in 1915, but it took nearly forty years before the court could muster the fairness to outlaw segregation in *Brown V. Board of Education of Topeka, Kansas* in 1954. Ten years earlier, Thurgood Marshall, a young lawyer, had successfully pleaded his case before the Supreme Court in 1944 (*Allwright*) in which the "White Primary" was outlawed. However, after the 1915 outlawing of the "Grandfather Clause" we must recognize a number of legal battles were being waged, some won, some lost. Nevertheless, legal challenges began to gradually chip away at the second-class citizenship of Black-Americans. That is, *de jure* segregation and its nefarious actions supporting white supremacy and white privilege began to lose some of its legal standing but *de facto* segregation and related terrorism against Blacks was hard to kill and in fact such behaviors did kill. From 1870 to 1950, *The New York Times* reported recently, more than 4084 Blacks were murdered or lynched in 9 southern states. To show the mindset continued in the "New South," these are the states that essentially voted against Barack Obama for President in 2008 and 2012. Most, if not all, voted for Donald Trump in 2016. Talk of "birds of a feather" and "Ties that bind."

Recently, a Southern "legal eagle" chronicled the nearly 4000 lynchings from 1870-1950. This showed racist white men intimidated Black American citizens and the federal government essentially remained silent. Throwing light on such developments, the courageous "legal eagle" established a Memorial and

FREDERICK MONDERSON

Museum in Montgomery, Alabama. This new institution commemorates the horror experienced by African-Americans in the "southern backlash" and listed the names of the identified victims. The gentleman also wanted to place a "Tourist marker" on each and every site of the horrifying ordeal, but current property owners raised "Hue and Cry" for such a designation would associate them and their property with the heinous acts of lynching of Blacks by whites.

In the period after securing the vote in 1865 until 1930 Blacks essentially voted Republican. Still, their plight was ignored by the party until the election of 1932 when Franklin Delano Roosevelt promised a "New Deal." Recognizing the significance of such a claim, Blacks then fled the Republican Party, that is, that portion permitted to vote, long before the later Voting Rights Act of 1965, and have voted Democrat ever since. Still, the door was opened so little it was difficult to get a shoe into it. In 1936 and again in 1940 they similarly voted Democrat. Throughout, A. Philip Randolph, a brilliant author and activist, protested treatment of Blacks and denial getting meaningful jobs. This injustice became highlighted as the nation inched towards World War II and Black citizens could not be permitted meaningful jobs in the War industry. In the summer of 1941 Randolph proposed a "March on Washington" to put 100,000 Black men on the streets and Great Mall of Washington, D.C. This move was not just to protest prevailing conditions but to embarrass the American government and show the world, the cousin to the

WHEN IS A "GANGSTER GOVERNMENT"? A "GANGSTER GOVERNMENT?"

scourge of Nazism and white supremacy was alive in America. Recognizing the threat of a significant "March on Washington," would send the wrong message to the world, President Roosevelt issued an Executive Order opening the war industry to Blacks workers, but the struggle was far from over.

This action did not, however, solve the problem that dragged on into the 1950s and 1960s witnessing the Rosa Parks incident on the bus and the resultant Montgomery Bus Boycott; the racist southern backlash that gave birth to and emboldened the Civil Rights Movement; the bombing deaths of 4 little Black girls in a Birmingham Church; the historic "Selma to Montgomery" protest march to the Alabama state capital; within the ensuing creative protests, numbers of Blacks were registered to vote against the machinations of the "Bull Connors," "George Wallaces" and men of similar persuasions. In this movement, Dr. King emerged as an effective Civil Rights leader particularly because he used non-violence as a tool that exposed American racism to the conscience of the world and as a result won concessions against *de jure* and *de facto* discrimination and segregation. Northern or liberal support that challenged the plight of Blacks ultimately led to the death of President John F. Kennedy in 1963; yet, as a show of "Continuity," President Lyndon Johnson, himself a Southerner, a Texan, forged through Congress passage of the *Civil Rights Bill* in 1964. The *Voting Rights Act* was passed the next year in 1965 and Malcolm X was killed that same year. Because "Negroes were fed up and won't take it no more," they kept up their peaceful protests. Still, others such as the Black Panthers insisted Blacks defend themselves in armed efforts. Yet, by 1968 Medgar Evers, Bobby Kennedy and Martin Luther King were also killed for racist reasons. Nevertheless, the civil right struggle remained strong and effective under the leadership of Rev. Joseph Lowery, Andrew Young, Wyatt Tee Walker, Rev. Shuttlesworth, Jesse Jackson, Rev. Abernathy, Fannie Lou Hamer, Amelia Boynton Robinson (1911-2015), and many others including activist soldiers such as Stokely Carmichael, Harry Belafonte and even Sidney Poitier.

The fascinating development is that more and more blacks began registering and voting and more and more Black representatives were being elected to local, state and national positions. Such actions highlighted the need for equality in the society. Still, as the Black voting rolls increased Democrats consistently and effectively courted this enthused and steadily empowered constituency, while Republicans orchestrated a multitude of efforts to nullify the Black vote.

Now we come to the realization, the American political system supports two principal parties, Democrat and Republican. The "educated voter" knows, because elected officials represent constituencies with particular interests, it is sometimes difficult to get things done in the halls of legislatures unless the people take to the streets to force legislative action and this can be in the form of

WHEN IS A "GANGSTER GOVERNMENT"?
A "GANGSTER GOVERNMENT?"

Initiative, Referendum, Recall or forced legislation, particularly at the ballot box, as they sought to address issues of concern. The government, in this case, federal, state and city or local, moves slowly if issues don't really benefit particular constituencies. So, a constant struggle "pushing the envelope" to bring about the necessary changes and social, educational and economic, even political rewards. Significantly, therefore, despite what may be said by the "uneducated voter," there are nearly 60 Black elected Democrats at the Federal level in Washington, D.C. and 2 or possibly 3 elected Black Republicans out of the 435 and the 100. Similar disparities exist between the two parties at state and city or local levels. Nonetheless, and reinforcing this fact, we should always reflect on Major Owens' previously stated view. More important and unmistakable, as stated, while Democrats try to "get out the Black vote," Republicans try to suppress or disfranchise the Black voter.

During the 2008 election in which Barack Obama was the Democratic Party Standard-Bearer, in the presidential election and again in 2012 the Republican problem was acerbated. That problem manifested in an avalanche of racist and disrespectful behaviors against the First African-American President and his Administration. Fact is, all manner of chicanery and misleading propaganda was perpetuated from the Republican playbook to nullify the Black vote. Significantly, as late as this age, during the Obama Administration, Attorney General Eric Holder filed suit against many Republican

FREDERICK MONDERSON

controlled state legislatures who devised strategies to deny the Black vote after the 2010 Census count.

Fact is, if you don't vote you don't count! Therefore, people must understand to make a difference everyone must vote. People vote for themselves, their children and their children's children as well as their communities. Only then will voters be able to leverage their strength against lawmakers who generally pay attention and disburse funds to people who vote or they have an affinity for. Either you vote or you don't count.

When is a "Gangster Government" a Gangster Government" Photo? Iconic image of Soldiers in "Charge!"

"Trump's actions forced the Constitutional Republic to protect itself." **Steny Hoyer**

WHEN IS A "GANGSTER GOVERNMENT"? A "GANGSTER GOVERNMENT?"

"Trump's craven rationalization is a pattern of wrongdoing." Steny Hoyer

16. THE GREAT CAPITULATION BY DR. FRED MONDERSON

First and foremost, we must understand, President Donald Trump does not own a golden throne but a golden toilet, gateway to his expressed place. A man's mind speaks to his place of refuge. At a recent "Fellowship" the Pastor spoke of "fishing in ankle-deep shallow waters" where weeds proliferate as the American air is swiveling under insensitivity and inhumanity. Notwithstanding, given the exemplary opportunity to lead a great nation, rather than manifest such extraordinary behavior reminiscent of the colossal Mosaic image we remember from the movie **Ten Commandments** or the Jesus figure high-atop the Brazilian landscape, Mr. Trump has devolved into a little image much unlike the towering figure the world acknowledges to be the American President who represents a caring, compassionate nation. Given "a child shall lead them," and in the current unfolding drama on the American landscape, Mr. Trump's recent Capitulation to remedy the unfolding kids at the border tragedy he created proved a failure, perhaps it was obfuscation from the beginning. So, incisively we recognize, the current Capitulation, same as the "Birther" retraction, was made out of fear of citizenry

FREDERICK MONDERSON

retribution, and so ultimately betrayed Mr. Trump's duplicitous behavior and nature. Much of this unfolded because of pressures people of goodwill generated in tandem, ultimately such actions underscored a weakness in Mr. Trump's masquerade, *al be it* false perception of his own invincibility. Given this hole in his false armor coating, never mind his "hot mouth," stark inhumanity and lying nature, in as much as Ronald Reagan smashed the wall and Trump plans to build his wall, it still seems out of fear of immigrants and so we are reminded of the beautiful lady in the movie **Chronicles of Riddick** who held, "**If he has weakness, he is unfit to be Lord Marshall**." Therefore, going forward, motivated activist pressures of all the people united will defeat the "little big-man" and without question the trash heap of history will welcome Donald Trump with open arms.

To predict the possible impending and ultimate political demise of Mr. Trump, one can look to historical examples that reveal, among other factors, America became successful because of its magnanimous heart, the creative nature of the nation's people and America's disposition in welcoming all, whose contributions helped power the nation to its premier position across the globe. Conversely, tyrants and oppressive systems have fared miserably over time, for given a long train of abuse, it becomes the duty and destiny of the people

WHEN IS A "GANGSTER GOVERNMENT"?
A "GANGSTER GOVERNMENT?"

to overthrow and destroy such oppression that vexes the soul and diminishes the humanity of the nation.

As such, it becomes apparent, amidst unmitigated harshness, brutality, seeming inhumanity, tyrants, bullies, men of questionable integrity, particularly those in failed leadership roles, often misguidedly think they are divinely ordained or that they are invincibly above the law. That is, until true reality steps in to shake their core and expose the fear and trembling within the fake overcutting. Sometimes an "act of God," but more often the moving, galvanizing force of the people in response to exceptionally egregious acts, find those same people coalescing, organizing, generating credible opposition, peacefully or otherwise, force such recalcitrants into realizing they are not really as invincible as such "legends in their own minds" think. Even the "Yes Men" and women who surround such false heroes, in fact "straw men," who not simply rubber stamp their pronouncements but go to great lengths to rationalize and justify whatever the expressed "party line;" as such these apologists are the first forgotten by history but more frequently the people of their age. Sure, "Judas got 30 pieces of silver," but contemporaries even settle for scraps of "chittlins," Malcolm X labeled it "Guts," as payment for their shameless and questionable yet approving resounding silence and consequently failure to act decisively and effectively in face of injustice. Therefore, in assessing all such scenarios, we must never forget, as an example, when the French Revolution began to consume itself, by 1792-93, the English Philosopher Edmund Burke in

FREDERICK MONDERSON

his *Reflections on the Revolution in France* wrote: "The only thing necessary for evil to triumph is for good men [and in this case women] to say or do nothing." Fortunately, in America galvanizing and antidote shibboleths abounds in good men and women who care more about people, pronouncements and rule of law than profits, power and privilege!

Today, appropriately and significantly across this great nation, a credible response to the ongoing negative and expanding cloud of poisonous language, condoning even encouraging proliferation of discriminatory and racist inhuman behavior, expressions seeming contempt for the rule of law, swilling at the public trough and the generated uncertainty in the future of the people are acts that mobilize the sternest opposition. In that, across the political landscape people are screaming, demanding accountability and working to bring about the much-needed change in the status quo. The question then is, how many rotten, "Humpty Dumpty" eggs will fall from the questionable wall and what happens afterwards. No less significant, today's caustic air in the environment motivated and fueled by pungent behaviors and practices emanating from the highest echelons of government is not new and like ultimate failures of the past, "the people united will never be defeated," nor will they go silently into the night. Clear thinking individuals have made their prognosis and prepared a prescription for the anti-heroes who think their "shithole don't stink." As such, a few

WHEN IS A "GANGSTER GOVERNMENT"?
A "GANGSTER GOVERNMENT?"

examples will suffice to demonstrate, like sand castles on the beach, the cleansing tide of history, in the people's interest, will wash away the grim, filth and odor of falsity and lies, to be replaced by honesty, value in the human person, good government and respect for the law. A few historic examples have and will show, as Malcolm X has indicated, not only is "History is a good teacher," but equally "How these people dealt with their situations."

From 1910 with the formation of the Union of South Africa until 1994 when the racist apartheid apparatus was dismantled, administrators of the oppressive system felt invincible. So, for nearly a century the government and its evil, racist, machinery of rich, white, particularly Afrikaner settlers, oppressed the native South African population unchecked. On the one hand, the segment of the population the system favored and represented got rich in its brutality and uncaring nature. On the other, in the passage of time and with Bantustan, nationalist and international activist mobilization, the system began to crumble and finally it capitulated but not without cost in death, despair and psychological and social desolation.

Ian Smith succeeded to rulership of "Southern Rhodesia" in a system that mirrored Apartheid South Africa's behavior, exploitation and white settler racist machinations. As the "Winds of Change" began to sweep across Africa and the Caribbean, the Commonwealth of nations pressured Britain for action against the pariah palatine. In response Smith

FREDERICK MONDERSON

declared **Unilateral Independence** for Rhodesia, rather than give way to Black rule. He insisted "white rule of Rhodesia" would continue "for a thousand years." Well, the "Boys in the Bush" had other ideas. Under guerilla and global pressure, according to the Mighty Sparrow, "Muzorewa took Ian Smith place," but ZANU and ZAPU would have none of it. Ultimately economic boycotts in divestment and moral, military and international pressures encouraged through challenged pressures of the Nkomo and Mugabe factions ultimately hurried Smith's demise to bring into reality the new state of Zimbabwe. This timely capitulation began to decrease the Southern African perimeter that was the extension of the shield giving South Africa breathing room in its struggle to contain armed struggle and effectively continue to oppress the people of the nation anciently called Azania. Now, added to Rhodesia's demise and with the fall of Mozambique and Angola even ultimately Namibia, South Africa suddenly found itself laid bear with threatening conflicts on its doorsteps and disdain and challenges at home from long festering discontent. Thus, with these now less-friendly states surrounding South Africa, the "boys" who went abroad to Libya and Cuba to learn "armed struggle," now stood poised on the border representing impending and serious confrontation more proximate.

Despite Ronald Reagan and Chester Crocker's "Constructive Engagement," the effectiveness of global mass mobilization in the anti-Apartheid

WHEN IS A "GANGSTER GOVERNMENT"? A "GANGSTER GOVERNMENT?"

movement, the divestment efforts led by the American Committee on Africa, encouraged by the work of Rev. Sullivan, David Dinkins, Percy Sutton, and Charlie Rangel, together with the driving forces of Basil Davidson and Carl McCall, AFSCME, 1199, the work of Randall Robinson and Trans-Africa, Cleveland Robinson's union organizing and street activism, Jitu Weusi's and Conrad Worrill's influence and efforts, Len Jeffries strategizing with the World Council of Churches, and a whole lot more including Winnie Mandela stoking fires on the home front, contemporary with the galvanizing creative influence of Stephen Biko, Oliver Tambo, Cyril Ramaphosa, Bishop Desmond Tutu, and Rev. Byers Naude, the beast now lay practically prostrate, but still dangerous. Therefore, in ultimate capitulation to avoid a rapid and complete collapse, Prime Minister DeKlerk sought an initial capitulating compromise in negotiating an end to apartheid, but this was rejected because "Prisoners do not negotiate." Finally, in full capitulation Nelson Mandela was released from Prison after 27-years of confinement. And so, the Black majority population, given a chance to vote, brought in a majority government and Africa was now finally free of the scourge of racist, white, settler, supremacy, minority rule.

In America, the arch-segregationist Governor George Wallace of Alabama, emerged as a super propagandist in response to the emergent Civil Rights Movement sweeping the nation throughout the 1950s and 1960s. As human and civil rights progress began to be made through mobilization for economic

FREDERICK MONDERSON

boycotts, lunch counter sit-ins, freedom rides, extensive voter registration and more, George Wallace in racist propagandist fashion, began proclaiming "Segregation Today, Segregation Tomorrow, Segregation Forever." In addition, and despite the unconscionable behaviors of the "Bull Connors," the water hoses, dogs set on to bite humans, mounted police charging gatherings as "storm troopers" and other harsh behaviors shaping developments as at the Edmund Pettus Bridge incident, unfolding in the Selma to Montgomery March, the power of the people prevailed. As people of goodwill, religious and civic leaders, black and white, put their shoulders to the movement's wheel of change, Wallace's great capitulation unfolded. Who could forget that iconic photograph as Jesse Jackson, Rev. Lowery and several others, stood over the Governor smiling as he "ate crow" in signing the historic legislation proclaiming Alabama desegregated!

Robert Duran, superior pugilist with "hands of stone" was a devastating force in the ring. He held a very impressive record until he met "Sugar Ray" Leonard. As the fight unfolded, Leonard continued peppering and frustrating Duran with footwork, jabs, uppercuts, left and right hooks and more. Confused and thrown off his game, the erstwhile champion gave up, capitulated with the now famous four words, "No Mas, No Mas!"

WHEN IS A "GANGSTER GOVERNMENT"?
A "GANGSTER GOVERNMENT?"

Dr. Brinkley, the Presidential historian once remarked, "If Donald Trump implodes it will be because of Twitter." The only thing greater than his lying record is his twitter volume! While this may be so, more probably it will be Mr. Trump's arrogance, reckless and insensitive nature that will force future capitulation as he realizes the forces arrayed against him are committed and so he will seek to recover lost ground and seek forgiveness. Too late for the big lie now clocked at 15,00; the insensitivity, racism, intolerance, shameful actions that all brought America to a new low at home and in puzzling eyes of the world. As Senator Flake termed it, "We have hit bottom!" Yet, we still fell further! With the knowledge of history, the people know the "Birther capitulation" was insincere and like so many instances "axle-grease slick" keeps moving the marker. This will then force the will of the people to truly actualize Mitch McConnell's famous objective, "We intend to make - Donald Trump - a one-term President."

"Biden is as good a man as god ever created."
Lindsey Graham

FREDERICK MONDERSON

When is a "Gangster Government" a "Gangster Government" Photo? Man of courage and fortitude, with the beauty and weight of the Capital Building "Watching his back!"

"We salute the moral courage of House Democrats. We never coerced. We emphasized patriotism and remain true to the vision of our founders. We have ensured that our children will always live in a democracy." **Jerry Nadler**.

17. AMERICAN LEADERS ABROAD BY DR. FRED MONDERSON

The mettle of an American leader is tested on a trip abroad which gives notice to allies as well as adversaries what type of individual they are dealing

WHEN IS A "GANGSTER GOVERNMENT"? A "GANGSTER GOVERNMENT?"

with, particularly if he or she aspires to the highest office of the land as President of the United States. The former among such leaders of nation states would welcome a personable American leader who is intelligent, knowledgeable about events they may agree on or disagree about; given the perceived perception questions whether this individual can be strong, decisive and if need be, can cooperate on important issues of mutual interest. Adversaries equally assesses such a leader to determine how experienced he is, and whether they can challenge his authority to determine how much they can get away with. However, while self-assured and decisive leaders on that first trip abroad may wow their audience and put adversaries on notice, weak and indecisive, irresolute and flip-flopping leaders often put their foot in mouth, embarrass or insult allies, or potentially offer a long leash to adversaries who are emboldened by amateur behavior. The classic case sketched above features Barack Obama and Mitt Romney, the former first as United States Senator, then President on the one hand, and the latter as former governor and later aspirant for the Presidency. In time perspective, when both leaders made their first trip abroad, America faced many challenges but each of a different nature. One thing is certain, their first trip sets the bar, high or low, of future expectations.

Barack Obama's first venture on the world stage, as all aspirants to the U.S Presidency would normally do, met with resounding success. Here was a Black man, a leader, senator of a great nation who was cool in demeanor; articulate in thought and speech; well-liked by his constituency; and possessed an ability to flourish convincingly in any argument or situation who proved attractive to great masses of people. In Europe he was an instant hit and received "rock-star" reception. The Germans wanted to elect him President of their country. In Kenya, the elders were flabbergasted and welcomed a "returning son." Those elders of his paternal heritage gave him the royal treatment, dressed him in traditional gear and reconnected his heritage endowed with the power of the spirits of creation first manifested in the land where "the gods first dwelt." Then they sent him forth. Perhaps the essence of this endowment made the difference in his election victory, except perception and false propagation of this particular reception showed how desperately ill-tempered the opposition could be.

As President, Mr. Obama visited friendly Canada, then with his beautifully fashionable wife had tea with the Queen in England and this encounter bowled over the British; from a tumultuous welcome by the Germans he then fascinated the French, disarmed the Muslim world and had time to surprise the troops in Iraq he led as their Commander-In-Chief. Moving on to Trinidad he stood up to Hugo Chavez of Venezuela and told Ahmenijhdad of Iran to behave or else! Now, having assuaged the world and changed its image of America, President Obama returned home to the wrath of Republicans, viz., McConnell, DeMint, Joe Wilson and all subscribers consistent with the "McConnell Mandate!"

WHEN IS A "GANGSTER GOVERNMENT"?
A "GANGSTER GOVERNMENT?"

In this journey Mr. Obama proved, leaders can and in fact achieve much without name calling and other agonizing behaviors that ultimately stain their image in history.

When is a "Gangster Government" a Gangster Government" Photo? Storefront portrait of Dr. Martin Luther King, a "Drum-major for justice!"

According to **Vladimir Putin**, "Thank goodness the US is blaming Ukraine for 2016 meddling," but this is an utterly false narrative, Russian propaganda.

FREDERICK MONDERSON

"The president's recklessness has led us to this Impeachment." **Nancy Pelosi**.

18. SPEAKING FOR GOD! BY DR. FRED MONDERSON

From time memorial a certain genre of men and women have professed to speak for god in revealing his thoughts, commandments and covenants. Within memory people have revealed they are god, sent by god or even spoken to god. However, even more recently, some have even claimed to speak for god and not being "men of the cloth," such pronouncements seems to trivialize the experience leading to skepticism in divine-human interaction, questioning whether god exists or whether people are really playing politics with god or exploiting politics in god's name. Despite misguided teachings, the general consensus is that god first appeared to Africans along the Nile at a time some 300,000 years ago. As one of the earliest organized societies with a record of religious belief and practice, the ancient Egyptians pinpointed god's earliest earthly home and the place of their origins. Accordingly, and purportedly, a 19th Dynasty nobleman's funeral book, states as to the origins of the ancient Egyptians, "We came from the headwaters of the Nile River at the foothills of the Mountains of the Moon where the God Hapi dwells." This area has been identified as the East African plains beside Mounts Kenya,

WHEN IS A "GANGSTER GOVERNMENT"?
A "GANGSTER GOVERNMENT?"

Kilimanjaro and Ruwenzori. It's generally believed the ancient Egyptian society experienced millennia of evolutionary development before the first dynasty's unification given c. 3100 B.C. though some scholars date this happening at least a thousand years earlier at 4241 B.C. when the calendar was generally believed invented. However, the people of Nabta Playa, a region to the south-east of Egypt who were unquestionably the first astronomers may have in fact invented the calendar sometime after 20,000 B.C. Within this time measured context, the Egyptians possessed a precession time cycle of some 26,000 years that some scholars have argued required two, three, possibly a fourth such cycles for measurement extending for a period of first 26,000; 52,000; 78,000; even 104,000 years of African star-gazing. Nevertheless, this is still less than the period of the 300,000-year intellectual and religious experience consciousness of divinely inspired recognition.

The ancient "Egyptian Bible," the New Kingdom *Book of the Dead* by way of the Middle Kingdom *Coffin Text* that evolved from the Old Kingdom *Pyramid Texts*, shows evidence of these African people's religious beliefs dating back millennia before Unification. One important early Egyptologist has argued, the earliest architects were priests, who, in contact with divinity was instructed as to what type of dwelling to build to house the God's corporal form on earth. Priestly functions grew into a powerful priest body, the Priesthood. As the king was considered the Son of God, his earthly representative and a god on earth, he had to officiate in the temples straddling the spiritual and temporal realms, between the divine and human forms. Since he could not perform all the rituals in all the temples at the same time, his stand–in became the priest. Each temple had a chief priest and the Priesthood as a national religious body had a chief or High Priest. In fact, there was a chief priest for each of the four principal religious centers where the four principal deities resided and were worshipped, viz., Ra at Heliopolis; Ptah at Memphis; Amun at Karnak; and Osiris at Abydos. At Asuit where Thoth, the intellect, chronographer and "legal eagle" of the gods resided as head of the Ogdoad, together these centers each had a priesthood that ritualized their god, interpreted his commands and spoke for him as did all the chief priests of the respective temples.

The king was recognized as the legitimate successor to the first God King Horus and strong pharaohs exploited this fact. These Pharaohs became imperial conquerors who won booty and tribute then endowed the priesthood by supplying food and bulls for sacrifice at the festivals as well as building temples for the worship of the gods. The kings also built temples to worship themselves, for upon death they joined the realm of the divine beings. Weak kings, on the other hand, were unsure of their own divinity and unsure how much the priests knew relative to their connection with divinity, and thus they trembled in the presence of priests who spoke for God and knew what god meant and wanted!

WHEN IS A "GANGSTER GOVERNMENT"?
A "GANGSTER GOVERNMENT?"

The reverence of these divine voices continued down through the ages though charlatans have exploited the position of author even giving bad decisions and advice. Some have become involved in the more mundane acquisition of wealth and social power. Dr. Martin Luther King railed against religious worship and secular materialism critiquing the classic admonition, "Praise God but pass the ammunition!"

America proved an animal of a different breed though the state was founded on the principles of a Christian nation. At the time of independence, practitioners of the institution of slavery denied the humanity of blacks, the mono-genesis theory, even denying these Africans were "children of god." This position was enshrined in the mentality of founding fathers who were themselves slaveholders. As Dr. ben-Jochannan has always pointed out, racism and religious bigotry is at the foundation of Western and Christian religious practice. Such practice was instrumental in forcing the creation of the African Methodist Episcopal Church in the early 19th Century.

In recent times, Reverends Jerry Falwell and Pat Robinson have claimed to be in communication with, even "spoken to" and "for god." While both are "men of the cloth," Jerry Falwell prognosticated on political matters but Pat Robinson practiced the craft, even seeking the U.S. Presidency. The newest generation of aspirants to this highest office added refinement, to the "speaking for god" spin.

FREDERICK MONDERSON

Michele Bachmann was out of the gates in the 2012 political primary season. Embolden by her Iowa Caucus win, she emphatically announced, "God told me to run" for the United States Presidency. One has to believe God's direct intervention into human affairs and became busy picking candidates for national leadership across the many nations of the globe. This being the case, he must have certainly expressed interest at the state and local level in America also. Finding no traction as her campaign began to falter in the Republican Presidential Primary, critics pounced, enquiring as to why god did not give Ms. Bachmann the wherewithal, viz., money, gifted advisers, stamina, volunteers in significant numbers, strategists, and all that was necessary for a god ordained victory. Observers could argue "God lost this one" as Ms. Bachmann exited the contest, yet struggled to remain visible and viable in events and issues surrounding the 2012 presidential election.

Ann Romney was another spokesperson for god when she proclaimed "God told" her husband, "Mitt Romney to run for the Presidency." Unlike Ms. Bachmann, inasmuch as Mr. Romney, viz., won the Republican contest, in a field of weak candidates, his track record in a previous run for the Presidency created a national campaign structure, possessing great wealth with an ability to attract supporters from the wealthy class, disarming many who questioned the legitimacy of his Mormon religion and in turn galvanizing the religious right possessing only one

WHEN IS A "GANGSTER GOVERNMENT"? A "GANGSTER GOVERNMENT?"

ticket to the big dance that being the "best of a bad lot!"

That is not to say Mr. Romney's Primary opponents had not sought the god connection, for Texas Governor Rick Perry was endorsed by a Bishop at a Baptist Convention while disparaging Mr. Romney's religion as a cult. So much so, the other Mormon in the race dismissed the Bishop as being a "moron" for criticizing Mormonism. Religion has always played a crucial role in American politics for, besides, kissing babies, candidates visit churches seeing pastoral endorsement and the visibility their presence gives among the congregation and potential voters. Equally, if the candidate is a member of a large church or a national religious body and affiliation this may have, it generally proves beneficial to the candidacy of the particular politician. However, while association may have positive benefits, there is a down-side as well.

In the 2008 Presidential Campaign, then Senator Barack Obama had been a member of a Chicago based religious institution headed by Reverend Jeremiah Wright. The media exposed excerpts from taped sermons of the Reverend which in inflammatory flourishes, Mr. Wright castigated America for past and present wrongs especially towards African people. Opponents quickly characterized these utterances as anti-American, never mind the context, and sought to tie the two individuals in an effort to derail Mr. Obama's candidacy. The rest is known. Fast-forward to 2012, both President Obama and Mr. Romney pledged to keep religion out of politics. However, while not slinging religion, these individuals attended church services as is politically customary, for a great theorist once said, "Politicians must be seen attending church on Sunday!"

However, while the "church angle" is good politics, ridiculously exploiting this connection smacks of nothing but ludicrous charlatanism. Case in point! At the Democratic Political Convention their platform plank seems to have unintentionally omitted the word God and even Israel. Republicans and other commentators pounced on this, what was called an "oversight" that was subsequently corrected. The propagated implication held Obama was "declaring war on God" and by extension, failure to mention Israel meant that he was throwing America's strongest ally in the Middle East, "under the bus." President Obama has consistently declared his religious affiliation as Christian while trumpeting America's tolerance for all forms of religious worship, and particularly in view of the most recent catastrophe having to do with falsely characterizing the Muslim prophet Mohammed.

Governor Romney stood with Pat Robinson to castigate President Obama in a shameless attempt to use religion for political gain because of the Democratic platform plank. Since Pat Robinson speaks to and for God, Mr. Romney should have first enquired of him whether God had any opinion on the matter. Another line of spurious attack on Mr.

WHEN IS A "GANGSTER GOVERNMENT"? A "GANGSTER GOVERNMENT?"

Obama was he had essentially abandoned Israel, though he expressed some disagreement with the Israeli Prime Minister. Even family members disagree, perhaps Mr. Romney has had some disagreement with his family members. However, this line of political pandering is below the pale since the former Prime Minister Ehud Barak had consistently offered the view, "Mr. Obama has been one of the most ardent supporters of Israel."

Perhaps the "war on God" attack line was a continuation of his insistence religious affiliated organizations must provide birth control support for their members. Let us not forget, in the beginning, Mr. Obama was accused of being a Muslim not against god and religion. In the Jeremiah Wright attack he was not accused of being against religion but being a member of a Christian church headed by a fiery preacher. Hardly a Sunday Mr. Obama is not observed attending church with his family. Clearly then, he is religious and as such, god-fearing. Therefore, how can he declare war on God. Therefore, some people shamelessly exploited God's name for political gain but astute observers see them, having "often peep their hole card."

"Trump betrayed workers. Hundreds of thousands in Ohio. He tried to bribe a foreign official for personal gain." **Senator Sherrod Brown**.

FREDERICK MONDERSON

"This president will only be in power a short time but excusing his behavior will forever tarnish your name." **Representative Amash** to his former Republican colleagues.

19.   Not 1979
By
Dr. Fred Monderson

A number of important developments resulted from the events of the 1979 taking of American Embassy staff hostage. Naturally, the failed helicopter rescue taught military planners some valuable lessons in conducting this type of mission that proved so successful decades later in the assault on Osama bin-Laden's compound. The award-winning ABC news broadcast **Nightline** grew out of the earlier version "America Held Hostage" under the leadership of news-broadcaster Ted Koppel. While the ongoing hostage debacle enabled Ronald Reagan, the Hollywood icon, to become President, the long-lasting dastard-deed and Reagan's persona instilled a fear that he would do the unthinkable and this forced the Iranians to give up their captives the instant he assumed the reins of power. However, while the Iranians continued to spew anti-American venom on their domestic platform, in the eyes of the international community the nation had crossed the line.

At the world leaders gathering for the 2012 annual United Nations meeting, the current Iranian leader

WHEN IS A "GANGSTER GOVERNMENT"?
A "GANGSTER GOVERNMENT?"

Mahmoud Ahmadinejad ranted anti-American and anti-Israeli flourishes while trying to extol the ancient nature of Iran's culture, etc. Interesting that, prior to the hostage taking, the modern world respected Iran as the earliest nation to respect and provide protection for diplomats and diplomatic missions in ancient times. The hostage taking and seizure of the American Embassy contravened that powerful and historical ideal they had given birth to. Nevertheless, all these events notwithstanding, for Governor Romney and his campaign personnel, in attacking President Obama in wake of the Libya assault and killing of the Ambassador and three other Americans, as they try to equate events of the two time periods is somewhat disingenuous, for a number of reasons.

First, while one event was sustained for more than a year and President Carter exhausted all reasonable options to not endanger the lives of the numerous hostages; the other was of very short duration and loss of 4 lives, the events that precipitated the outburst were completely different.

Second, the world had changed tremendously between 1979/1980 and 2012 technologically, shrinking of the globe and the manifestation of a revolution in people's thinking and though that there is a war on terror; therefore, the notion of the embassy remains inviolate.

FREDERICK MONDERSON

When is a "Gangster Government" a Gangster Government" Photo? Iconic image photographing a photographer on the manicured green lawn photographing the Capital Building from its side.

Third, while there was a principal, albeit religious, figure coordinating events in Ayatollah Khomeini who solidified the Iranian revolution and opposition to American support for the Shaw Riza Pahlavi, there was no such uniform figure in Libya. A hodgepodge of militant groups, militias, held-over from the revolution they had coalesced in opposition to the Khadafy regime. Thus, though they were in the process of consolidating the government, the revolution was far from solidifying leadership with armed hotheads crisscrossing the country establishing rules of law to their liking.

Fourth, while in Iran anti-Americanism gave vent to the revolution before a captive audience and Americans could only watch from a distance; the

WHEN IS A "GANGSTER GOVERNMENT"?
A "GANGSTER GOVERNMENT?"

deceased Ambassador and his team had been instrumental in guiding the success of the rebels, and after their victory in helping to formulate policy, cementing foreign relations and helping to shape Libya's future.

Fifth, in Iran the revolution and seizure of the hostages was championed and directed by a domestic movement with participation from the national military apparatus, many of whom changed allegiance, and in alliance with some disaffected soldiers, students and mullahs of the Ayatollah's brigade. This was not so in Libya. While the Iranian revolution was a single and isolated incident in a vast region, the revolt in Libya was part of an international rebellious movement dubbed the "Arab Spring" where success in one country emboldened other participants in another. Equally, while the thrust of the Iranian rebellion was a domestic revolt against the status quo, the United States and NATO forces aided the Libyan rebels and this contributed to their success. Again, the Libyan revolt involved foreign fighters of which elements of Al Qaeda were participants. Thus, once victory was assured, the drawn-out process of creating a national military force with accountability as part of the nation's goals and responsibilities had not been accomplished and purportedly armed militants with ties abroad may have been instructed to launch the assault because of recent American gains against the war on terror, particularly around the time of the anniversary of "September 11th." Like a cop investigating a crime, no nation's intelligence can predict every course of action by opponents nor "friendly fire" developments. One of the reasons why the perpetrators of 9/11 were successful, America always guarded against foreign attacks and the insidious filmmaker blind-sided the nation with his smut. The lurking "dark forces" took advantage of this as well as the legitimate protests and launched their assault.

Sixth, America was not at war in the throes of the Iranian revolution but was during the "Arab Spring." There were forces deployed in Iraq, Afghanistan, elsewhere in Africa and challenging Somali Pirates, albeit successfully, in all theaters of operation. Thus, it is sophistry to claim a lack of leadership at this time.

Seventh, while the Iranian nation stagnated in their anti-Americanism rancor during the hostage crisis, so much so, in three decades they were suppressing their own people seeking change through the ballot box. In Libya, the people stood up, challenged and chased the militant perpetrators of the crime. Unlike Iran, the Libyans became enlightened, perhaps the great loss of the American Ambassador's efforts and they themselves remembering how the world aided their cause. Thus, they chose a more rational and constructive path rather than be constrained by the archaic albatross of militant beliefs the civilized world frowns upon.

Eighth, while President Jimmy Carter didn't have to face the military challenges posed to Barack Obama and so had no such success in this respect, Mr.

WHEN IS A "GANGSTER GOVERNMENT"? A "GANGSTER GOVERNMENT?"

Obama could boast of his efforts to contend and end the Iraq and Afghanistan conflicts, decimation of Al Qaeda and killing of Osama bin Laden all the while curtailing Somali Pirates' activities. Certainly, this is demonstrated leadership.

Ninth, while President Carter could not boast of any equally world challenging activities on his watch, Mr. Obama's realization of the role Islam plays in the modern world, his outreach for better relations and calls for justice therein in Turkey and Cairo speeches must get him some credit for encouraging a climate that spawned the "Arab Spring" which disengaged dictators in Tunisia, Libya, Egypt, forced changes in Yemen and encouraged, though not successfully up to his time, the aspirations of the people of Syria, certainly Mr. Obama's stature gets some credit. In the movie **Ten Commandments**, despite its falsity and misguided representation, Joshua told Moses, "Stand on the high ground and extend your arms so the people will see your silhouette and have hope;" the story of Mr. Obama's influence in these developments has hardly been told. It was leadership that changed the world's perception of America after the Republican tenure. It was leadership that rescued the nation's economy from its downhill plunge in bank failure, Wall Street contraction, escalating housing industry hemorrhaging, the rising numbers in job losses, runaway credit card interest rates, troublesome numbers in student loans, etc. Despite what has been said, stimulus dollars saved the day and Wall Street bailout enabled the Dow to rebound three times to what it was when Mr. Obama first took office. It was the same leadership that has allowed Vice President Joe Biden to boast, "General Motors is alive and Osama bin-Laden is dead!"

Tenth, it is amazing leadership that Mr. Obama could conceive of and campaign for and pass affordable Health Care Reform that Republicans facetiously and maliciously call "Obama Care" as well as the equally significant Lilly Ledbetter law giving women equal pay for equal work despite the work of headhunters as McConnell, DeMint, Santorum and Gingrich. Thus, when Governor Romney sought to equate events of 1979 with development of 2012, perhaps he should have read this piece, otherwise he needed better advisers or he should have stuck to the things he knew well such as fixing the Olympics, outsourcing under Bain Capital, banking overseas and maintaining accounts in the Bahamas and Switzerland as well as changing his position on issues as a chameleon changes his colors.

"I cannot turn away from the Sacred Pledge. The Founding Fathers placed their lives, fortune and Sacred Honor to create the democratic Republic we must now defend." **Larry Hogan Seer**.

WHEN IS A "GANGSTER GOVERNMENT"? A "GANGSTER GOVERNMENT?"

"It is impossible for me to condone and overlook the long train of abuse." **Larry Hogan Seer**.

20. "HERE AS 'EYE CANDY'" BY DR. FRED MONDERSON

After making his address to world leaders at the United Nations, President Obama, accompanied by his wife Michelle, visited **ABC TV**, Chanel 7, New York, "**The View**" as he said, "As Eye Candy!" This is because *The View*, hosted by four ladies, is thought to be "a ladies show" and Mr. Obama has consistently advocated on behalf of women, particularly so in the Lilly Ledbetter Equal Pay for Equal Work legislation; appointment of two women to the Supreme Court; his insistence on employer supplied birth control prescriptions; the Health Care Reform Law that substantially affects women; plus the fact he is handsome, charming, has a beautiful smile, all buttressed by his glamorous wife Michelle; and in New York, given these factors, this is the place to be! The President's opponents wanted to make "hash" out of the fact he did not meet with world leaders on a one-to-one basis after his speech. He does this all the time. He just finished addressing the world leaders and his strategists believed meeting with a leader, eight leaders, a dozen leaders, would not have been sufficient. So, therefore, don't meet with any leaders individually. Of course, there was a fundamentally strategic reason for his not meeting with any head of state at this time. However, his "Eye

FREDERICK MONDERSON

Candy" line did not disturb Michelle for like Bess said in her song in **Porgy and Bess**, "I've got my man!"

There is no question the 2012 political campaign was one of chest-like strategy and Mr. Obama proved an expert at the game given his 2008 winning campaign. He has also managed to keep Republican wolves at bay as they sought to effectuate the "McConnell Mandate." Given every move he made, they countered, not in the interest of the people's business, but rightfully earning the title "Party of No!" Since he met with no world leader and they criticized him, if he met with any number, they would end up insisting he probably meet with every leader present whom he addressed, meet with at the G-8 Summit, practically any day at the White House or on trips abroad.

Fact is, Mr. Obama remained cognizant of the multi-million-dollar individual donations into his opponents' coffer to take his job. However, there is an old saying, "When an opponent is self-destructing, say nothing, just observe!" In this case, young, fit and fashionable, Obama decided to play "Eye Candy" games while Romney did his thing! Even more important, however, Obama wanted to stay in touch with his people, the "grass-lawn roots" by emphasizing how different he was to Governor Romney who would have sought, if he became President, to eradicate every meaningful piece of legislation President Obama enacted, whether Health Care Reform, Dream Act legislation, Don't Ask,

WHEN IS A "GANGSTER GOVERNMENT"?
A "GANGSTER GOVERNMENT?"

Don't Tell, equality for all Americans regardless of their sexual orientation. Mr. Obama's position was thus clear, "that all Americans play by the same rules, have equal opportunity on a level playing field" relishing in the hope-filled thought that the American Dream is attainable for all who so aspire. Insisting Congress pass his jobs bill, placing great emphasis on educational opportunities, hiring and retraining more teachers as well as first responders - fire and police, Mr. Obama continued to lay the foundation for a brighter American future. Compare this to Mr. Romney's "Taking America Back" to Pre-Health Care Reform Status; insisting Hispanics "Self deport;" giving more to those like himself who have too much will cause nothing but bitterness in contrast to Mr. Obama's "Candy," "Eye" or otherwise; discarding nearly half of the American electorate in his disrespectful downgrade of their social status, rather than **DACA** and the need for comprehensive immigration reform, etc. We could add his insult of America's greatest ally, the British, in his Olympics gaffe and his insensitivity to Mr. Obama's delicately but effectively sailing the American ship of state through the changing, challenging and sometimes rough waters of the new reality in the game of nations.

"Each man, each woman must look into their own soul to find courage." **Larry Hogan Seer**.

FREDERICK MONDERSON

"Declaration of conscience and stories of courage should be our watchword." **Larry Hogan Seer**.

21. OBAMA CARES
By
Dr. Fred Monderson

Throughout the Republican Campaign, line and staff advocated the Mantra to "Repeal Obama-Care." All along, from Day One, Republicans in and out of Congress had a principal goal to "Deny Obama a Win!" This was part of the many-pronged Grand Strategy to deny Mr. Obama a second term, or as Senator McConnell put it wearing that never-forgotten smirk on his face: "My job is to make sure President Obama does not win re-election." To accomplish such they had to obstruct every move the President made, block every legislative action he proposed, not applaud every good idea he presented in the **State of the Union Addresses** he gave, and to portray him in every respect as a weak leader with whom the American people would become disenchanted and he won't be re-elected. Even blind persons could see there was racial animosity undergirding Republican strategy against Mr. Obama. The surprising thing in all this, the political games notwithstanding, the effete Michael Steel and Allen West shamefacedly hid and remained silent as President Barack Obama was verbally assaulted, called the most insidious names, NIGGER, and such likes, perhaps, not given permission to speak, these "Republican leaders" remained silent as

WHEN IS A "GANGSTER GOVERNMENT"?
A "GANGSTER GOVERNMENT?"

expected. By Edmund Burke's yardstick, during the backlash of the French Revolution in 1792-93, he wrote: "The only thing necessary for evil to triumph is for good men to say silent." Thus, in Mr. Burke's vein, we ask: "Are Michael Steele and Allen West good men?" But Obama is bigger than "these two little men," many times over. Brushing aside the flakes of their *ad hominem* attacks he once admonished, "I know Politics is a contact sport" so let them come." Significantly, and with that powerfully disarming smile he laughed off the "circus criers" because he knew he was the reality of power in Washington, DC!

It was sheer brilliance for Mr. Obama to see the need for Health Care Reform, formulate a strategy to sell it across the American political landscape and once elected, pass it into law. This legislative accomplishment that eluded presidents for some six decades was indeed significant; and there is no need to reiterate Vice-President Biden's platitude about the big event; for we can clearly see how Lilliputian Republicans are for rather than applaud this social edifice, like their assaults on Mr. Obama, they seek to tear it down, despite the fact untold millions of Americans stood to benefit from its provisions.

This accomplishment troubled Republicans that a Black Democrat could achieve this milestone, rescue the millions possessing no health care and show more of an identification with the 99 rather than the 1 percent. Therefore, Republicans doubled down in the fiercest obstructionist strategy as the "Party of No" demonstrated, blocking all legislative effort by the President. In this strategy, they unfolded a forked mantra of denying Mr. Obama a second term and propagated falsely about Health Care Reform to win support to gain congressional advantage and overturn "Obama Care."

Setting faith in the sanctity of the Supreme Court they took him there. With an oftentimes majority on the bench, Republicans were assured Affordable Care Act would fail. Picture the "losers" Newt and Michele Bachmann sitting in the Court's pew.

There is something about Chief Justice Roberts when facing President Obama. Need I say more. Notwithstanding, rather than overturning "Obama Care" the supreme jurist ruled Health Care Reform was constitutional, even if it was a tax that even Mr. Obama's team had not envisioned. Nevertheless, in that great disappointment, Republicans in and out of the court's chamber, viewed Chief Justice Roberts as tantamount to being a "traitor" for "giving the Black guy a win!" Thus, losing in the "Court of Legal Opinion," Republicans launched a new strategy to persevere in the same "Court of Public Opinion" in the hopes of winning a Congressional majority in the next election and then overturning the law, legally.

Dr. Leonard James long believed, "As a Black man in a racist society, I expect to be knocked down, but as long as I answer the bell, that is all that matters!" As such, President Obama had made it clear earlier on, "Politics is a contact sport." In the wake of the

WHEN IS A "GANGSTER GOVERNMENT"? A "GANGSTER GOVERNMENT?"

recent Middle east debacle, the insulting film and widespread backlash, Mr. Obama made his position clear at the United Nations.

When is a "Gangster Government" a "Gangster Government" Photo? Another iconic image of the Capitol Building as a backdrop to foreground greenery.

"Rudy Giuliani is facing a lot of trouble. He was involved in an attempt to take over a Ukraine Gas Company; there were campaign contributions made from Ukraine; He was involved in the situation of Ambassador Yavonavich." **Leon Panetta**

FREDERICK MONDERSON

"We are a nation of laws, not men. The Constitution is not a parchment but a beautifully crafted architecture of democracy." **Adam Schiff**

22. THREE AMIGOS AND HEALTH CARE
BY
Dr. Fred Monderson

Very few men in significant public life have had a champion of substance who made a difference in his quest for the great prize. Barack Hussein Obama was fortunate to have two such stalwarts in his corner. The argument is plausible that Senator Teddy Kennedy, the "Lion of the Senate," who, in endorsing the young Obama felt he had passed the torch to capable hands and with the wherewithal of his campaign wizardry, the young leader became President of the United States, a significant accomplishment for an African-American. Former President Bill Clinton added the icing on the cake to make that first win possible.

The second time around, Bill Clinton loomed large in his support for President Obama. He understood issues, had seen Barack's plans and strategies, having been there and done that he put his full weight behind the President's re-election. Mr. Clinton bolstered this publicly affirming he strongly believed the President would be re-elected! How fortunate Mr. Obama had been to have two champions praising his cause as they discerned the "Presidential timber" in the

WHEN IS A "GANGSTER GOVERNMENT"? A "GANGSTER GOVERNMENT?"

mountain of a man, Barack Obama. However, recognition and support did not come easily. Mr. Obama had to demonstrate courage, wisdom, foresight and steady nerves to convince the decision.

Not only had President Clinton been able to understand Barack's playbook, perhaps because some of the advisers of the one supported the other. Even more important, Republican strategy of scorched earth and obstructionism against Barack Obama proved a carbon copy of their attacks on Bill. And, just as he weathered that storm and turned back the opposition in fighting the good fight, Barack Obama trumped his opponents returning their punt for a touchdown.

When is a "Gangster Government" a "Gangster Government" Photo? The "House of Representatives side" of the entrance to the Capitol Building.

"We had a fair process in the House of Representatives." **Adam Schiff**

FREDERICK MONDERSON

"Mitch McConnell has declared; he is not an impartial Juror but will take his cues from the White House!" **Adam Schiff**

23. MITCH MCCONNEL "PLOTTER" BY Dr. FRED MONDERSON

Back in October 2013, the analyst and commentator "Sizzlin Cillizza" exposed the conspiracy against Barack Obama spearheaded by then Minority Leader Senator Mitch McConnell. Some four years earlier at the end of 2008, right thinking individuals had suggested as much given the Senator had publicly announced his intent "to make Barack Obama a one-term president." Anyone expressing the same sentiments about the current occupant of the office will certainly tee-off Mitch. However, his views notwithstanding, "What goes around comes around." Nonetheless and significantly, Mr. McConnell failed in his quest as Barack Obama "fought his way back" to be re-elected to a second term.

No less significant though serious, the Senator racked up an impressive record of foul behavior and attitude, some say racist, even hypocritical actions toward the first African-America President, Number 44.

1. McConnell's first outing as stated, his intent to make Barack Obama a "one term President" was

WHEN IS A "GANGSTER GOVERNMENT"? A "GANGSTER GOVERNMENT?"

deemed "Racist" by the actor Morgan Freeman on CNN's Piers Morgan's **TV** program.

2. During the Budgetary "Debt Ceiling" debacle, the conscionable Barack Obama "compromised" in face of the "Party of No's" holding the government and people of America hostage. Coming out of the negotiations, sparkle-eyed and beaming, Mitch McConnell gave a "thumbs up" to the cameras, many interpreted as a signal to fellow plotters observing off-screen, seeming to say, "I got the Nigger in the White House." Concomitantly, Mitch's partner, John Boehner, House Speaker, after it all boasted, "We got 98 percent of what we wanted." Still, Barack Obama accomplished his mission of administrative leadership.

John Boehner lost his job and is now getting rich peddling marijuana options. Mitch McConnell, on the other hand, went on to finally accomplish his life-long mission of becoming Senate Leader. From that position many aspire to become President but such seemed not the desire of our boy. Dr. Leonard James often told his student, "The higher monkey climb, the more he exposes himself." Today, with miles still to go, Mitch McConnell is being labeled "hypocrite."

Despite Republican negativity and opposition Barack Obama appointed two women to the Supreme Court. Then Justice Scalia died and President Obama nominated a respectable jurist, Merrick Garland, to replace Mr. Scalia. Out-front championing opposition to Mr. Garland was none other than Mitch McConnell who argued, with the 2016 Presidential Election looming, the American people should decide who should replace Justice Scalia. At a later gathering Senator McConnell gleefully boasted, "I looked Barack Obama in the eye and said, 'Mr. President you will not get this judgeship.'" Strange, how "What goes around comes around," another judgeship became vacant on the eve of the 2018 Mid-Term election and Senator McConnell, now in the Senate leadership, did everything in his power to have the seat filled, contrary to prior arguments about the looming election.

Fate sometimes plays tricks in front of our faces. In a relaxed frame of mind, a gleeful and boastful Senator McConnell was asked the question, "If another judgeship becomes vacant on eve of the 2020 election, what would you do?" Instantly, the Senator responded, "I would fill it!" The double hypocrisy in this statement, is that (1) Mitch McConnell as Senate Majority leader cannot fill a judgeship, this is the responsibility of the President; and, (2) Mr. McConnell's answer goes against the one he offered when it was President Obama's opportunity to appoint Merrick Garland. Therefore, we are correct in asking, "Was it about party loyalty and opportunity, Mr. McConnell's ego, or Mr. Obama's skin color, which harps back to Morgan Freeman's conclusion about Mr. McConnell's initial racist pronouncement of his intent to "Make Obama a one-term president." As Mr. Freeman publicly declared, this statement was racist and so, *ipso facto*, we have

WHEN IS A "GANGSTER GOVERNMENT"? A "GANGSTER GOVERNMENT?"

a racist as Senate Majority leader. Sadly, his undetached stance is no different from that, essentially of the entire Republican party particularly in its state of genuflecting to President Trump especially in face of the untold number of actions, pronouncements and behaviors many have deem "beneath the dignity of the Office of President of the United states."

When is a "Gangster Government" a "Gangster Government" Photo? Another view of the Capitol Building enhanced by its manicured lawn in a beautiful Green, White and Blue kaleidoscope.

At the **Michigan Rally** on the night while the House of Representatives was Impeaching Donald Trump, he was "Red in the face, Going off the Rails."
Jim Acosta

FREDERICK MONDERSON

When is a "Gangster Government" A "Gangster Government" Photo? Mythical figures in the fountain beside the Jefferson Building.

"Trump wants to punish Europe, but American businesses will suffer." **Jenny Lawcourt**

WHEN IS A "GANGSTER GOVERNMENT"? A "GANGSTER GOVERNMENT?"

"President Trump undermines the discipline of our fighting forces. Our fighting force must have discipline. Discipline is essential to an effective fighting force. The President's interference undermines discipline. He takes a callous approach to the rule of law. He undermines the rule of law."
Leon Panetta

24. "ONLY I CAN" VS "YES, WE CAN!" BY DR. FRED MONDERSON

What's wrong with this title? The first is self-centered, egotistical and problematic in terms that essentially down-plays the efforts of others. The second is inclusive, encourageable and potentially success oriented. Or, in another way, one seeks to ride the wagon single-handedly taking credit for getting there, perhaps even driving the vehicle into a ditch. The other encourages all persons to place their shoulders to the wheel and push. That is, having more persons involved provides input as a problem-solving strategy. Well, the first proposition was spoken by President Donald Trump while campaigning, whereas the other was spoken by Mr. Obama in his effort to become President and fulfill his exemplar role in the White House. The interesting thing, when words are spoken, they can become a "Call to Action" admonition and in-time, the effectiveness of the thought and its results or consequences becomes manifest. Later, we saw how such expressions benefitted the author or speaker and the subsequent impact on the universe that hears such words; how the recipients have been moved to action; and finally, how their lives have been impacted by the words of the great men.

More than a decade ago, America arrived at a historic crossroad with tremendous baggage, viz., banks were facing bankruptcy; the housing industry was hemorrhaging tremendously with foreclosures rising rapidly; the auto industry had lost and continued to lose market share; unemployment rates were high; while "Wall Street" was on a downward spiral, "Main Street" was sneezing and "Back Street" caught pneumonia; first responders' and educators' jobs stood on the chopping block, even as Affordable Health Care rapidly became more out of reach of untold millions of Americans. Two wars were being waged in Iraq and Afghanistan. To this we could add America's efforts to combat climate change and more particularly to curb Iran's nuclear ambitions then pivot towards the economic potential of the Pacific Basin amidst the challenges of an aggressively expanding China, both economically and militarily. Thus, the world's image of an America of high ideals, demonstrated practices of principles of ethics, good government and, opportunities for individuals had plummeted for, though they commiserated with the nation over 9/11. As was evident, the world did object to the administration's go it alone strategy to topple Saddam Hussein.

WHEN IS A "GANGSTER GOVERNMENT"?
A "GANGSTER GOVERNMENT?"

In the 2016 Presidential Election, Donald J. Trump emerged successful; demolishing, first an extensive list of Republican competitors, then the Democratic candidate Hillary Clinton. Let's not go into "Russian interference" in the election in its numerous methods. Nevertheless, a number of statements made by Donald Trump before and as a candidate for the Presidency, then as President, that should have been truly studied and rejected for the inflammatory rhetoric and ultimately failure to produce successful results. Everyone knows Donald Trump created a great deal of political traction by fanning flames of a concocted "Birther" malady grounded in falsity.

Once he arrived, he began characterizing himself as "The Only One" who could solve any and all issues facing the nation, economic, foreign policy, infrastructure, unification, law enforcement. Interesting and first of all, the things Mr. Trump got credit for were a result of tremendous input by many others. For instance, appointment of federal judges and especially that to the Supreme Court were orchestrated through the machinations of Senator Mitch McConnel, Speaker of the Senate. Sadly, a number of "non-crediting Trump" legislation was and are still being blocked by the Speaker. In this particular issue, some have accused Senator McConnell of stealing the first Trump Supreme Court appointment. That is, because, among other issues, he publicly boasted, "I looked Obama in the eye and said, 'Mr. President you will not have this seat.'" This was not surprising given Mr. McConnell was part of the conspiracy against Mr. Obama's government and then there's that famous "Thumbs up" signal after the debt ceiling meeting where a smiling McConnell signaled, many interpreted, his handlers, "I got that Nigger in the White House."

Some even argued; the Senator may have been a part of the strategy that orchestrated Mr. Trump's unrelenting campaign to roll back practically every accomplishment of President Obama. Many view Mr. Obama's legislative, even foreign policy, achievements and assiduously negotiated diplomatic agreements, as truly beneficial to Americans and American interests. Hence, people wonder at the pathological pursuits of Mr. Trump, particularly given the evidence reflected in his unrelenting and false "Birther" quest.

Competent observers have determined, Mr. Trump's anti-Obama tirade was fueled by racial animus and efforts to placate a base who "saw no evil, hear no evil, and demonstrated deaf ears to Trump's spoken evil," because they see themselves like him. Even more, sadly, evangelical moralists have lost their way, their moral compass, ignoring some 15,000 lies and mis-statements, insults, even prejudiced and demeaning views spoken by President Trump simply because he appointed conservative judges. This itself is an oxymoron, for judges should not inherently be conservative or liberal, since their rulings must withstand the test of fairness, challenges and time. That Wall Street is booming and unemployment rates are low, they proclaim, "Trump's our man," even though the great bulk of Americans do not truly

WHEN IS A "GANGSTER GOVERNMENT"?
A "GANGSTER GOVERNMENT?"

benefit from Wall Street gains or employment numbers and more important, the economic foundations Mr. Obama put in place. So true to his character, Mr. Trump takes credit for everything. He even took credit for a Hurricane striking Louisiana even though the Weather service initially expressed this was not so!

Whether climate change, environmental realities, clean air initiatives, global trade pacts, even arms control successes Mr. Obama negotiated, Donald Trump has or is in the process of overturning because he projects, "I'm the only one who can do it." His is an immediate manifestation of recent Republican legislative strategy and insistence, "Don't give the Black man a win!"

Thus, as Mr. Trump and his Republican defenders, enablers and supports, "Cut their noses and spite the American face." Their "I alone can" mantra is proving problematic today, and for the future. On the other hand, Mr. Obama's working philosophy that held, "Yes we can," is a manifestation of an ancient African aphorism, "If you want to go fast, go alone; if you want to go far, go together." However, the manner in which the two positions are viewed, the more inclusive approach is and must be more effective, since "two heads are better than one." Hence, time will certainly reveal which course of action is more in the interest of the one (percent, that is), the few or the many. In reality, one can only see some 180 degrees, while two or more can see the full gamut of 360 degrees.

FREDERICK MONDERSON

When is a "Gangster Government" a "Gangster government" Photo? The front face of the Capitol Building as seen from the Jefferson Building.

When is a "Gangster Government" a "Gangster Government" Photo? Another view of the Marble Terrace from the rear of the Capitol Building.

"Andrew Johnson was not elected. Bill Clinton was re-elected. Donald trump is facing re-election."
Laura Coates

WHEN IS A "GANGSTER GOVERNMENT"? A "GANGSTER GOVERNMENT?"

Rick Santorum says "Wait!" But, "While the grass is growing, the horse is starving!" The Courts will take too long! **Fred Monderson**

25. "SELLING ONE'S SOUL" BY DR. FRED MONDERSON

In Western civilization, the soul is a tremendously important part of the personality, particularly because the belief it is involved in the afterlife experience. Some cultures label this development "The Judgment." As early as in Ancient Egypt, the conception of Kingship was a hall mark of the state. In that reality, a principal admonition of the king was to administer the state, within the philosophic axiom of Ma'at, meaning truth, justice and righteousness, balance, order; that is, correct behavior. Now, after a life of rule, service or experience, the king died and was ultimately buried and his "Ba" or "Soul" began a journey to the place of Judgment in the Hall of the Double Ma'ati. There, the belief system insisted, the heart should be weighed against a feather of truth. In that early age, the heart was considered the seat of a physical and conscience personality manifestation. Then, all things being equal, the king was declared "True of Voice," or "Justified." There he was permitted to exist for eternity as a spirit, soul or entity in the Elysian Fields or heavenly abode.

FREDERICK MONDERSON

In Christendom, a beneficiary of the Egyptian, African, religious and philosophical belief system, practices dictated one live by or keep the **Ten Commandments**' admonition principally to, love thy neighbor, act as a reputable civic-minded individual, even practice the **Sacraments**. In the intellectual, civic, even political experience on a global plain, at some time actors begin to wonder how history will judge their behaviors given the opportunity to function in the public behalf on the legal landscape.

In the Meridian Park section of Washington, D.C., there is a memorial to President Buchannan who "walked on the mountain tops of the law." In today's reality, Attorney General William Barr, the nation's highest-ranking lawman is the actor who is the legal subject of study. This two-time Attorney General, as many have argued, is tremendously versed in the law. Beyond execution of his duties, he should also be concerned with how history views his time at the bar. Such an outcome of intellectual historical scrutiny through discussion and analysis, can for argument sake, be equated with the above sketched Egyptian quest for everlasting heavenly bliss; the Christian desire for resurrection; and the opportunity to exist beside the divine right hand in the many mansions of the heavenly father and his son.

In another, somewhat sarcastic though not so, context, an individual was quoted as saying, "I'm working flat-out for the devil." Thus, in essence, this

WHEN IS A "GANGSTER GOVERNMENT"? A "GANGSTER GOVERNMENT?"

individual, in an equally sarcastic rejoinder has been accused of "Selling his soul to the devil." Some commentators accused Attorney General Barr of essentially "Selling his soul to the Devil!" Other commentators argued Attorney General Barr "Sold his soul to the Devil."

Responding to the manner in which Mr. Barr handled the "hot button" Mueller Report and his testimony before Congress in uttering the charged term "Spying," House Speaker Nancy Pelosi first described Attorney General Barr as being "off the rails." Evidence seems to clearly indicate, he was "not acting as the nation's attorney general" but essentially as "Trump's Attorney General" or as "Trump's lawyer." Mr. Barr first wrote a missive giving President Donald Trump cover for his actions beyond the scope of this still enormous powers as Chief Executive. When Barr's predecessor Jeff Sessions reclused himself from the Muller Inquiry and Mr. Trump became vexatious thinking Sessions should have acted as his lawyer as if he did not have sufficient legal eagles, then that Attorney General was toast. However, there stood Mr. Barr, a Trump apologist and so, having kissed Trump's ring, Barr got the Attorney General position despite much pushback from many who disagreed with Trump and Bush renderings. Strange, he did promise those who conducted his confirmation hearings for the position that he would be impartial, but this has not been his position. He has done what Sessions did not do.

FREDERICK MONDERSON

The Muller Report has generated much discussion, pro and con. However, while many Republican and pro-Trump commentators have argued Mr. Barr exercised correct judgment in his deliberations and announcements, many have faulted him for a biased determination. His summary of the Muller Report has been deemed inadequate and a gross distortion. His Press Conference before release of the Report has been deemed unnecessary and problematic. Like all historic figures, Mr. Barr's prior stint as Attorney General, upon scrutiny, has been deemed skewed to protect his former boss, President George H.W. Bush, Number 41.

As all such circumstances, prior action oftentimes in similar situations, whether it's an arsonist returning to the scene of a fire he had set or an armed robber robbing the same liquor store time and time again, a pattern of behavior becomes evident. Thus, and though, Mr. Barr pledged to be objectively neutral and professionally unbiased in the volatile setting he inherited, critics claim his promises were betrayed and thus, in the words of former District Attorney Elie Hornig, "Mr. Barr's credibility is now in the gutter."

After the four-page release of the Summary of Mr. Muller's Report, implying that the March 24 letter completely misled, Nancy Pelosi indeed remarked the Attorney General is "off the rails;" "Acting not like the people's Attorney General, but Mr. Trump's lawyer" is a view from an experienced hand. However, while the special counsel team never

WHEN IS A "GANGSTER GOVERNMENT"?
A "GANGSTER GOVERNMENT?"

intended to make a procedural ruling against Mr. Trump because Justice Department standing policy maintains, "A sitting president cannot be indicted," Muller yet intended the final decision be left to Congress, not the Attorney General. After all, Mr. Muller must have been familiar with Mr. Barr's prior statement about the President not being subject to any court proceedings, based on the Department of Justice traditional view. They argue further, while the inquiry found "No collusion," and chose not to bring charges against President Trump because of such policy; yet, in this respect, Mr. Muller equally stated, "Neither do I exonerate him." However, while beyond this statement Mr. Muller has remained silent, and as such, in "running interference," Mr. Barr has enabled President Trump to falsely trumpet, "No Collusion, No Obstruction," which is simply not correct. Mr. Barr has not publicly corrected nor emphasized the "No obstruction" portion thereby enabling Mr. Trump's base to believe it is true. Sadly, this base s comfortably at home in falsity.

While Presidential advisers quoted "Alternative facts" and others have placed Mr. Trump in an "Alternative universe" one should wonder after the *Washington Post's Fact Checker* reports, "Mr. Trump has made 14,440 lies or false statements" so far; the question becomes, "does he ignore such a claim or does Mr. Trump congratulate himself for this unbelievable accomplishment mired in falsity? Sad to say, his evangelical moral supporters not simply have egg on their faces; this is under layer full of lies, deceit, self-interested gain and a propensity characteristic supporters' unquestioned loyalty. In a strange twist, the Muller Report indicated only because people around the President refused to accede to some of his illegal requests, he was saved from blatant "Obstruction of Justice." Still, the Muller Report did document some 10 instances where Mr. Trump obstructed justice.

Right after Muller, Attorney General Barr launched an inquiry into the FBI and equally into actions against Mr. Trump. In fact, Mr. Barr began canvassing the world to find dirt under which ever rock so as to clean the stain from the ominous clouds engulfing Mr. Trump. In the Ukraine scandal, Mr. Barr's name was mentioned synonymous with Mr. Trump's other lawyer Mr. Rudy Giuliani. Caught in another net, when the Inspector General Report insisting, if door number one and door number two had no dirt, perhaps a more favorable door number three would turn up something. Thus, all such behaviors smacks of "Selling one's soul to the Devil." Such behaviors go to the heart of whether Mr. Barr believes in anything other than he is attorney general.

"The House has voted to defend its institutional responsibilities." **Tim Naftali**.

WHEN IS A "GANGSTER GOVERNMENT"? A "GANGSTER GOVERNMENT?"

"President Trump does not understand Health Care."
Abby Philips

26. "HOW THE SNAKE LOST ITS TAIL" BY DR. FRED MONDERSON

One day a snake was slithering along in the grass and came upon a piece of meat which he tasted. Liking the new morsel, he continued chewing and enjoying every bit of it. He then turned and realized he was chewing his own tail. Donald Trump relishes recounting the tale of a woman who found a badly wounded snake by the roadside. She took it home, treated its wounds and nurtured it back to good health. Unexpectedly, one day, the snake bit the benefactor. Surprised, she asked, "Mr. Snake, after all I have done for you, how could you bite me?" To this he responded, "When you took me in, you knew I was a snake. I snake!" Since Mr. Trump so often speaks in aphorisms, parables, double speak, he was probably telling his supporters, "you voted for me knowing I'm a snake!"

Barack Obama did a wonderful job putting the nation back on a firm footing. He cleaned up the mess he inherited from the previous Republican administration. Because a Black man succeeded 43 white men in the Office of the Presidency, a whole slew of movements sprang up in opposition, questioning, generating a climate of racial animus and disrespect, even sabotaging his administration. Many in this nation prayed for relief in the sort of "a great white hope," who would "roll back Obama's progressive accomplishments."

In Donald Trump's emergence as a serious political figure, he gained notoriety with the fabricated "Birther" controversy. This questioning of President Obama's nationality and birthright was born out of a propensity for self-aggrandizement and to appease a virulent segment of the American population of angry and jealous individuals who expressed ill-favor that a Black man could and did decide for the Presidency, then wage a credible campaign to win, twice. Thus, the anger camouflaged in racist garb and jargon found favor with persons of an anti-black bent and disposition as demonstrated in the disrespect and racism directed toward the Black man as President. Donald Trump, with his latent racist inclination and a host of other anomalous proclivities found "Birtherism" to his liking and pursued the fool's errand with a tenacious ferocity that excited a segment of the American electorate very receptive of such damning and insensitive political spice and intrigue. And so, Donald Trump achieved his political platform to express an aspiration for the longest he held of the Presidency. He climbed to the Presidency through insults and on the character of a Blackman he insensitively and maliciously maligned.

During the Republican Presidential Primary in 2016, a field of 16 other candidates characterized the

WHEN IS A "GANGSTER GOVERNMENT"?
A "GANGSTER GOVERNMENT?"

Trump image in unflattering terms. This criticism crescendoed into a full-blown realization, so that many felt he was "unfit for the office." That is, given the belief, the Presidency of the United States represented, for the most part, a high standard of moral and intellectual fortitude, wherein its actions and thought were to be emulated and Mr. Trump's behavior and mannerism then and now did not meet this threshold. Such an individual in this leadership position must be beyond reproach in many respects. Thus, the high bar of thought and action associated with the leadership of such a position was to be respected and his authoritative expressions were indicative of what the people of the American nation stood for. Like a great shining beacon in a storm, in this respect, the world looked to American preeminence in awe and wonder, reflective of the highest humane, moral, ethical and intellectual standards such actions represented. Much of this has dissipated and found wanting under Donald Trump, in perceptions abroad and at home. That is why world leaders laughed at President Trump at the United Nations world forum in New York. Silly fellow; he thought and acceded, they were laughing with but not at him. There was no mistake when recently the Canadian, British and French heads of state, in a huddle, laughed at the President of the United States. So much like the school-yard bully, Mr. Trump took his ball and net, then headed home because he did not like what happened.

Sure, adversaries were permitted to entertain their own negative perception of America, even some

Americans themselves; but when allies and associates began to experience the ascorbic nature of contemporary American thought and deed, such actions become disturbing. Between Ted Cruz describing Donald Trump as "a sniveling coward" and Jeb Bush pointing out "Donald Trump is insulting his way to the Presidency" all during the Primary; and Donald describing brilliant Neurosurgeon Ben Carson, "now turned," as "low energy," and Marco Rubio as "little Marco," these were clear signals to Republicans, Democrats and Independents alike, Mr. Trump was unpredictable; "Low IQ," perhaps insanely dangerous, Michael Moore called him an "evil genius." Maybe!

Nevertheless, in all the hoopla following the Trump electoral victory, fervent expectations of economic gain, particularly in the Stock Exchange, growth in the GNP, more jobs to lower the unemployment rate, rejection of international agreements signed by prior administrations, viz., NAFTA, the Iran Nuclear Deal, Paris Climate Change Agreement, PTP, rejection of climate change arguments, loosening of air quality control restrictions at home and more; through it all, Mr. Trump's base was steadfast in its support, refusing to be critical for any transgressions. Surprisingly, his earliest Republican critics easily feel in line once he seemed firmly in control of the party as its leader. Such actions are arguably out of fear of the voting strength of his base or hopefully to receive some sort of support in their own agendas. In talks at face value, the Trump behemoth seemed invincible as it sailed along, not realizing he was

WHEN IS A "GANGSTER GOVERNMENT"?
A "GANGSTER GOVERNMENT?"

cruising for a later bruising. However, as elders have long insisted, "Be careful with whom you associate" or "Don't join gangs. You will own their doings."

Well, as events unfolded, Mr. Trump's overt shenanigans, viz., attacks on the Press as "fake news" and "enemies of the people;" "Mexico will pay for the wall;" attacks on NFL players who "took a knee" in protest of police behaviors towards Blacks and the same type of venom directed at Congresswoman Maxine Walters; disrespecting the wife of a Black soldier killed in military action in Niger, West Africa; believing white supremacists, KKK, Neo-Nazis were "very fine people;" African nations were "shithole countries;" berating allies Canada, German and Britain; while praising Xi, Kim and Putin; but even those actions did not seem to dent the perceived armor surrounding Mr. Trump. That dent did not come as a gift in the Muller Probe despite persons of the "Rogues gallery" surrounding Mr. Trump who could and did ultimately reveal inner workings of his mentality and organization.

First, the National Security Adviser to President Trump General Michael Flynn, that "Lock her up" guy, lied to the FBI probing his contacts with Russian operatives seeking to have an impact on the 2016 Presidential election. Faced with the embarrassment, Mr. Trump fired Flynn who later pleaded guilty to lying. Next, George Papadopoulos pleaded guilty to lying to the FBI. Paul Manafort, political operator, a savvy operative and for a time Mr. Trump's campaign chairman, was the next domino to fall. But first, the FBI raided the office, hotel room and home of Michael Cohen, Mr. Trump's long-time lawyer who described himself as Trump's "fixer" and who promised "to take a bullet for Mr. Trump." Now, with all Mr. Cohen's data in Special Counsel Muller's hands after the raid, Paul Manafort went to trial and despite his bravado, he was found guilty on 8-counts. Concurrently, Cohen pleaded guilty to two charges, equally implicating Mr. Trump in payments to women for sexual favors where such actions were considered election law violations. However, while Mr. Cohen had "flipped" Mr. Manafort "stood fast" and the President praised him for not being "a rat." Some argued, this was "mob talk." And so, Manafort prepared for his next trial with a lot of jail time hanging over his head and more to come.

Meanwhile, a recording between Mr. Cohen and President Trump to not simply pay Stormy Daniels, the porn actress, but to recover "all the data" from Decker, Publisher of the National *Enquirer* became public. Turns out, as revealed, Mr. Decker, a prominent ally of Mr. Trump, over the years, would "buy" negative stories about Trump in a "capture and kill" operation, proved very troublesome for Mr. Trump. That is, once secured, Decker chose not to publish such stories but tuck them away in a safe. With Decker granted immunity from criminal prosecution and "cooperating with Muller," the safe's contents were turned over to the Inquiry. Alan Weisenbaum, long the Trump Organization Financial Officer also mentioned in the Cohen tape of Trump became Muller's "next canary." And so,

WHEN IS A "GANGSTER GOVERNMENT"?
A "GANGSTER GOVERNMENT?"

commentators Bob Baer, John Dean, General Clapper and many others agreed, Mr. Trump has lots of trouble. However, as the proverbial aphorism held, like "Water running off duck's back," Mr. Trump seemed to have weathered storm after storm. But, as odds go, "a big one is due." As it turned out, this was the Ukraine scandal forcing Mr. Trump to confess, "I never thought a phone call would lead to my Impeachment!" Sort of like the gunslinger in **Rio Brave** said to John Wayne, "I never thought a cripple would beat me."

If that was not enough, and reassessing his position "out there," the "Manafort dam broke" and he agreed to cooperate with Mr. Muller to avoid the perils of the first guilty trial and to avoid the challenges and perils of the second trial. All the while, Rudy Giuliani, who gained fame as a District Attorney and later Mayor of New York City during the 9/11 disaster, but twice rejected as a presidential candidate, emerged as President Trump's "Outside lawyer." In this new role, some determined, Rudy is Mr. Trump's "attack dog" to the Mueller investigation. No less significant, his outrageous expressions caused some of the best legal minds, while commenting, admitted to being ashamed of Mr. Giuliani's actions, sayings and assessments of the fast unfolding events involving the President. In essence, while SS Donald Trump began to sink, Rudy's explanations, contradictory at times, were simplistic at best, tremendously problematic for Trump at worse. Such positions, supposedly a strategy, are reasons critics felt "Rudy is losing it."

To add to the President's woes, *The New York Times'* "Anonymous Op-Ed" followed by Bob Woodard's *Fear: Trump in the White House*; Craig Unger's *House of Trump, House of Putin*; Michael Di Antonio's *The Truth About Donald Trump*; Michael Wolff's *Fire and Fury*; *A Higher Loyalty* by James Comey; and Rick Nelson's *Everything Trump Touches Dies*; all painted a disturbing picture of the man National Security Adviser General Kelly called "an idiot" and former Defense Secretary General Mathis "a 5th or 6th grader" who was running "Crazy town." Afterall, while Donald Trump Co-authored *The Art of the Deal* with Tony Schwartz, Trump has not credited him with any of the thought-provoking ideas in its content. As such, as a self-promoting showman who used muscle, trickery and potentially illegal behavior or bitterness, spitefulness and "nasty" behaviors led some to say, "He is not fit to be President." To have amassed his wealth, and given he has demonstrated considerable evidence that he functions on a low intellectual level, conjecture would conclude he did more than step on other people's toes, and there have been countless claims of people being short-changed or "beaten" in one way or the other by Mr. Trump.

In this and all the hoopla aside, the Trump base who had prayed for a "great White Hope" to counter the Presidency of Barack Obama, must now own Mr. Trump's "more than 999 problems."

WHEN IS A "GANGSTER GOVERNMENT"?
A "GANGSTER GOVERNMENT?"

Thus, because of Trump's erratic actions, we're back at the negative global perception of America preceding President Obama's election in 2008. And so, the woes a man sows produces the headaches he reaps and Mr. Trump is a great sower of chaos and insensitivity who is driven by questionable behaviors. Contempt for the rule of law, potential "dangling of pardons" for cohorts under legal sanction, possible witness tampering in pending court cases and all such activities border on "obstruction of justice." We must remember. Contrary to Trump and Barr's pretzel-like views, "Muller did not exonerate" Number 45. Assessing such developments, Former CIA Director Leon Panetta explained for clarity, "Donald Trump does not take time to understand actions he intends to take." That is, "he does things by instinct, not thinking things through." Typical examples of this form of behavior is his decision to rescind the Security Clearance of Mr. Brennan and then he published an "enemies list" which generated much "pushback." In addition, functioning "off the rails," he promised to declassify the FISA warrant information on Carter Paige, something deemed harmful to the country. Thus, he held back on the latter. Not surprising, like most bullies, when faced with credible challenges, "he caves!" Asked whether he thought such actions can precipitate a Constitutional Crisis, Mr. Panctta responded, "We are already in a Constitutional Crisis."

Hence, in responding to how the snake lost its tail, it was because of the actions he perpetrated, the unsavory characters he associated with and when caught, called upon, these cohorts turned against the man they practically swore loyalty to. Thus, while the snake may not have lost its tail as yet, that tail still faces jeopardy and not the Alex Tribeck's game shows.

When is a "Gangster Government" a "Gangster Government" Photo? Iconic entrance to the Capitol Building. Notice the symbol of **Declaring Independence** just below the flag on the cornice or piedmont above the columned capitals.

"Donald Trump is not a great deal maker." **Linda Chavez**

WHEN IS A "GANGSTER GOVERNMENT"? A "GANGSTER GOVERNMENT?"

"Donald Trump has joined an exclusive club he does not want to be a part of." **Kirstin Powers**.

27. COUP VERSUS CONSPIRACY
BY
DR. FRED MONDERSON

In his false characterization of the **Muller Report** as "No Collusion, No Obstruction," Mr. Trump described the investigation as a "coup, a takedown" by angry democrats which failed! The interesting thing about Mr. Trump's "base," especially after he declared, "If I shoot someone on Fifth Avenue, I would not lose a vote;" the reality seems to be, if he further indicates "Today is Sunday," even though it is Thursday, such a base of followers would agree with him. Much of this has to do with the false reality **Fox News** and other **Right-Wing Media** feed these people on a daily basis. An equally and meaningful comparison that makes a point is as follows: Some years ago, *Newsweek* Magazine featured a cover article entitled, "Why are Obama's Critics so dumb!" Perhaps the same can be said for Mr. Trump's base who loves him beyond reason especially after he told them, "Don't believe what you hear. Don't believe what you read. Don't believe what you see, that's not happening. Believe me!" Notwithstanding, **IMPEACHMENT** is happening! So, he conned these people and kept referring to critical media as "fake news" while accepting the

FREDERICK MONDERSON

false factory mill "Fox News" as genuine because they praise him and stroke his ego; "Kiss his ring!"

Given such, this day, "Don't believe I'm being Impeached for Abuse of Power and Obstruction of Congress" is not a correct refrain. I'm reminded of the commercial showing the couple and their dog sitting in the living room with the water rising and they, reading their newspaper, remained seemingly oblivious to what was happening.

The Washington Post newspaper's **Fact Check** apparatus assessed Mr. Trump committed more than "14,440 lies or false statements" in his first three years in office. The Trump people belittled Michael Cohen because he told a lie or three and is now serving time for it. They claim he was under oath when he testified in Congress, which is true. Mr. Trump told thousands of lies. He did not testify under oath to the Muller Inquiry, 'Does that make his testimony questionable and therefore "Collusion" not correct?' Mr. Trump promised to release his taxes and has not. Was this promise a lie? It probably is! Saying he is worth 10 billion dollars when in fact it is probably one billing, having gorged at the public swill, when he leaves office he can then say, "See, I told you 10 Billion!"

The morals of Mr. Trump's base and evangelicals in particular is such they do not see a problem with his lying. Trump has stained the once "sacred" Oval Office with his behavior and these people are still committed to "four more years." At the current rate

WHEN IS A "GANGSTER GOVERNMENT"? A "GANGSTER GOVERNMENT?"

for the remainder of his term he may double the lies. Given the same rate of lying, over a second term, he would out-perform the Dow Jones industrials with his falsity. Thus, since Mr. Trump's base and especially evangelicals do not see his behavior as problematic, then as Christians seeking heavenly redemption, one has to wonder how this religious right would square such behaviors with Saint Peter!

A glaring contradiction in Mr. Trump's interpretation of the Muller Report is that Muller cleared him of "Collusion" which is ok for his base; but Muller did not clear him of "Obstruction" which is what happened. Yet, Mr. Trump tells just the opposite. Actually, the President continues to say to his followers, "No Collusion, No Obstruction, Folks" and since Fox News parrots such, this is all these poor folks know. Recently James Comey, the former head of the FBI reminded, the Russian leader Joseph Stalin once affirmed, "If you keep repeating a lie it becomes the truth!"

Sad to say, Mr. Trump's accept this false characterization despite the numerous assessments to the contrary. All this notwithstanding, Mr. Trump, in decrying the Muller Report, characterized the findings as a "Take down, a coup against his presidency that failed." "Witch Hunt" is also a term he uses frequently. This is the term he used in regards the Ukraine scandal. Collectively he uses these terms to characterize the Impeachment charges leveled against him. Sadly, his "base" and Twitter

FREDERICK MONDERSON

followers" are left with Mr. Trump's alternative, though false, reality.

Strange that an evangelical pastor proposed giving Mr. Trump 2 years in office as "Reparations" for the "hardships" created as the Muller investigation proceeded. How sad that "Men of the Cloth" could entertain such over the cliff views. I'm again reminded of the Florida "Koran burning Pastor" and the Arizona "Pastor praying for Obama's death." These men live in the **Twilight Zone**. Today it's called **The Matrix**. The contradiction rests in the fact, when Mr. Trump addresses his political rallies, he boasts of appointing Supreme Court and other federal judges, passage of the biggest tax cut in history, takes credit for Wall Street gains and lower unemployment figures because he is "doing a good job." To cap it off, his questionable boast of "No Collusion, No Obstruction" despite interpretations to the contrary, one wonders what has become of true leadership in this country. All this notwithstanding, two issues are tremendously important as per the above. All the while Mr. Trump enjoyed being president; he golfed; visited Mar-O-Lago and enjoyed all the attendant amenities of his office. Of course, he's on twitter all the time!

First, how ridiculously misplaced is the idea of Reparations for Mr. Trump when denied to the African-American community claiming such having been victimized in being subject to slave trade, slavery, racial terrorism, and institutional and all forms of discrimination, still having a psychological

WHEN IS A "GANGSTER GOVERNMENT"? A "GANGSTER GOVERNMENT?"

impact to this day. That is, providing free labor under duress for this nation's building enterprises. All such behaviors contributed to extreme forms of psychological, economic, and educational social maladies resulting in deleterious and irrepressible lacerations on the psyche of the legitimate claimants for Reparations who were oppressed simply because of their race, which is Black. Thus, given the totality of the Muller Report, the pastor's suggestion and Mr. Trump's claims, these are all outrageously simplistic and false. Naturally, these may find justification in Mr. Trump's alternative universe.

On the one hand, President Barack Obama was victimized by the "real coup and conspiracy" that failed as perpetuated by Mitch McConnell and a number or high-ranking Republicans who sought to sabotage the man and his legally elected and constituted administration. The animus and racial prejudice galvanized against Mr. Obama was principally so because of his race, however rationalized; to the contrary, notwithstanding. Many of the highest-ranking Republicans who today cry foul and defend Mr. Trump were around during Mr. Obama's baptism under fire, yet they were silent in face of the continuous assaults. This is because many of these are today carrying the torches that were lit during Mr. Obama's time. No less significant, on the other hand, and while Mr. Obama's slate was clean, the Muller Report brought indictments and convictions, jail time, against and to several high-ranking individuals who were connected to the 2016 Trump Campaign and administration in the orbit he created. Mr. Obama was never subject to the shamefulness that characterizes Mr. Trump's behaviors. That is, not simply the indictments against his top operatives but the "almost criminal behaviors" committed by the "best" people he promised to hire who had to resign or be fired.

The evidence is irrefutable, upon Mr. Obama being elected in 2018, Mitch McConnell (R. Kentucky), then Senate Minority leader, publicly affirmed, "I intend to make Barack Obama a one-term president." Hardly a Republican spoke out against this outrageous intent. However, one man did speak, that is; on **CNN's Piers Morgan**, Morgan Freeman the actor, condemned the statement as being "blatantly racist."

Unbeknownst to all, though some clear-sighted thinkers postulated the view, for working with others as the newly formed "Tea Party" comprised of Republican activists, in and outside government, these individuals orchestrated a systematic campaign of sabotage to undermine every legislative initiative Mr. Obama proposed, particularly the Affordable Care Act (ACA) mischaracterized as "Obamacare." This very effective obstructionism earned Republicans the title "Party of No." Yet, Obama passed Lilly Ledbetter Act and several far-reaching initiatives that benefitted the American people.

Sometimes it is not good to broadcast one's intentions. After Mr. McConnell's boast, President Obama, placed all his adversaries on the hood of his

WHEN IS A "GANGSTER GOVERNMENT"? A "GANGSTER GOVERNMENT?"

car to keep an eye on them as he drove off to tackle the nation's challenges he inherited. And so, ignoring the "Good ole boys," mantra, he affirmed, recognizing "Politics is a contact sport!"

Beside his elegance of mind and nobility of spirit, what set Mr. Obama apart from his challengers, as reported, was his enormously driven work ethic fueled by an unmatched intellectual capability that dwarfed all as Gulliver to his challengers or the giraffe to the tortoise. So, Mr. Obama addressed Wall Street stagnation, bank bankruptcies, housing industry foreclosures and decline, rising unemployment rates, collapsing national infrastructure, all addressed through strong economic and fiscal policy regulations and leadership daring. In the Movie **Gladiator**, the king spoke of "busy bees" meeting in the dark of night. And so, Senator Mitch McConnell "plotted" with his collaborators from their "under-ground cell." Still, to many, there was no doubt the original admonition and charge had changed in a meaningful way. Adding more fuel to his fire, Mr. Obama kept turning out hit after hit after hit, despite the "Party of No's" full court legislative press to "Not give the Black guy a win!" As such, as Denzel Eli would ultimately confess, **The Book of Eli** was "Bruised, but it will still do!"

Come Mr. Obama's 2012 Presidential re-election, on October 6, 2013, *The New York Times* newspaper published "a big write-up" about the plot against the Obama Presidency. The article named Ed Meese and high-ranking Republicans, some 20-heads of Republican managed NGOs and individuals in and outside the legislative arena who were involved. Mr. McConnell, named as a "plotter" by Chris Sicciliza, who, for fifty years in politics had engaged in such behaviors. CNN later did a feature where the faces of the Anti-Obama "Cabal" were shown and this "Coup and Conspiracy" then became fully fleshed out. No one did or said anything. No one, especially Mr. McConnell was charged or prosecuted.

We are then forced to consider and compare whether the Muller Report and its findings against Mr. Trump and his campaign was legitimate FBI investigation of a possible Russian conspiracy or Republican behavior against Mr. Obama and his administration which was a domestic and treasonous act against the legally constituted American government and people. No one is talking about opening an investigation as to what Republicans did to Mr. Obama. A popular Republican refrain especially as articulated by Representatives Jim Jordan and Collins is that Democrats hate Donald Trump and wanted to overturn the will of the American people. These hypocrites remained silent when McConnell and the Republicans "gave Obama the business!"

WHEN IS A "GANGSTER GOVERNMENT"?
A "GANGSTER GOVERNMENT?"

When is a "Gangster Government" a "Gangster Government" Photo? Majesty in magnificent architectural column, capital and ceiling of the Supreme Court building.

When is a "Gangster Government" a "Gangster Government" Photo? The message is clear "Pray for Your Leaders!"

"The President has weaponize himself." **Charlie Dent**

FREDERICK MONDERSON

"Don't do that, I told you not to do that." **Jake Tapper** on **Nancy Pelosi** after she read the first recorded Impeachment Resolution and signaled this was no time for celebration by her colleagues.

28. STAND STILL ...
BY
DR. FRED MONDERSON

"Stand still and witness the Salvation of the Lord!"

Word has it, the Trump Administration had considered revoking former President Barack Obama's Security Clearance, but this ridiculous and possibly vindictive idea was shelved. This act began the breech of his oath of office to serve, support and defend the Constitution and as such, as a model of justice and equality for all Americans. Nevertheless, such a decision comes after Donald Trump's championing the "Birther falsity" he "red herringed" that grew legs and ultimately was instrumental in projecting him to the United States Presidency. Meanwhile, in his capacity as President during his tenure, despite the avalanche of attacks on his personality and administration, Mr. Obama remained fully-engaged at the well-known critical junction of the nation's history.

The Obama Administration was unique in a number of ways but principally as the first African-American

WHEN IS A "GANGSTER GOVERNMENT"?
A "GANGSTER GOVERNMENT?"

President of the nation. Number 44 challenged failing norm practices and created economic and financial policies that placed the nation's economic structure on a sound footing. He rescued banks and "Wall Street." The auto and housing industry as well as state and local governments shortcomings were given a tremendous "shot in the arm;" while remaining committed to the war on terror, Iraq and Afghanistan and much more. Now, while the Obama Presidency created a reservoir of pride and dignity for the Black experience at home and much goodwill to the American cause abroad, all were because of the man's elegance of mind and nobility of spirit recognizable in thoughts and deeds. This and more are reasons today people love Obama.

As all this unfolded, Sunday after Sunday and intervening week-days, Saintly grand-mothers and grand-fathers, their sons and daughters and grand-children gathered in church houses to pray for Barack Obama; a man on a divine mission to save America tottering on the brink of financial and economic ruin; joblessness; housing collapse; upholding high the nation's moral and ethical standards; and managing its involvement in global conflict creatively. President Obama, with his head down and eyes focused on the issues began turning the battleship of state away from the threatening waters of doom and he did it successfully. Yet, in challenge, he had to contend with the masquerading evil and racist implications of "I intend to make Barack Obama a one-term President" refrain spouted and prosecuted by Mitch McConnel; the disrespectfully shocking

FREDERICK MONDERSON

"Birther King" Donald Trump consistently asking for birth certificate and college transcripts, as if he never had such.

But they were not alone. After Obama orchestrated the Affordable Care Act, Senator DeMint insisted Republican colleagues create his "Waterloo;" Michele Bachmann accused him of running "a gangster government" in a city where, the FBI is head-quartered along with some 22 other American security agencies including the CIA, NSA, Etc. All the while, Senator Grassley declared Obama "stupid;" Rick Santorum accused him of "poisoning the well;" "Lipstick on a Pig" Sarah Palin had charged he was "palling around with terrorists." Nevertheless, in the general society because of his policies, people were returning to work, banks began lending again, the auto industry regained its market share, housing starts picked up, then Obama deployed his "primary weapon" Michelle Obama on the world stage in which she "floored the Queen," "wow" the Germans; "disarmed" the French, all the while earning the moniker "Mighty Michelle."

Still, out of jealousy, full of racial animus, the "Tea Party" gathered in nefarious fashion; Militias paraded threateningly under false pretexts; all the while Ted Nugent sang his poisonous chorus of "The Nigger in the White House." Yet, undaunted the grand-mothers prayed and prayed for President Obama and oh, what a glorious transference of religious and spiritual nourishment and empowerment such efforts were for their hero on a mission. Nevertheless, Obama

WHEN IS A "GANGSTER GOVERNMENT"?
A "GANGSTER GOVERNMENT?"

continued to swim among sharks, barracudas and piranhas but remained wary of their bite. After all, he admitted, "Politics is a contact sport." Sadly, on their knees in conversation with their god, Dylan Roof entered that Holy Sanctuary in resplendent KKK, Confederate and Nazi regalia then killed 9 in "Mother Emanuel." No less alarming, the surviving Saints, similarly as Jesus on the Cross said to the Centurion, "We forgive you. We don't want to be burdened with your hatred." Similar messages are being sent to Donald Trump. The Black prayers were to bless, protect and propel President Obama, while the white practitioners prayed and gave mulligans to President Trump to forget and offset his sinful ongoing ways.

And so, as the wheels of truth, justice and righteousness - Malat, rolled on, President Obama "fought back to be re-elected." This "come-back" in favorability was against the coordinated assaults, disrespect, the climate of racist animus and deceit generated as a result of McConnell's failed quest; the coordinated strategy of Ed Meese aided by some 22 CEO's of Republican NGOs, who all mobilized against the ACA they maliciously misnamed "Obamacare." Joe Wilson could not resist and so injected his "You lie," as the President of the United States delivered the State of the Union message in the Hall to the Members of Congress. And the Elders prayed on for Obama and the nation, generating tons of spiritual, ethical and emotional strength and goodwill the oppressor could not counter. Contrast this with prayers and Mulligans for Mr. Trump; still

FREDERICK MONDERSON

Donald Trump needs "1000 Mulligans for Christmas 2019." Nonetheless, this gift may be difficult even insufficient since Donald Trump is not on **Santa's NICE LIST!** Yet, they do not seem to be working!

Then the "Lord of Hosts" decided to intervene! Still, baffled, he began weighing the requests of Evangelicals even while noticing Blacks on their knees, enjoining to bring good into the world. These oppressed persons had good reason to engage their god, especially after the deaths of Trayvon Martin, Michael Brown, Eric Garner, Gurley and more as a climate of questionable public and private behavior unfolded. But who could question divine design and intent? Still, the black-white divide began turning into a chasm.

Who knows, perhaps the divine decided to chastise America and so allowed Donald Trump access to the Presidency in the cosmic realization, "You only get one shot." Even if, "The chosen one," he betrayed divine intent with his lies and misdeeds. In the resulting tumultuous celebratory exuberance from under every rock came an emissary. The glitter of "new penny jewelry" blinded everyone. Moving quick under promise of hiring "the best people" President Trump began rescinding Obama's Executive Orders, engaging corporate entities on the economic and financial pedestals Obama crafted, enabling Wall Street to begin its historic climb, on a platform bequeathed by one President to another. As the economic wonder unfolded, Republicans were

WHEN IS A "GANGSTER GOVERNMENT"? A "GANGSTER GOVERNMENT?"

elated and touted each success. As they saw it, Mr. Trump boast was reality, given "Only I can do it!"

And so, the base, which actually means "bottom" loved their President. It was as if relieved of "Black rule," the "Great White Hope" had arrived, not fully realizing, their pet was actually a "Great White Shark!" And so, this "Bull in the China House" began rampaging rough-shod over everyone, insulting the media, touting "fake news" claims, even evoking Obama's name at every turn trying to sully his legacy. Through it all and beyond, the Saints remained on their knees, praying a fallen angel, disciple of the devil, will not consume all.

Meanwhile, given "Absolute power corrupts absolutely," Donald Goliath began trampling across the social and political landscape of the nation, cutting food stamps so the needy can suffer more. Even more, the grinch continued sowing confusion, denying everything, lying like no other, still he must have had a sense or some inkling the Avenging David was on the way.

As myriad of events began unfolding the questionable Trey Gowdy chose to "run" and "fight" in another arena; "Stupid" Grassley, discombobulated and speechless, to this day, remains dumb-founded; Wishy-Washy Senator Graham is proving a master of zig-zag; and only Bob Corker has stood to deliver! While embarrassing no one but

FREDERICK MONDERSON

himself, Speaker Mitch McConnell, in face of 14,440 Donald Trump lies, misstatements, plus insults, racist rants and more, fail to do the manly thing as the people's representative for as John Brennan has indicated, Mr. Trump is "drunk with power." And so, the behemoth spread, like the librarian in **BLADE**, spewing darkness across the American moral and ethical landscape while having political implications that continue to divide the nation, it forced avenging angel Jerry Nadler to descend among men focusing on the blasphemy of Trump, Giuliani and Perry having invoked the divine's name in vain. Many of the President's "best people" fell short and were removed from office or ran afoul of the law. For example, Michael Cohen – pleaded guilty – 8 counts; Paul Manafort – guilty – 8 counts; Michael Flynn – guilty – lying to the FBI; George Papadopoulos – guilty – lying to the FBI; Scott Pruitt – 14 investigations into his tenure; Tom Price – HHC boss - fired; Steve Bannon forced out; Jeff Sessions – Recluse - Omarosa Manigault-Newman – turned traitor. Then there is Rob Porter, fired for spousal abuse. Strange that every time one of these things happen, the President describe these as "good people;" or, "I don't know;" such persons as Sondland as he did with Michael Cohen, the "coffee boy Papadopoulos," "Manafort only worked for me a short time;" even "I never met Pranas" yet in the displayed photographs they are together and this denials is consistent with his statement about Stormy Daniels, Karen McDougal and equally with the 17 women who accused him of improper sexual

WHEN IS A "GANGSTER GOVERNMENT"?
A "GANGSTER GOVERNMENT?"

behavior, even rape. As David Axelrod exclaimed, Mr. Trump is "offensive to the truth."

Nevertheless, despite Mr. Trump's claims, Special Counsel Robert Muller's investigation was a "witch hunt," the inquiry into a myriad of evidence, successfully brought 191 criminal charges against 35 defendants while securing 5 guilty pleas. A generally philosophic belief, "one man can become a majority if his truths are immutable." In light of the 2016 election claims of Russian interference, Trump making nice with Russia, one man "called out" the President and in viewing the overt evidence pronounced "the king is naked." Naturally he braced for the backlash but his many years of service to the nation made John Brennan immune to Trump's water pistol. Perhaps that water falling to earth germinated the prayers of the Saints on their knees which began the budding opposition to injustice and tarnishing of the American ideal. Perhaps their prayers will continue to be answered. After all, those saintly people who identified with the Black man in the White House, had suffered so much from the insults, humiliation, even racist climate directed toward President Obama.

Mr. Trump needs to be reminded, "Whom the gods wish to destroy they first make mad." In this regard, Martin Luther King reminded, "The arc of the moral universe is long but it bends towards justice." In the streets of New York, we are told, "What goes around comes around." Perhaps the conviction of Mr. Manafort and Mr. Cohen were part of the "Big

FREDERICK MONDERSON

Payback" answer to prayers for the years of Obama persecution, insults to Black women, sports personalities, Mexicans and other Latinos. Mr. Trump has shown no concern for diversity, a pillar in the strength of America. Let's not forget the "Central Park 5" whom he tellingly disparaged, which all seem to indicate for Mr. Trumps, while the "Cows are not there yet," the "Chickens have certainly come home." In this coop, these birds are cackling up a storm in Ukraine Impeachment! Thus, in comparing Obama and Trump, we see Midday and Midnight. You go figure, who's who!

President Trump has his many plates full. He lit many fires creating an enormous smoky cloud that has settled across the American skies. This threatening overcast has unsettled him terribly. This is a man in crisis. His base chose to be oblivious to such developments because in his utter contempt for the rule of law, he kept insisting, "Don't believe what you read. Don't believe what you see. That is not what is happening." However, Impeachment has indeed happened! In his "alternative universe" of evasions and untruths Mr. Trump's repeated "No Collusion" proved incorrect. In that "out of this world place," his Adviser Kelly Ann Conway offered "Alternative facts" and his attorney Rudy Giuliani insisted, "truth is not truth." Such pronouncements were naturally unrealistic. In this regard, the award-winning journalist Carl Burnstein spoke of the "sewer seeping up from the White House swamp." Nevertheless, like lemmings in Trump's "alternative universe," his supporters still seem clueless and bent

WHEN IS A "GANGSTER GOVERNMENT"?
A "GANGSTER GOVERNMENT?"

on following him over the cliff. What is the truth, however, is that after President Trump suspended John Brennan's Security Clearance, he then published an additional "enemies list" of ten names whose clearance he was considering suspending?

When is a "Gangster Government" a "Gangster Government" Photo? Symbolism for "Equal Justice Under Law" and "Sanctity" the **Constitution** represents as guide to the nation's behavior and those taking the oath to defend it.

For a man who secured several military deferrals due to "bone spurs" and who is now Commander-In-Chief of the nation's armed forces and whose "enemies list" consist of many who have given more than 300 years of service defending this nation, the insult was unbearable. So, Admiral William McRaven (Retired), who oversaw the raid to eviscerate Osama bin Laden considered Trump's

FREDERICK MONDERSON

description of the press as the "Enemy of the people," forms the "greatest threat to our democracy." In response, he wrote, "Suspend my clearance so I can stand next to John Brennan." Then 15 intelligence personnel penned a letter in support of Brennan and the Admiral. These were joined by 60 others and again by another 175 American service patriots, who essentially told the President as did Admiral McRaven "you have embarrassed us before our children, humiliated us on the world stage, and worst of all, divided us as a nation." Evangelicals should take note.

Naturally, in their jubilation of false triumph, his base never saw and still does not see this coming, nor did they see the avenging angel in the person of Jerry Nadler. In fact, they fail to see the big picture facing a worried Trump who has been obfuscating in voluminous texting. As he feared the specter of Muller, McGhan, Omarosa, Cohen, Manafort, Gates, Stormy Daniels, Karen McDougal, Vladimir Putin, Kim Jung Un, China, Iran, and an unleashed Brennan, Clapper, Hayden, he has now come face to face with Adam Schiff, Anonymous, a whistleblower, Ambassador Sondland, Colonel Vindman and finally the chairman of the judicial Committee Jerry Nadler, and still more, much, much more to come. One man against a football team. He must certainly be worried for Impeachment is not a nice word, but full of historical stain. Significantly, this man of spite, bigotry, racism and homophobia, in the words of Omarosa, "Trump has met his match." Matching this, many have argued, "Corruption is the

WHEN IS A "GANGSTER GOVERNMENT"? A "GANGSTER GOVERNMENT?"

feature of the Trump Administration." So, we ask, 'Where is Michele Bachmann' to trumpet "A gangster government" run by Donald Trump.

However, whatever may be said of Omarosa, she has brought home the bacon! We heard about, even speculated about Donald Trump but now she has recorded goods on him in the form of video, recordings, pictures, emails. Added to this, Donald Jr. is also in trouble for lying, even meeting with an American adversary's representative. In all this, Paris Dennard, Ben Carson, Kanye West, the Cleveland Pastor, Mark Burns, Kelly-Ann Conway and all the Trump apologists, loyalists, his "best people," many of whom were fired for criminal and unethical activities, are now saddled with and must deny "Trump's sh-t don't stink." Fact is, these people are so far in, they're in the Perfume room."

The real question is will Donald Senior and Junior share the same cell, having played past Muller but crashed into the Schiff and Nadler Wall. Meanwhile, as the Saints continue praying, they "Stand to Witness the Salvation of the Lord" in all its magnanimous retribution.

FREDERICK MONDERSON

When is a "Gangster Government" a "Gangster Government" Photo? Immense grandeur intimating wealth of knowledge and power housed in the Jefferson Building of the Library of Congress, as seen from its rear.

When is a "Gangster Government" a "Gangster Government" Photo? The Majesty of columnar architecture of the Madison Building.

On the Obstruction of Congress Resolution – "No President has ever said I will not provide any document to your request nor allow my people to respond to your subpoenas." **Jeffrey Toobin**.

**WHEN IS A "GANGSTER GOVERNMENT"?
A "GANGSTER GOVERNMENT?"**

"The flick of the hand along with the look." **Dana Bash**

29. DINKINS AND OBAMA AND RUDY AND DONALD BY DR. FRED MONDERSON

"History, I contend is the Present." James Baldwin (1924-1987, Quoted in *Emerge* January 1990)

In 1993 David Dinkins, the first African-American Mayor of New York City, faced re-election against the Republican challenger Rudy Giuliani. The "ancient Malcolm X" often expounded, "History is a good teacher" and despite the "modern Kanye West's" ignorance of Malcolm's significance, the "old master's" insightful wisdom is ever-potent as a tool for anyone seeking to understand the profound predicament America faces today.

Bubbling in "law and order propaganda palaver," the former federal prosecutor Rudy Giuliani deployed law enforcement related thugs who discombobulated the Dinking campaign through "storm trooper tactics" and racist behaviors that ultimately enabled him to seize the prize of becoming Mayor of New York City. Full of obfuscation and chicanery resulting in polarization of the city along black-white lines, through racial attitudes, actions and behaviors,

FREDERICK MONDERSON

destiny ultimately began sucking Mr. Giuliani into a negative downward spiral chasm. In calamitous irony, the devastation of 9-11-2001 happened and with the blessings of the nation's and the world's goodwill, Mr. Giuliani was able to salvage his reputation, to become "America's Mayor," but only after earning the title "Brutaliani." However, rather than relinquish his term-limited position after two terms of service in 2001, the Mayor arrogantly argued he was "the only one" who could lead the city at that time. This insistence therefore necessitated he be given a third term of service which was rejected.

As District Attorney for the Southern District in New York, before he became Mayor, sadly Rudy Giuliani did not hire "Black DAs" despite there being more than 100 slots. While there were many who did significant work in the "post-911 recovery," Giuliani hogged the media spotlight as often as possible whether as DA or as Mayor and this visibility contributed much to him being labeled "America's Mayor." David Dinkins once remarked, the portraits of himself and his wife Joyce to whom he was married for 42 years at the time, "depicted her hair jet black and his, all white." Word had it, as one iota of Giuliani's insidiousness, this portrait, hung in Gracie Mansion as a Mayor's tribute, was removed by Giuliani when he took over as mayor.

WHEN IS A "GANGSTER GOVERNMENT"?
A "GANGSTER GOVERNMENT?"

Today, following the 2016 election, in which unfolding actions and evidence increasingly mirror "1984" the "Animal Farm" activists come to power. Then many of the new rulers began exhibiting "beams of political incorrectness." Such actions, in comparison are profoundly being manifested by the current administration. Yet, as we assess contemporary developments and look to the future, we saw a special prosecutor methodologically and painstakingly sugaring "Molly" the white horse beside the fence as he seeks insider information in an effort to do destiny's work of dethroning "animal rule."

Equally significantly, now that we are faced with Donald Trump and Rudy Giuliani back together in close relationship publicly, an interesting but profound observation has emerged as we reflect on history. Yogi Berra, the well-known baseball icon, known for his entertaining wit, first offered, "You can see a lot from observing" and more appropriately, "Looks like Déjà vu all over again," as the two amigos huddled, befuddled and confused and incessantly parrot conspiracy theories, "Made in Russia!"

Increasingly, as contemporary revealing evidence seems to indicate, the imagery of "1984" has returned and "Old Major" and his boys, having ousted the "humans" are now running the "farm." It is apparently interesting, as history reminded us, when Barack Obama, the first African-American President

FREDERICK MONDERSON

held the reins of leadership of the nation, a falsely concocted heavy cloud of racism and disrespect descended upon the efforts and personality of a man whose work ethic was exceptional; still, all because his race mattered. In that unfolding hostile age, many people and movements coalesced. There we say, Republicans, Blacks, Men of the Cloth, Evangelicals, Militias, and more than a gaggle of racists, white supremacists, "Tea Party" radicals and others as "Lipstick on a Pig" Sarah Palin; "Joe the Plumber" the "socialist" architect; not to exclude "Waterloo DeMint;" "Go for the Jugular" Billy Krystal; "You Lie" Joe Wilson; "Poison the Well" Rick Santorum; "Gangster Government," "God told me to run" Michele Bachmann; "I intend to make Barack Obama a one-term President;" and even Allen West, now gone like the Do Do Bird, and more, all intensely focused on the "mole in the President Obama's eye," his singular tree. Today, no one notices Donald Trump's beam, his forest of lies, insults, threats and intimidation matched by his "dangling of pardons!"

So much so, they Caucused in the halls of legislatures; did TV advertising and "Robo Calls" to discredit Obama and his programs; the Devil was at work in Bible study gatherings; he was sent threatening gestures in Military style militia training camp exercises; Obama's integrity became a campaign issue; one guy, half naked, kept jerking his middle finger up and down in front of the White House as the Secret Service watched helplessly; many others massed and protested on the Great Lawn

WHEN IS A "GANGSTER GOVERNMENT"?
A "GANGSTER GOVERNMENT?"

and streets of Washington, D.C.; *The New York Times* reported some 20-odd NGO administrators were involved in training operatives to fan-out across the nation and negatively portray the ACA falsely labeled "Obamacare;" while still others gathered, posturing on the steps of the Capital Building to focus on that speck magnified, in Mr. Obama's Demeanor; all such actions naturally ignoring his integrity, work ethic, elegance of mind and nobility of spirit the world saw but Republicans did not. Today a mighty oak beam and Donald Trump's demeanor and actions, thoughts. has fallen across the roadway in Ronald Reagan's "City on a Hill," yet and hypocritically, no Republican again seems to notice. That is, the same Republican persons who hounded Mr. Obama for purportedly ethical issues which were never evident, have turned a blind eye to all transgressions particularly in the case, so far, of "Trump's 14, 440 lies to Obama's supposed 18."

We see such questionable behaviors highlighted, manifesting in grabbing women's private parts; representative spokespersons who twist the fact and never listen to themselves as they spew distorted messages to the American people through the media platforms, especially Fox News and other Right Wing Media; high rates of personnel turnover in the current administration in association with abusive unethical even border criminal behaviors; associates pleading guilty to misconduct or being fired as public servants; "porn stars" now becoming respectable household names juxtaposed to "fixers" awash in questionable money, smelling of sleaze business, forcing investigators to follow the money into the swamp; Russian oligarchs as players in American political and financial dealings. Many among the young can now ask their parents, "Can I now tell lies since the President does it frequently?" Altogether these confluences of ethical and suspicious activities raise questions of conspiracy and issues of credibility; or, as one Fox News anchor called it, "Swamp stink!" In fact, administration apologists most vehemently defend the rotting log lying in the swamp. Strange, while Biblical lore holds, "If God be for you who could be against you;" today, many religious groups hold the position, "If the Devil is giving out goodies, then what do we care!" What is clouding this alarming attitude and, importantly more compelling, according to an old African proverb which holds: "A log can lie in water for any length of time, but it still will never become a crocodile." Yet, appropriately, however, "having lain in the water for some time, without question the log has begun to rot and stink."

As is becoming increasingly clear, now that Mr. Giuliani has joined Donald Trump's legal team, they seem to have rekindled many decades of friendship. Well, given the success of Mr. Giuliani's rambunctious discombobulation of the Dinkins campaign in 1993 which brought him success as candidate for mayor; and Trump was active then, so let's not forget the "Central Park Five" and that unfortunate incident; is it now not so-farfetched that he instructed and encouraged his buddy to apply the

WHEN IS A "GANGSTER GOVERNMENT"?
A "GANGSTER GOVERNMENT?"

same strategy against the first African-American President in which the "Birther" charade falsity was born and perpetuated.

Men of wealth generally seem to want everything even possess aspirations to achieve high political office. Everyone knows, Donald Trump rose to political prominence on the "Birther" falsity and whether supporting the charade, goaded on by admirers, or simply ignoring this travesty in silence; as Abraham Lincoln reminded, "Silence in face of wrongdoing embodies culpability" for which Republicans are guilty in condemning this wrong. So, "one lie grew into 14,440 lies," and the lying behemoth gets taller and taller, leaving us to wonder, what's next? Assessing such behaviors has become tremendously important; for, given the previous high moral standard associated with being American as viewed on the world stage; and most assuredly the morality associated with the Office of the Presidency of the United States; in such a tumbling Humpty Dumpty world this reputation, high position and morality standards are fast becoming lusterless.

"Republicans were shaken by David Holmes' testimony. Republicans are not leading but are lagging indicators." **John Kasich**

FREDERICK MONDERSON

"There was not going to be an **Impeachment** except for Ukraine." **Charlie Dent**.

30. OWNING TRUMP BY DR. FRED MONDERSON

Now three years into his Presidency, the people of Mr. Trump's "base" and others who enable his over the top behavior, whether enabling "white supremacy," cuddling with and falling in love with the world's most odious tyrants, while simultaneously treating American opponents and institutions with contempt, even disparaging allies and threatening long-held alliances; such individuals must now own the record Trump orchestrated. Having stepped into the "Shithole," Mr. Trumps now leaves odious footprints, as for example, "enabling white supremacy;" his "Send her home" mantra; even taking photos with an orphaned baby and gleefully exploiting such, for after all, Melania "Does not care, Do you!" Interesting that Rudy Giuliani, Kellyanne Conway, even Kayleigh McEnaney and equally Paris Dennard and Ben Carson among other enablers are not out there defending his actions. Strange, when this ultimate "con artist" hears a large crowd clambering, he exclaims "The people cheering him on," when in fact, they are expressing outrage at his presence and behavior. Case in point, the recent world leaders' gathering where Macron, Trudeau, and Johnson laughed at Mr. Trump as did the United

WHEN IS A "GANGSTER GOVERNMENT"?
A "GANGSTER GOVERNMENT?"

Nations did when he addressed them, then explaining "They were laughing not at but with him.

When Donald Trump became President, and despite the pro and con propaganda associated with his campaign, he made several controversial statements as continuation of his equally outrageous pronouncements as with, viz., the "birther" fallacy controversy; impugning Mexicans, the disabled and even LBGT; the attacks on Megyn Kelly and Rosie O'Donnell, even Senator Warren as Pocahontas. Then there was the diatribe against Ben Carson and even Blacks "not being smart enough to vote for him." Let us not get started on Colin Kaepernick, NFL players, and athletes who declined the White House invitation. Equally, we can mention the Johnson widow, Maxine Waters, the Gang, Elijah Cummings, and so much more. Meanwhile as in the beginning, when his minions, Corey Lewandowsky, Kellyanne Conway, Paris Dennard, especially Kaylee and others took to the air waves as well as high-level Republican spokespersons such as Jennings, and Torres, even Cuccinelli who went to great lengths to defend the new President against legitimate criticisms of his words especially as they emanated from the mouth of the President of the United States and "leader of the Free World;" we now focus on these enablers' moral compasses. Sadly, as these people spewed their convoluted rhetoric, they seemed unaware persons were paying attention to the seemingly outrageous things they themselves were saying as defenders of a man unfit to be President of the United States. However, as fate would have it, their statements became more outrageous and they doubled down in defense of their hero, no matter how ridiculous his pronouncements became.

Fast forward, Trump fabricated the "Obama bugged my Campaign falsity." In a TV interview with Mr. Lester Holt, Donald Trump expressly mentioned, the firing of FBI Chief James Comey had to do with "the Russian thing;" then a seeming racist propensity in the "Birther Mold" Mr. Trump began to overturn every legislative and negotiated agreement former President Obama achieved, viz., Paris Climate Agreement, Trans-Pacific Partnership agreement, DACA, Research and Development emphasis on clean, non-fossil fuel energy. Then he threatened and withdrew from the Iran Nuclear Deal. And so, Mr. Trump proceeded with his "Anti-Obama tirade" in guise "only he can be patriotic" and Obama can't. Let's not forget Obama was more intelligent, better prepared regarding issues requiring presidential leadership; after graduation did not seek-out Wall Street but became a "Community Organizer," as he simultaneously taught and practiced law and was never self-aggrandizing in promoting his interest over America's at home or abroad. Mr. Obama maintained a respectful and constructive relationship with America's global allies, and never gave in to challenges by America's adversaries abroad.

As we know, at the Republican National Convention, former New York City Mayor Michael Bloomberg, who must have had some knowledge of Mr. Trump's

WHEN IS A "GANGSTER GOVERNMENT"? A "GANGSTER GOVERNMENT?"

behaviors, candidly exclaimed, "I know a con when I see one." Unfortunately, no one took him seriously and Mr. Trump's base encircled him even more after that. Sold and handed out, MAGA hats were seen everywhere, meanwhile the Stock market essentially rose from Obama's c. 18,000 to Trump's c. 26,000. An 8000 point rise, the unemployment numbers began to come down but lost was the fact Mr. Obama inherited the Stock market at c. 6500 and by the end of his tenure it stood at 18,000; as a result of sound financial and economic policies and regulations that addressed Wall Street, bank failures, rise in foreclosures in the housing industry; equally combatting the reality of teachers and first responder's jobs tottering on the chopping block. Because of a drop in revenue, state and local governments faced hardships as they tried to deal with the situation and so Mr. Obama's policies and regulations helped alleviate these concerns.

One thing is unmistakably clear, while Obama could claim dispatch of Osama bin-Laden; Al Zawahiri and the Isis leader have evaded Mr. Trump. Thus, it seems there's one Obama achievement, capture of terrorist masterminds; President Trump can't match. Recently, however, Al Baghdadi was captured and Donald Trump milked it for a great deal.

"One man, One Vote. A five-minute Vote!"

FREDERICK MONDERSON

When is a "Gangster Government" a "Gangster Government" Photo? Majesty, power, beauty and architectural symbolism manifesting Law and Constitutional Order, as the Hallmark and underpining of American Democracy!

"Using United States assets as collateral is wrong."
Rex Tillerson

31. SOUTH CAROLINA
BY
Dr. Fred Monderson

"The state of South Carolina produced the likes of John Jackson, Chancellor Williams, Dr. John Henrik Clarke, Samuel Carson, Sonny Carson and so many, many more stalwarts in quest for freedom and upliftment of African people!"

WHEN IS A "GANGSTER GOVERNMENT"?
A "GANGSTER GOVERNMENT?"

A number of democratic presidential hopefuls descended on South Carolina to attend this year's (2019) **Black Economic Forum** ostensibly to pitch their program to the State's Black electorate. In the earliest contest in the cycle, South Carolina comes after Iowa and New Hampshire, but more important, there's a broad swath of Black democrats in this state's voting population. As such, a good showing in this contest can project a candidate in a meaningful position on the road to the convention. Jesse Jackson in 1984, Al Sharpton in 2004 and Barack Obama in 2008 won here but other candidates also campaign in the state to create an image of Black support for later contests. James Clyburn's "Fish Fry" is another significant attraction for those seeking the significant Black vote of this state. In some respects, James Clyburn is politically the most powerful Black person in the nation, even more-so than Barack Obama, who, essentially is sidelined. This power position is manifest because Mr. Clyburn presides at the pinnacle of power in the House of Representatives. The question then becomes, "How did South Carolina earn the position and the popularity it now shares?"

In the first case, not simply luck of the draw but reorganization of the primary calendar accounts for this pole position. In regards the second, South Carolina was home to one of the largest enslaved populations during slavery and with the coming of the vote, candidates began courting these voters whose strengths equally became objects promoting gerrymandering and legal actions. However, as in many southern, particular the "lynching" states, the vote did not come easily nor was it easy to hold on to. Thus, in the Pre-Independence periods, the Pre-Civil War Period, Post Civil War to the 1965 Voting Rights Act; and the age of the voting Rights Act to today; no other group in this country faced the problems of the Black voter, not even women voters who equally had to fight for the franchise. Even in that unfolding spectacle, the Black female seem to have been victimized twice. Yet, they persevered and as a result of vigorous activism, Black women have been elected to a variety of national, state and local offices. In 1972, Shirley Chisolm ran for the presidency, and though unsuccessful, she made an imprint and paved the way for many black and white women, especially with her "unbought and unbossed" mantra.

During slavery in the Pre-Independence Period, Blacks had no civil, human and certainly no voting rights. The record is replete with Blacks who fought in the Revolutionary War but had no voting rights. Many fought in their master's stead and this was certainly a contradiction for they were defending the South, a bastion of slavery. Nevertheless, in this period voting privileges depended on economic status and a miniscule number of Blacks being wealthy, were permitted the franchise. This state of affairs generally continued until the Civil War's end. Then, there was the exceptional case of Blacks were who freed by their masters and an equal few who were fortunate to purchase their freedom. Still, by virtue of color their status was tenuous.

WHEN IS A "GANGSTER GOVERNMENT"?
A "GANGSTER GOVERNMENT?"

The Civil War came and went with Blacks fighting, for the most part, on the Union side. The known fact is, President Abe Lincoln issued the **Emancipation Proclamation** freeing enslaved Africans effective January 1, 1863. However, not until war's end in 1965 did the **Radical Republicans** successfully enact the 13th Amendment which officially freed those Africans held in bondage. The Radical Republicans next passed the 14th Amendment which gave citizenship to person born in the United States. Finally, in 1868 Congress passed the 15th Amendment granting the right to vote to all male citizens and so Black men became entitled to exercise the franchise. This political empowerment enabled Blacks to play a major role in Reconstruction by electing their choices to state governments, the House of Representatives and the Federal Senate. During Reconstruction the Black voting rolls expanded to unprecedented levels and so African-Americans were involved in re-writing State Constitutions in the South. The 1876 election saw the southern candidate Rutherford B. Hayes succeed to the presidency and with political machinations set in motion, the new administration brought Reconstruction to an end. This new reality began efforts designed to bring about the reemergence of "Southern Supremacy" that took the form of an unleashed systematic campaign to drastically reduce the Black voting rolls. Employing a wide array of strategies including intimidation; tar and feathering; even lynching, as Blacks were systematically purged from the voting rolls. And so, the newly freed Africans lost much, if not all forms of civil war Amendment rights. Therefore, disfranchisement proved one of the many strategies employed in the South, for which the African-American scholar Rayford Logan characterized as "The Nadir."

Joanne Grant in *Black Protest* (New York: Fawcett Books, 1968: 111) provided startling documentation emphasizing the unfolding reality. In this she wrote: "In Louisiana in 1896 there were 164,088 whites registered and 130,344 Negroes. In 1900, the first registration year after a new constitution had been adopted, there were 125,437 white and 5,340 Negroes registered. By 1904 Negro registration had declined to 1,718, and white registration was 106,360. This represented a 96 percent decrease in Negro registration, and a four percent decrease in white."

"In Alabama, Mississippi and South Carolina disfranchisement began earlier. In 1883 in Alabama there were only 3,742 registered Negroes out of the 140,000 formerly registered. In South Carolina Negro registration decreased from 92,081 in 1876 to 2,823 in 1898. In Mississippi the decrease was from 52,705 in 1876 to 3,573 in 1898. Systematic exclusion continued up to through the present time [1968]. Between 1920 and 1930 about 10,000 Negroes voted in Georgia out of a potential Negro electorate of 369,511, and in Virginia the Negro vote at any time in that decade was 12,000 to 18,000 out

WHEN IS A "GANGSTER GOVERNMENT"? A "GANGSTER GOVERNMENT?"

of a voting-age-or-over and literate Negro population of 248,347."

It took vigorous activism, the Civil Rights Movement, much coordination and creative alliances that secured, held fast and helped assure, not simply South Carolina, but many Southern states housing Black voters, to secure the hard fought-for sacred franchise.

When is a "Gangster Government" a "Gangster Government" Photo? "Laying down the Law" in sort of "Mosaic fashion!"

"Republican Senators are the only people with power to restrain the President." *New York Times* Editorial.

FREDERICK MONDERSON

"What is in the interest of the nation? Trump peddles Russian efforts. There is not one ounce of truth in the Russian narrative. This fictional theory helps Russian interest. The President and those who peddle such falsity are undermining our strengths at home and abroad. We are not protecting Ukraine but handed it to Russia as we did in handing Syria to Iran. He undermines the discipline of our military. None of us anticipated this undermining of our national security. Trump is undermining the values of the United States." **Leon Panetta**

32. STAR SPANGLED BANNER AND BLACK NATIONAL ANTHEM BY DR. FRED MONDERSON

Recently at my child's graduation June 19, 2019, "Juneteenth," we sang the Star-Spangled Banner and we also sang the Black National Anthem. Interesting, the psychological and social connection these two symbols represented and the emotional and spiritual effluence both evoked were powerful emotions of a "double consciousness" as W.E.B. DuBois first pointed out. It is an extraordinary sign that these two motifs, can converge at this important ceremony to underscore the intellectual journey to achieve and recognize the potential significance of two such symbols combining to create a greater experience for this nation in its quest for further and sustainable evolution towards a more perfect union. This

WHEN IS A "GANGSTER GOVERNMENT"?
A "GANGSTER GOVERNMENT?"

combining is significant for who can measure the importance of each element's contribution though, paradoxically, each seems on a different track. Still, one within the other, that is to say, while beginnings are not always pleasant, milestones along the way and final destination can become even more important and rewarding. Hence, each component in the experience must be awarded appropriate recognition and acknowledge the earned equality of all participants while pinpointing "cons against the pros."

Much more significant, the constituency the **Black National Anthem** represents from the inception has fought not simply to uphold the ideals the Star-Spangled Banner speaks to but to defend the freedom and cultural integrity this powerful expression represents. However, the dividers, the racists and other such miserable oppressors' actions must not enable us to forget the efforts of the Haitian Revolutionaries who fought at the "Battle of Savannah," in the initial great war, the Revolutionary War, to become the genesis, the nucleus of what America is today. Upon return to their homeland, Haiti, these early African nationalists quietly affirmed: "We have learned the ways of the white man. We have learned how to load the muzzle at the breech and how to fire the cannon with remarkable effect. Belief in our African gods will bring us victory!"

FREDERICK MONDERSON

During the Obama Age, "Tea Party" activists made their statements time and again. The Blacks have remained silent through it all, but the millions of black veterans have been trained and are aboard this ship. Harking back to *The New Yorker* Cover story seeking to disparage Michelle Obama as a warrior woman, many of those millions of veterans may be prepared to fight under her command. But who wants conflict, whether racial, educational, political, social or religious? It is not too much to ask for respectable equality. This land is our land and its success or failure affects us all. Jerry Rawlins, former president of Ghana, in West Africa, once told the Brooklyn Activist Sonny Carson, "Black America is Africa's greatest ally in the world! Its 'Trojan Horse!" We know malevolent forces have killed our leaders, Martin Luther King, Malcolm X, Medgar Evers, and more, though we suffered the agonizing trauma, yet we forgave rather than internalize the millstone of hatred, bigotry, and more important, racism and discrimination in their many guises. Dylan roof killed nine praying in Mother Emanuel Church in South Carolina. This much violent behavior is too high a price to pay, day in and day out.

In this challenged and troubled time, African-Americans want to move forward under the philosophic construct of the fatherhood of god and the brotherhood of man manifested in the act of being human and in American citizenship. Today, when America's enemies, viz., Russia, China, North Korea, Iran, etc., threaten our way of life, is it time to exclude Blacks? African-Americans proudly carried the

WHEN IS A "GANGSTER GOVERNMENT"?
A "GANGSTER GOVERNMENT?"

banner, performing exceptionally well in all military conflicts America has engaged in. In these engagements the American veterans learned well! As in all the great conflicts America faced, malevolent miscreants be told, as Barack Obama did to Russia when he discovered they were "misbehaving in American Elections," he told them "Cut it out!"

There has been a long history of failed promises towards African-American, simply form the time of the Civil War, such as, viz.,

1. The promises of "Juneteenth;"

2. "40-Acres and a Mule" that were never delivered;

3. Social conditions needing a "Civil Rights Movement;"

4. More than "4000 lynchings in the South;"

5. The "Mother Emanuel Martyrdom;"

6. "Racial hatred and disrespect directed towards Barack Obama," the first African-American President;

7. More than "a century of systematically engineered political disfranchisement;"

8. References to our ancestral lands as being "Shithole countries;"

9. Not to discount decades of "high unemployment rates," and a "criminal justice system" run amok;

10. "Educational opportunities challenged, lack of quality health care;"

11. "Black on Black" and other forms of "violence" visited on the Black National Anthem's constituency;

12. Let us not forget "I intend to make Barack Obama a one term President" and "I looked Barack Obama in the eye and told him, 'Mr. President you won't get this seat on the Supreme Court' Mitch McConnell who thinks Reparations is not "a good idea."

These then are some of the issues African-Americans experienced and must contend with and confront.

"Whether or not Donald Trump recognizes Separation of Powers, it is a sad day for America but a great day for Constitutional Democracy." **Laura Coates**

WHEN IS A "GANGSTER GOVERNMENT"?
A "GANGSTER GOVERNMENT?"

When is a "Gangster Government" a "Gangster Government" Photo? The "Colonnade Hall" of the Jefferson Building of the Library of Congress, indeed a work of art that needs to be showcased.

When is a "Gangster Government" a "Gangster Government" Photo? Another view of the front face of the Capitol Building from the Jefferson Building.

FREDERICK MONDERSON

"The Founders did not want Power in the hands of one person! There has to be a counterweight and they created the Impeachment option!"

33.   LOW IQ
BY
DR. FRED MONDERSON

During the 2016 Republican Primary and Convention, former New York City Mayor Michael Bloomberg referred to then candidate Donald Trump's strategy as "a con." In fact, he said, "I know a con when I see one." Nonetheless and strange, Mr. Trump's base has been so "conned," if he tells them "Sunday is Tuesday," they agree. Additionally, they believe all the news is fake and more than a dozen women who accused Donald Trump of sexual harassment are all liars. That "claim of denial" is perpetuated by a man who has been clocked at 14,440 lies and mis-statements in a three-year period. These Trump supporters are the same people who did not believe by the age of 16-years Kim Jung Un had authored 104 books. In assessing this propaganda, they perceive the North Korean people to be idiots who believe such; but as Donald Trump's supporters they appear to be "clear-eyed and bushy tailed" in view of their revered leader, especially disregarding his lying ways. So, we ask, 'Who are the idiots?'

Mr. Trump expresses a number of popular refrains he trots out every so often. These include "We'll see what happens;" "He's a good man;" and "No

WHEN IS A "GANGSTER GOVERNMENT"?
A "GANGSTER GOVERNMENT?"

Collusion, No Obstruction folks," which he particularly obsesses over in response to Muller's Report findings. Factually known, this is false! Conversely, when he wishes to characterize opponents, he accuses them of having "Low IQ." The whole notion of "Low IQ" is a state of mind.

A most pointed accusations in reference to "Low IQ" is one he leveled against Don Lemon, the CNN Anchor of **Don Lemon Tonight**, aired weeknights, Monday to Friday at 10:00 – 12:00 PM. Much of this stem from Mr. Lemon's consistent focus on Mr. Trump's aberrations. There he invites a number of extremely informed and highly analytic guests who markedly point to Mr. Trump and his pitfalls. Sadly, Mr. Trump's base never watches Don Lemon Tonight to see their "Dear Leader" "without clothes" and not with "the coat of Fox News falsity!" Trump also accused Lebron James and Rosie O'Donnell of being "Low IQ." LeBron did pushback, claiming, as a member of a championship team, "You bum, coming to the White House used to be fun until you got there." This is not "Low IQ" to challenge, in this manner, the most powerful man in the world, but LeBron has stature and gumption or "balls," Republicans in Congress seem to lack in fear of calling out Donald Trump's moral bankruptcy.

In the "Birther Charade," beyond the "Birth Certificate" requests, Mr. Trump also asked to see Mr. Obama's College Transcripts. However, in this quest Mr. Trump would not reciprocate by either

FREDERICK MONDERSON

supplying his Birth Certificate, College Transcript or Tax Returns.

This Birth Certificate and College Transcript request, "Show me yours, I'll show you mine." No! Mr. Trump hid everything, from his Tax Returns to his closest aides' testimony. This was a strange request of a man who is an Ivy League graduate, twice over, Columbia and Harvard, and elected President of his Alma Mata's Law Review, as well as a practicing attorney and teacher of United States law. Imagine such a request of a Constitutional Scholar, and all the attributes that propelled him to the American Presidency, twice. Mr. Obama had a low administration turnover rate and no scandals attached to his time in office. Conversely, imagine such a request of an individual who first promised to release but refused to turn over his Income Tax Returns, for fear it would reveal his shortfalls and entanglements with questionable characters and unsavory entities. Mr. Trump would not, even if he was paid, turn over his College Transcripts for this would reveal the depths of his thinking as such behavior equally hides his business and Income Tax Return entanglements. He does seem to be profiting from his Presidency.

Ask any Republican what Mr. Trump discussed with Russian Representatives, whether Vladimir Putin or the Foreign Minister, in more than a dozen meetings, and they have nothing. His meetings with Kim Jung Un, the Egyptian, Turkish and Philippine leaders and so all America is in the dark about Mr. Trump's meetings with these global "bad boys."

WHEN IS A "GANGSTER GOVERNMENT"?
A "GANGSTER GOVERNMENT?"

Mr. Trump has often boasted of attending the best schools, standing ahead of his class and essentially what a genius he is. Word has it, Mr. Trump functions at a 5th or 6th grade level giving rise to the view he achieved real estate success not through brilliance of thought, hard work and strategy but through uncivil and unconscionable, perhaps illegal, practices of threats and intimidation, keeping any and all beneath his shoe like chewing gum. Still, it's generally agreed overuse of particular terms signals the user is challenged grammatically and linguistically and "We'll see what happens" is one overuse phrase just as "He's a good man" of all departing associates entangled in some illegal activity. It is common knowledge Mr. Trump does not read! John McCain was a voracious reader and we know at Christmastime the Obama White House published his reading list. This has not been done for President Trump. Equally, a generally agreed postulate is that educated persons function ethically, morally, civilly and analytically above the norm. This may entail respect for persons, use of admirable language and refrain from repetition in communication. Further, we must not lose sight Mr. Trump is ignorant of and holds contempt for the Constitution and as such demonstrated a profound ignorance and a failure to understand the implications of the First Amendment protections in the Bill of Rights; and equally what constitutes Impeachment or the Emoluments Clause. Naturally, the educated person generally stays on the right side of the law avoiding unsavory associations and illegal entanglements. None of these "high concepts" Mr. trump grasps or utilizes and so wallows in actions and deeds subject to scrutiny and criticism, even legal challenges.

Clearly Mr. Trump's language, behavior and actions are of a "Low IQ" nature. Upon becoming President and with revelations of Russian involvement in aiding his election, he has unleashed unending and venomous accusations and denunciations of the FBI, CIA, NSA, the Justice Department, the Attorney General, the Deputy Attorney General, the Mueller Probe, Mr. Mueller himself, foundational American institutions, even the Pope as well as Merkel, Trudeau and Macron. Yet he sees China's Xi; North Korea's Kim Jung Un; and Russia's Vladimir Putin as good guys and "strong leaders" whom he wished he could emulate, seeming to indicate he can stay in power longer than permitted as the Constitution dictates. Perhaps it is because these individuals, with no checks on their power, can do what he cannot. That is, rule ruthlessly and without compunction and this is because the American system does not tolerate dictatorship, but has a system of Checks and Balances. Dr. Martin Luther King reminded, "The arc of the moral universe is long but it bends towards justice." That is to say, while some persons may bend, stretch, even break the law; in America, that law ultimately catches up with law-breakers, as the Impeachment debacle that will stain Mr. Trump's legacy forever. No matter how he rationalizes as with "No Collusion, No Obstruction, folks;" once Speaker Nancy Pelosi gaveled in, President Trump has been **IMPEACHED! THERE'S NO TURNING**

WHEN IS A "GANGSTER GOVERNMENT"? A "GANGSTER GOVERNMENT?"

BACK! If it walks like **Impeached**; talks like **Impeached**, it must be **IMPEACHED**!

Assessing the man, Mr. Trump sees Neo-Nazis, White Supremacists and KKK members as "very fine people" because they are on "his side." In his anti-media tirade, to brand **CBS**, **NBC**, **ABC**, **CNN** as "fake news" and "enemies of the people" and the major culprit Fox News is not, means Mr. Trump does not understand what **Freedom of the Press** means and this is certainly "Low IQ" behavior. And so, like co-opted lemmings Mr. Trump's followers, Republicans especially in Congress, whose job as a separate branch of the government is to serve as a check on the President in this democracy; we could, perhaps separate "Intellectual gentry" not fully understand Mr. Trump and Republican defenders "confusing speak;" and so, these people never seem to question any of his actions.

Right thinking military strategists often avoid fighting on two or more fronts. Yet, despite his boasts of his intellectual prowess, Mr. Trump attacks on numerous fronts except against those considered his base, and still none dare "march out of step." He has a fetish about receiving loyalty but does not reciprocate. Anyone unfortunate enough to point out as much as a Trump "White lie" or any form of criticism of his actions that may show disloyalty is subject to a full-court press of vindictiveness and vilification. He is a hater! He does not forgive nor forget and he certainly refuses to apologize, even when blatantly wrong. Essentially, he dishes on any and every one and expects they will take it without retaliation. That is "Low IQ" thinking. Then he tells his base, this "boy who cried wolf," that "people are out to get him." Naturally they agree and choose to see the "Mole not the pole" or the "Tree not the forest" of lies, insults, unconscionable behavior.

As the 2012 Republican candidate, John McCain, without batting an eye, told the disgruntled woman, in reference to Barack Obama's birth certificate issue, "No Ma'am, he is a citizen, a decent family man, we simply have disagreements over policy issues;" Mr. Trump refuses to recognize it is not him but his actions people object to. Given all, Mr. Trump wishes to sees "a lot of Trump," therein lies his conundrum. We have heard of "ducks lining up" but Republicans who line up behind Mr. Trump and see no evil, hear no evil, and cannot speak to and condemn evil, and so are enablers of a lost cause. What these people do not seem to realize or even care about, many listen to and observe their behavior, pro and con. Like an impending hurricane bring the wrath of the people, Mr. Trump and his associates have been warned. For people who like to invoke the divine's name, they must be reminded, "cleanliness is next to godliness" in thought and deed. Mr. Trump needs be careful, "An angry god may wield a thunderbolt at him" while he looks up! The "Chosen One" mantra, a la Perry, Giuliani, Trump, themselves questionable characters, notwithstanding. We must

WHEN IS A "GANGSTER GOVERNMENT"? A "GANGSTER GOVERNMENT?"

equate Mr. Trump's words and deeds, however sad and misguided, as comparable with the Pope spewing such venom from the Vatican. This is and should be Unthinkable. Philosophically speaking, perhaps Jerry Nadler is that "visiting angel of vengeance" for Trump, et al., having taken god's name in vain!

Day after day as he makes those unforced errors and attacks opponents to sow chaos, yet Mr. Trump expects to not be visited with retribution, and this is certainly "Low IQ thinking," if it is thinking at all.

When Robert Mueller was chosen as the Special Prosecutor to conduct the investigation of the attack on the American election process in 2016, he was described as fair and decent but not a saint. Fairness aside, to be villainized day after day while doing one's job, can certainly lead one to defend one's integrity. Mr. Trump lives in a glass house yet he throws stones and expects none of these projectiles will boomerang. Mr. Mueller, taking his responsibility seriously, chose to be fair, in process followed each and every lead into its most logical conclusion and much of this points to Donald Trump's wrongdoing. It's an accepted fact, "Whom the gods wish to destroy they first make mad" and possessing a "Low IQ" mentality invites "hurry sundown." Poor Mr. Trump!

FREDERICK MONDERSON

When is a "Gangster Government" a "Gangster Government" Photo? Entrance to the Jefferson Building of the Library of Congress.

"It is a tragic day for people who voted to impeach Trump!" "Lots of things get said in a campaign" **Rick Santorum**

When is a "Gangster government" a "Gangster government" Photo? Another view of the front face of the Capital Building from the Jefferson Building.

WHEN IS A "GANGSTER GOVERNMENT"? A "GANGSTER GOVERNMENT?"

"The sheer volume and degrees of his lies is staggering. There is a foundation of lies. Daniel Dale the 'Lie Detector' counted 5 lies per day when he started. Today he is doing as much as 22 lies per day." Jake Tapper.

34. TRUMP LEAVING OFFICE BY DR. FRED MONDERSON

Recently, Bill Mahr, appearing on Chris Cuomo's Prime Time, CNN Show: **Let's Get After it**, raised the seeming growing concern that if not re-elected in 2020, President Donald Trump will refuse to leave office, claiming the election was rigged. This is carrying "Schoolyard bullying" beyond the next level. Naturally, this was before **IMPEACHMENT**! Nevertheless, what options remain to the great body of Americans in the pro and anti-Trump camps? We must be realistic to the fact Donald Trump has upset the American applecart and in doing so, at this time, much of the fruit have rolled away not to be recovered. In that case, if we accept the merits of the first proposition, the Democratic campaign now in progress should be suspended, Mr. Trump himself should cease all such related activities and we should crown him instantly. As the argument holds, let us suppose Mr. Trump loses the 2020 presidential election which requires him to vacate the White House at 12:00 Noon, January 20, 2021. Let us further assume he claims victory in 2020 election, chooses to occupy the White House another 4 years, will he then vacate the office on the exact date in 2025?

Let us for argument further say, he loses and claims he was cheated, then refuses to leave January 20, 2021, to get to 2025, he has to obliterate all adherence to law throwing the nation into chaos. Does he in his alternative universe mind expect to the be only one disobeying the law, or are Americans also allowed to follow suit, resulting from the simplest, viz., disobeying traffic laws, stop paying bills, refusing to accept the sanctity of one's neighbors' personal space and property rights. Thus, we come to the absurd conclusion, many have enabled the ogre in the White House to fracture the American system beyond repair. There is an alternative however.

At Noon January 20, 2021, either "Men in White Jackets" or "Men with handcuffs" will be visibly waiting to jump into action.

Interesting, but there should be several teams of the above not simply to greet Mr. Trump but equally his sycophants, viz., Bill Barr, Steve Mnuchin, Mitch McConnell, Jim Jordan, Collins, and more. Then again, there's still another scenario.

At the recent 75th Annual celebration of D-Day, President Trump represented the American nation heaped praises on the veterans who stormed the Normandy Beach on June 6, 1944. There he unrolled a previously unexpected behavior which seemed a

WHEN IS A "GANGSTER GOVERNMENT"?
A "GANGSTER GOVERNMENT?"

flicker of "Presidential Timber." Soon, however, he reverted to "rotten wood" behavior by attacking Speaker Nancy Pelosi using the most unimagined vile diatribe. Sadly, the white crosses that marked the graves of Normandy's revered dead stood as a backdrop to Mr. Trump's slap in the face of these veterans who gave their lives to uphold the ideals, laws, customs, institutions and aspirations, that he refused to serve; yet represents what America stands for and have propelled this nation to the stature it previously held in the world.

The horrible behavior aside, this "war dead" backdrop inclusion is remindful of another, the Korean War memorial in Washington, DC. There, a platoon of soldiers in a "rice paddy" procession is shown on patrol. However, a wall to the side projects a powerful and meaningful message. Engraved in the marble are the images of many of these soldiers' comrades who were lost to combat seemingly preferred to admonition somewhat similar to what in the movie "Saving Private Ryan" Captain Miller asked of the young soldier whose mother had "given four sons as sacrifice on the altar of American freedom." He said, "Live and uphold the ideals this nation stands for." Paradoxically, for a now Commander-In-Chief whose "Bone spurs" kept him from serving during Viet Nam, he has consistently trashed and will abrogate if the above scenario materializes.

The American hero Senator John McCain is a useful example, ironically, to make a point. His father and grandfather were veterans who served to uphold American institutions and ideals. There are thousands, millions in and out of uniform who are troubled by the unfolding scenarios and one has to believe "after a long train of abuses, it is the duty of the American people to abolish such a government and its perpetrators" associated with lying, vulgar and disrespectful language, indictments, convictions, cozying up to Russia, perpetuating debunked conspiracy theories, and much more.

Now, if we begin with the 700 former Attorney generals who signed the letter pointing out Donald Trump did commit obstruction of justice and the 300 retired Admirals and Generals who signaled their disapproval of President Trump denying clearance to General Clapper among others as well as an increasingly agitated and mobilized electorate perhaps reality will finally come to Mr. Trump's understanding. He may even choose to relocate to Moscow at the end of his tenure.

What is significant, however, as Rev. Sharpton said to Kanye West after his Trump escapade, "Donald Trump will not always be president and we will remember your behavior." This is the question to be posed to short-sighted supporters who refuse to see or smell Mr. Trump as he wallows in the "Shithole" he created. We know Paris Dennard, Mark Burns, Rev. Darrell, even Omarosa, have all disappeared from the radar. We also know history will not be kind to Mr. Trump. What will become of his followers is

WHEN IS A "GANGSTER GOVERNMENT"? A "GANGSTER GOVERNMENT?"

the question, for the American people have long memories.

When is a "Gangster government" a "Gangster government" Photo? Still another view of the Marble Terrace at the rear of the Capitol Building.

"There is much talk about the 63,000,000 people who voted for Donald Trump, but no mention of the 67,000,000 who voted against him."

FREDERICK MONDERSON

When is a **"Gangster Government"** a **"Gangster government Photo**? View of the entrance to Union Station with a few people milling around and the "God Bless America" flag nearby.

"The President does nothing but project unto others his own lack of morality." **Adam Schiff**

35. AMERICA AS LAUGHING STOCK BY DR. FRED MONDERSON

For the most part America is driving in the opposite direction on the world's superhighway stage and people in "Red Hats" called "the base" are in jubilation not realizing the real wall is immanent! On the world stage adversaries are making tremendous gains at this nation's expense; competitors are making gains, meddling in and exploiting our economic basket; and allies are dumfounded by this nation's rejection of present reality as they too have

WHEN IS A "GANGSTER GOVERNMENT"? A "GANGSTER GOVERNMENT?"

begun trumpeting "we first, too!" This means, they are moving towards preserving their own special interests, security, without consideration or involvement with America. That being said, all across the globe people and their nations are beginning to have different, *al be it*, negative views of the once great American nation, champion of democracy and moral, even scientific thought and experimentation.

For years, this nation has admired and appreciated individuals of superior minds whose understanding of the workings of contemporary socio-political dynamics proved enlightening yardsticks. Their observations and deductions regarding events and issues created under President Donald J. Trump's thoughts and actions as well as policies are generally unheeded particularly by Mr. Trump's base but especially elected Republican members of Congress who refuse to recognize the catastrophic downward spiral of the nation's morality and its impact on America's longstanding norms and institutional practices as well as its perceived role in the world.

Some have argued, Republican legislators may realize the President is guilty of wrongdoing but are afraid to speak-up or challenge the President because of the base's support for Mr. Trump. They are afraid if he utters a word against them it may jeopardize their hold on the elected position they now occupy. How sad. Again, Edmund Burke reminded, "The only thing necessary for evil to triumph is for good men to do or say nothing." *Ipso facto*, there are no good men or women in the Republican Party. As we stand today, shame of Senator Kennedy (R. Texas), for his dismissing Russian meddling in the 2016 election and trumping the discredited "Ukraine involvement" Ambassador Jovanovich determined was false; a Russian manufactured talking point. Sadly, individuals as Senators are abrogating the oath of responsibility to the Constitution they swore to uphold and so are disappointing the nation and people who believe, as Conservatives love to tout, the "Strict observance of the Constitution."

One of the great minds whose insights have been enlightening to the American understanding due to his many years in high-level decision-making positions in government is Leon Panetta. Without fear and in objective assessment relating to Mr. Trump's behaviors indicated "they were not in the nation's interests" but designed to serve the President's narrow self-interest.

Panetta first pointed out, Mr. Trump peddles a Russian narrative, talking point, in which there is not one ounce of proof to substantiate such claims. The President's fictional behavior undermines the nation's interests. Mr. Trump's failure to protect Ukraine has handed Russia a win both in this brave but vulnerable nation as well as in Syria. His intervention in a military judicial matter undermines the discipline of our armed forces. No one anticipated his undermining the security and values of the United States. Mr. Trump's failure to recognize and acknowledge he only represents one of three

WHEN IS A "GANGSTER GOVERNMENT"? A "GANGSTER GOVERNMENT?"

branches of government of equal stature is undermining the values that made America great. That is, an America that has always been great and there is no need for the "again."

Donald Trump says "Republicans passed the biggest tax cut in history." False! It is actually the eighth. He says "We have the cleanest air and water." This too is false.

Bernie Sanders rightly calls Donald Trump "A pathological liar."

When is a "Gangster Government" a "Gangster government" Photo? Colorful photo of the bustle outside Union Station.

"We cannot name managers until we see what is said on the Senate Side." **Nancy Pelosi**.

FREDERICK MONDERSON
36. ANOTHER SNAKE STORY
BY
DR. FRED MONDERSON

We know the story of how the snake lost his tail. More important, however, President Trump in the exuberance of his rallies often told the story of the snake. In actuality, a lady traveling a road came upon a badly wounded snake. She took the snake home, treated its wounds and nourished it back to health. After some time in the comfort and luxury of the good Samaritan's company, the snake bit its benefactor. Immediately, the lady asked, "Mr. Snake, after all I have done for you, how could you bite me?" To this the snake responded, "I'm a snake. I snake!"

Now, with his new revelation that he has "Insurance," Rudy Giuliani has signaled *writ large*, if as some have intimated because of the numerous times his name has been mentioned in the ongoing Impeachment Inquiry, "If President Trump seeks to throw me under the bus, I have insurance."

Even the three monkeys who "See no evil, hear no evil nor speak no evil," could realize this is snake medicine, that is potential blackmail!

Ok. So, Donald Trump and Rudy Giuliani go way back. They are both New Yorkers. Trump is a billionaire real estate magnate. Giuliani, a former Federal Prosecutor who gained fame prosecuting the

WHEN IS A "GANGSTER GOVERNMENT"? A "GANGSTER GOVERNMENT?"

Mob. He eventually became Mayor of New York City, though he savaged former Mayor David Dinkins; and in so doing, removed his photo from its conspicuous position in Gracie Mansion, the Mayor's residence. During his campaign he had signs posted in the African-American community that read "Rudy G. fights racism." Sadly, however, many thought Rudy a true and unrepentant racist.

Unfortunately, however, yet fortunate for Mr. Giuliani whose fortunes were on a downward skid, the attack on the World Trade Center 9-11-2001 happened. As so often, in times of calamity Americans showed true patriotism and rallied to New York City suffering nearly 3000 deaths inflicted by Osama bin Laden and his henchmen. With support flooding the city and with Rudy Giuliani at its head, the reality became "New York Strong" and Rudy got over "like a fat rat." So much so, Mr. Giuliani became "America's Mayor." However, and to the contrary, Rev. Al Sharpton who had followed Rudy for years added insightfully, anyone placed in so supportive a position would have performed as Mayor Giuliani did. Nevertheless, when the Mayor tried to run for President; on two occasions, the American people resoundingly rejected his candidacy. Maybe they saw Rudy's underbelly same as Al Sharpton saw earlier on. Well, forward to Muller's Inquiry and Rudy Giuliani emerged as a big-wheel lawyer for Mr. Trump.

FREDERICK MONDERSON

When is a "Gangster Government" a "Gangster Government" Photo? Another view of art and architectural magnificence in the Jefferson Building of the Library of Congress.

"Democrats are outraged over Mitch McConnell's speech on **Fox News**, to underscore what he put on the table will be a fair trial. They don't believe McConnell will have a fair trial." **Phil Mattingly**.

When is a "Gangster Government" a "Gangster Government" Photo? Gold Star "Price of Freedom!"

WHEN IS A "GANGSTER GOVERNMENT"? A "GANGSTER GOVERNMENT?"

"Donald Trump declares his lies are true. We haven't seen anything like this." **Mary Macklin**

37. DEMONIZING WOMEN BY DR. FRED MONDERSON

Beyond his relentless pursuit of the "Birther" issue, Donald trump next most foul engagement has been to consistently attack and dishonor women. Some have argued, given one's mother is among many things as one's first teacher, and most impressive role model, to entertain a negative attitude towards women in general means, perhaps, the individual early entertained a hatred for one's mother. Its general knowledge Donald Trump had this "thing" with his father, but any reference to a relationship with his mother is based on pure speculation.

When is a "Gangster Government" a "Gangster Government" Photo? Another view of the mythical figure in front of the entrance to the Jefferson Building of the Library of Congress.

FREDERICK MONDERSON

When is a "Gangster Government" a "Gangster Government" Photo? The Garden at the Smithsonian Museum.

"This is a somber moment. It is the first time two parties controlled different houses. We are witnessing something historic." **Tim Naftali**.

"Donald Trump was concerned about corruption but he remained silent on the issue of corruption in the Ukraine phone call."

38. FLAILING THE MESSENGER BY DR. FRED MONDERSON

The Donald John Trump Presidency has made one thing unmistakably clear, Mr. Trump and his minions and Republicans in general, particularly in this age, have "this thing with the truth." As E.F. Hutton's

WHEN IS A "GANGSTER GOVERNMENT"? A "GANGSTER GOVERNMENT?"

Pitchman often stated, "If it came up, slap you on the bottom and stated, I'm here, you probably won't believe it anyway." Malcolm X, on the other hand, often reminded, "History is a good teacher." Thus, and because American history is so ingrained in the nation's academic curriculum, as in the past, the Trump era will be a consistent subject of analysis and debate. As such, not simply Republicans *writ large* but persons such as Congressmen Jim Jordan, Collins and Devon Nunes will come in for their dose of scrutiny and seemingly it may be a perpetual intellectual or academic flogging for their failing to recognize the truth but steadfastly choosing the other path of flogging or flailing the messengers who have testified before their committee under oath. Their blind devotion to destroy truth to defend the indefensible is tantamount to malfeasance in regards to their Congressional oath to defend the Constitution of the United States.

In Representative Nunes' introductory remarks at Ambassador Sondland's testimony to the Congressional Committee investigating the President's potential impeachment actions, he used very colorful language to state his views though much seemed incompatible with the facts as presented, not simply by this witness but others as well.

Strange, but this Ranking Republican Member, Mr. Nunes' view of events seemed not consistent with his behavior when Republicans controlled the House of Representatives and he chaired this Intelligence

Committee. Then, as some characterized, his behavior seemed more President Trump's man in his actions rather than an objective Republican Member of Congress who swore to uphold the Constitution, whether from foreign or domestic threats to the tenets of this sacred American document.

It is and should be that an elected Representative reflects the thoughts and actions of his Constituency. Therefore, every decision should be answerable to the people he or she represents. As was said in one of the "Danny Ocean movies," "You of all people should know, there's always someone watching." And so, Mr. Nunes was observed visiting the White House at Midnight, purportedly to share secrets his Committee had uncovered that had relevance to the ongoing Muller Investigation. Many believed, rather than remain objective and consistent with his oath to defend the Constitution, by his actions, Mr. Nunes was thereby proving to be Mr. Trump's lawyer. One of them that is. As faith would have it, American voters denounced Mr. Nunes's and Mr. Trump's behavior in general and essentially "Gave the House to the Democrats."

This time in the **Impeachment Inquiry**, Representative Adam Schiff is the Intelligence Committee Chairman and Mr. Nunes is the Ranking Member. Now at the Sondland testimony, as Mr. Schiff chose to "run a tight ship" as opposed to Mr. Nunes' "leaky boat," the Ranking Member assailed the witness and the process of investigation in the most caustic and fault-filled manner. That is to say,

WHEN IS A "GANGSTER GOVERNMENT"? A "GANGSTER GOVERNMENT?"

Mr. Nunes' behavior was not inconsistent with the time when he did his "Midnight Run." Explaining this latter is difficult for Midnight is no "Tea time," and there is generally no meeting held at that time. He is certainly no Paul Revere! Therefore, such surreptitious actions, though not to be observed, represented an action inconsistent with the objectivity demanded of a Chairman of a Congressional Committee as prestigious as Intelligence.

"If the phone call was so perfect, why is the president blocking everyone who could exonerate him from testifying." **Wajahad Ali**

When is a "Gangster Government" a "Gangster Government" Photo? Art in monumental form!

FREDERICK MONDERSON

When is a **"Gangster Government"** a **"gangster Government" Photo**? What more can be said!

"Limits of partisanship have been reached and surpassed." **John Lott**.

39. I WANT A TRIAL BY DR. FRED MONDERSON

Following the recent Impeachment hearings in which objective witnesses have delivered testimony under oath, and commentators expressed, the cumulative evidence painted a bleak picture of President Trump's Abuse of Power, Obstruction of Justice; Bribery; and "Obstruction of Congress." In

WHEN IS A "GANGSTER GOVERNMENT"?
A "GANGSTER GOVERNMENT?"

pushback, the next day, Mr. Trump declared, "I want a trial."

The founding fathers designed a system so that no one can be considered above the law. That is, above the Constitution. As such, they agreed upon a system of Impeachment to remove a President for malfeasance in office. Such behavior is translated as treason, bribery, and high crimes and misdemeanors. To determine such, in this case, the House of Representatives' Intelligence Committee must conduct an Impeachment Inquiry to determine the fact of the case that is then turned over to the Judiciary Committee which, based on the evidence uncovered in their deliberations next draw up the Article or Articles of Impeachment. The following step in the process is for the evidence to be turned over to the Senate to conduct a trial in which the Supreme Court's Chief Justice presides. Apparently, Mr. Trump seems to have more confidence in the Republican majority, controlled under his leadership, perhaps by fear of his retaliating against them and perhaps encouraging a challenge in any primary, that they will exonerate him regardless of the evidence. He truly believes the Senate will vote against Impeachment and removal from office as opposed to the now revealed facts as supplied by witnesses who testified under oath to tell the truth, the whole truth and nothing but the truth.

In the movie, **The Shawshank Redemption**, the young convict was told, "Everyone here is

FREDERICK MONDERSON

innocent." However, a classroom situation recounts, some students began playing dice in the back of the room as the teacher tried to teach. The teacher then took off her shoe and threw it at the students. She was removed from the school on a claim of student abuse. Offered the option of resigning, she chose a trial because she thought her actions were justified. Unfortunately, she was found guilty of child abuse upon which she was fired and lost her pension.

When is a "Gangster Government" a "Gangster Government" Photo? The National Archives, emphasizing "The Ties that Bind" engraved above the Pediment.

"Party loyalty must have its limits." **John Lott**

WHEN IS A "GANGSTER GOVERNMENT"? A "GANGSTER GOVERNMENT?"

When is a "Gangster Government" a "Gangster Government Photo? The United States Government Printing Office.

"This is not about Ukraine. This is about our democracy. This is about our national security and whether the American people have the right to expect that the President of the United States will act in their interests with their security in mind and not for some personal or political reason. If we don't care about this, we can darn well be sure the President will be back at it doing this all over again." **Adam Schiff**

40. JETTISONING TRUTH TELLERS BY DR. FRED MONDERSON

In days of old pirates would make opponents, people they disliked, "Walk the Plank" into the sea. Today,

FREDERICK MONDERSON

President Trump, disparages anyone who speaks out against him to further bamboozle the minds of his "base" who believe "he walks on water." These people; yet, like "the three monkeys" – "See no evil; hear no evil; and Speak no evil" in regards President Trump. Nevertheless, discount every facet of truth leveled against their "hero." How sad; America is at a dangerous crossroad and "The Red Hat nation" refuses to see the danger, the world and a great many Americans glaringly notice. Much of the truth as well as the long-standing institutions of American government represented in honesty, integrity, truthfulness, empathy, good government, etc., Mr. Trump particularly tramples in spewing lies as he traverses the White House Lawn on way to waiting helicopters.

When is a "Gangster Government" a "Gangster Government" Photo? Entrance to the Treasury of the United States.

WHEN IS A "GANGSTER GOVERNMENT"? A "GANGSTER GOVERNMENT?"

During Mr. Trump's political dawning as the Republican Campaign unfolded, many, especially his party opponents were flabbergasted by the loose language of a man who aspired to the highest office in this land, many viewed with august respect. Former Florida Governor Jeb Bush often reacted, "Donald Trump is insulting his way to the Presidency." However, though not as far-fetched yet seeming not to be insulting, Mr. Trump's behavior and his base's emerging acceptance can be compared with the behavior of a Priest, while not really interjecting religion in this analogy. No less significant, we must regard the role of a priest with great reverence. That being so, the long train of abuse emanating from the mouth of Mr. Trump who could be equated with a priest standing at the altar, naked yet seeming to function. In such a case Mr. Trump's base would probably rationalize, the reason his is naked at the altar is because his luggage did not arrive as yet. Such absurdity, notwithstanding, Mr. Trump's loose lips did sink his Republican opponents' ships, as in the case of "little Marco;" "Black are too stupid to vote for me;" disparaging of Ben Carson; his attack on the Gold Star family member Mr. Khan and his wife; the American Judge considered not objective because he is of Mexican heritage; is sort of arguing men of British, Irish or Scottish heritage cannot be loyal and objective in their American relations.

FREDERICK MONDERSON

When is a "Gangster Government" a "Gangster Government" Photo? The White House, where the President lives, at 1600 Pennsylvania Avenue.

"Rudy Giuliani is the quarterback for the Ukraine scheme." While John Bolton believed Mick Mulvaney and Ambassador Sondland were concocting a 'drug deal;' he felt Rudy Giuliani was a "'hand grenade' that will blow up everyone."

"Forget about President Trump. Will any one of my colleagues on the other side say that it is an abuse of power to condition as an official act? Is any one of my colleagues willing to say that it is OK for a President of the United States of America to invite foreign interference in our elections **Pramila Jayapal**?"

WHEN IS A "GANGSTER GOVERNMENT"? A "GANGSTER GOVERNMENT?"

41. MINIONS FOR TRUMP'S TYRANNY BY DR. FRED MONDERSON

In response to CNN's Wolf Blitzer's question in asking for commentary on the behavior of those Congressmen who stormed the Democratic Impeachment Inquiry, Representative Jackson simply described such individuals as "Minions for Trump's Tyranny." How strange, that many of these "new recruits" to Congress, would as "fools rush in where wise men fear to tred," staunchly demonstrates defense of a President even Michele Bachmann refuses to categorize as heading "a gangster government." Not only is such outlandish behavior unprecedented it is ethically questioned and potentially a serious infraction of Congressional, particularly, national security rules. How sad, that these individuals would choose, for the historical record, to be stained by an albatross of moral filth and illegality attached to Mr. Trump's name going forward. I'm amused by a political cartoon depicting Mr. Trump's appearance at a Cleaner or Laundry with stains splattered across the front of his clothing. The Cleaner's response was, "I can't get that out," meaning the **Impeachment**!

Perhaps these gentlemen need be reminded of what Rev. Al Sharpton said to Kanye West after his escapade with Trump. "Mr. Trump will not always be president and African-Americans and the world will remember your behavior into the future." Untold righteous people must remember, Congressional Republicans especially, the American people took notice when Donald trump received the pushback he deservedly received and he was vociferously and adamantly defended in the Impeachment Hearing. Now we are being told by the *Washington Post*, regarding the Ukraine scandal, "Putin told me!" Clearly this is akin to "a mark" caught in a "long con," perhaps not dissimilar to Mike Bloomberg's "I know a con when I see one," at the Republican National Convention.

Notwithstanding, the issue is not so much the Congressmen broaching the security regulations in entering a secure location with electronic devices that makes the area vulnerable to external listening devices at Mr. Trump's urging, but their disruptive and obnoxious behaviors is a further example of the "ugly American" at home, this time defending a pathological liar. Even more significant, these individuals are now tied to, own Mr. Trump's outlandish behaviors or from the elevator ride to his calling Republican critics "scum." We can add to this Impeachment, and especially the scatter-shot attacks on everything and all, including the Dingell family.

Objectively speaking, his public behavior, his incessant lying, attacks on the legitimate work of the press, his secretive nature that questions discussions with certain foreign leaders, the emoluments questions, behaviors of his children in his administrations' responsibility to the American idea

WHEN IS A "GANGSTER GOVERNMENT"?
A "GANGSTER GOVERNMENT?"

and ideal of governance, not to mention *ad hominem* name calling and attacks on Democratic members of Congress, as well as his refusal to comply with Subpoenas and so much more, recognizes the "Ship of State" adrift in turbulent waters. Just as significant, regarding Mr. Putin's influence on Donald Trump, it's important to remember, they met more than a dozen times and there is no transcript of anything said between the two men. Given Mr. Trump's preferential treatment of Mr. Putin and Russia, one has to wonder, yet his Congressional backers "follow the dear leader."

"There is no advantage to Trump in a long trial. He does not want witnesses testifying to the whole nation." **David Axelrod**

FREDERICK MONDERSON

"We must be clear. No one, not even the president is above the law. Unlike President Trump, we understand our duty, first and foremost is to protect the Constitution and to protect the interests of the American people. That is why we must take this solemn step today." Jerry Nadler.

42. RIP VAN WINKLE IN RED OUTFIT BY DR. FRED MONDERSON

As the Republican base slumbers in the harmonious and soothing yet potentially dangerous music of Pied Piper Donald Trump, their ultimate realization mirrors Rip Van Winkle lengthy sleep to awaken in a different age. While blind men can see, and drunk men are yet conscious, Donald Trump's base is deniably jubilant and oblivious to the numerous facts pointing to a predicament all but these folks choose to see. Case in point, Mr. Trump attacked critical American institutions even denying Russian espionage against the nation and the President denies this fact reported by the American Intelligence Community. In an effort to reflect this Russian intervention undermining the American electoral process, Trump began parroting Russian talking points such as blaming Ukraine for this blatant attack. Finally, it come out, regarding Ukraine's potential role in hacking the American political process, purportedly he stated: "Putin told me."

WHEN IS A "GANGSTER GOVERNMENT"? A "GANGSTER GOVERNMENT?"

Granted Republicans sent Mr. Trump to Washington to "Rock the boat," but he has been so resolute we are now feeling the effects of "Shaking Baby Syndrome" as the President has upset and abrogated all norms of the accumulated history of presidential leadership, behavior and administrative responsibility. Mr. Trump, knowingly and unknowingly compares himself and his acts and results, with all other presidents. For example, when he touts, "Republicans," under his leadership, "have passed the biggest tax cut in history," but this has been proven incorrect, yet his people gobble it up. Of course, like so many among the wealthy, including himself, who have benefitted from swilling at the public trough, while he eats high up on the hog, his base yet have to fight for parts of the chittlins.

He again touts the "lowest unemployment figures in history." Nonetheless, in a dogged refusal to credit former President Obama who not rescued the American economy from its devastating decline, he "pulled the car from the ditch," repaired its disfunctional parts and set the vehicle on its path to create the foundation from which Mr. Trump has launched "his Wall Street and unemployment numbers success, he still chants the "Only I" mantra.

In a disingenuous and ungrateful tirade rather than thank Number 44, Number 45, savages his predecessor at every opportunity with the same vituperative animosity he demonstrated in the "Birther" escapade of shameless falsity. Of course, devoid of conscience and empathy, Mr. Trump, elected Republicans and Mr. Trump's base celebrated his despicable and disgusting performances by dismissing his every act on the pretext people don't like him. Who likes a liar, an abuser, a sexual predator, according to the 17 women who accused Mr. Trump of inappropriate sexual behavior, even rape?

In 1936, as Italy invaded Ethiopia, this forced Emperor Haile Selaisse to appear in protest at the League of Nations. There he cautioned, with the historic words, if the League did not act to rectify the situation and condemn Italian fascist aggression against his nation, then, "Today for me; Tomorrow for you." In that bold admonition, Haile Selaisse foreshadowed World War II and its catastrophic impact on western civilization.

In many respects, the unbridled enthusiasm of Donald Trump's base seems poised to experience a tremendous disappointment when the full ramifications of the President's actions are truly revealed. Many people vigorously ad valiantly claim to be patriots but put to the test, "they settle" and this, particularly Republicans in government, can be seen in their response to the situation consistently unfolding at 1600 Pennsylvania Avenue, Washington, DC.

1. President Trump is a hyper-pathological liar so far clocked at c. 14, 500 lies and this does not seem to concern his followers particularly the Evangelicals

WHEN IS A "GANGSTER GOVERNMENT"? A "GANGSTER GOVERNMENT?"

who preach morality on a daily basis, especially on Sunday.

2. President Trump has a history of abusing women, saying and doing things to and about them. Some 17 women accused the President of sexual misconduct, even rape and the base response is less than a ripple. Saying Nancy Pelosi's "teeth are falling out" and is attacks on Representative Dingell is so "gutter," "low IQ," "low life!"

3. Though the Department of Justice has a standing policy, not a legislative fiat, that a sitting President cannot be indicted, Mr. Trump has been linked to questionable individuals and actions and that same base has brushed this off. Despite 10 cases of Obstruction listed by Muller, none of this has registered on Trump's base's radar. Mark Galli, Editor of **Christianity Today**, who called for Mr. Trump's removal from office, argued, "Given the opportunity and vision of the American people to make it more noble, more humane;" in this Mr. Trump has failed!

FREDERICK MONDERSON

When is a "Gangster Government" a "Gangster Government" Photo? "Here Sir, the sword to defend our Republic!"

When is a "Gangster Government" a "Gangster Government" Photo? "We must stand firm to defend this sacred land!"

WHEN IS A "GANGSTER GOVERNMENT"?
A "GANGSTER GOVERNMENT?"

When is a "Gangster Government" a "Gangster Government" Photo? "There. There! We must be ready to do battle in defense of our way of life"

When is a "Gangster Government" a "Gangster Government" Photo? The **Ark of the Covenant** as spiritual force guarding the entrance to the Capital Building.

FREDERICK MONDERSON

When is a "Gangster Government" a "Gangster Government" Photo? "We must forever be vigilant in defense of our freedoms!"

WHEN IS A "GANGSTER GOVERNMENT"? A "GANGSTER GOVERNMENT?"

When is a "Gangster Government" a "Gangster Government" Photo? The **Tabernacle**, another spiritual power guarding the entrance to the Capitol Building, where the laws are made!

"This is a political decision. We know how impeachment divides the country, so we have to be strategic in terms of what is it that, based on the evidence, is easier for the people of this country to understand. We need to bring the public with us, and these are clear, explicit, undisputed evidence that shows how [Trump] obstructed Congress and how the president abused his office." **Nydia Velazquez**

FREDERICK MONDERSON

"The prospect of not having a trial is a good for Mitch Mc Connell. Public sentiments can change when people pay attention." **Preet Bahara**

43. "THE SACRED OATH I TOOK" BY DR. FRED MONDERSON

Increasingly, these days, one by one people are beginning to grow and show they have "balls" in a sort of confrontation with the President of the Unite States, Donald John Trump. The newest sequel of the classic movie, **The Magnificent Seven** stars Denzel Washington. Now, after the chief villain had done his ghastly deed of killing many of the town's folks, including the heroine's husband, she went to get help and returned with seven gunfighters. They took the town and erased the villain's "deputies" who were holding the town as ransom. After that first scrimmage, she hailed the town's people to come out then explained, "I brought these men to help." One of the cowed but now brazen men of the town asked, "Who gave you permission to speak for us in bringing these gunfighters here?" She responded, "I was the only one with balls enough to do so!" Such a bold statement from a woman, seemed alarming even to the seasoned and tough gunfighters present.

Recently in a New York City school, a 6-year old led the Pledge of Allegiance to the flag, much to the joyous delight and approval of the parents gathered

WHEN IS A "GANGSTER GOVERNMENT"?
A "GANGSTER GOVERNMENT?"

in the Auditorium for the Award Ceremony, "Student of the Month." In the military, soldiers take an oath to defend the country from foreign and domestic enemies. Equally too, elected officials, in Congress and in government, take an oath to defend the Constitution of the United States of America and as the pledge states, "One nation under god, with liberty and justice for all."

In a recent incident involving a Navy Seal, the Secretary of the Navy clashed with the President who fired him for abrogating the "chain of command" in regards to the Seal found guilty of an improper behavior that goes against the Uniform Code of Military Justice (UCMJ) which is designed to instill and maintain a uniform and consistent system of discipline in the nation's armed forces. In departing, the Secretary penned a letter to the White House explaining his reason for quitting because unfolding circumstance contravened "The sacred Oath I took!" The "balls on this fellow" to rebuke the President of the United states over the inherent honor of the oath, sent shock waves across all spectrums of American society, the good, the bad and the ugly.

A number of persons hold the view one cannot take a position, hold to an argument, even fight a battle over "Principle," but this is what men of honor do, demonstrating spine and backbone in challenging unjust laws or behaviors.

For the longest, Republicans particularly those in government have held to high principles of morality, honor, discipline, patriotism and issued challenges to many and all who demonstrate the slightest deviation from such an established standard. In this age of Trump lacking worthwhile standards of morality, truth, honor, the backbone of the world's perception of the ideal of America is not even a back-burner issue. The "fish stinks from the dead down;" if the President of the United States, the Commander-In-Chief, "Leader of the Free World," is seen as a liar, a pathological liar, a man whose word equals a wooden-nickel with a hole, not only will the world view America differently; all the roaches will emerge from within walls; America's enemies will extend an inch into a yard! Regarding the Phone call to the Ukraine President; Mr. Trump implores, "Trust me!" How does one trust or believe a pathological liar, who in three years uttered nearly 15,000 lies or false statements.

The Navy Secretary's action and letter in bucking the President is reminiscent of similar men in or of uniform who spoke to perceived contravention of principles and right as emanating from and reaction to action of President Trump. Mr. Trump may be extremely wealthy, a big man but he acts little. In a nation where the Constitution guarantees free speech, even he speaks of his right to free speech, yet he denies the privilege to anyone who seeks to speak to criticizes him, given he has a thin skin. Because of his orthodoxy from the inception people were alarmed at the President's behavior especially his Anti-Muslim, Anti-Immigrant, mocking of a disabled reporter, and so much more. He then cracked the

WHEN IS A "GANGSTER GOVERNMENT"? A "GANGSTER GOVERNMENT?"

door to lying, finally holding it ajar. In fact, he removed the door!

When is a "Gangster Government" a "Gangster Government" Photo? The Place from which Power emanates, with Tabernacles sandwiching the entrance and exit as sentinels of spiritual power on guard!

FREDERICK MONDERSON

When is a **"Gangster Government"** a **"Gangster Government" Photo**? Another view of the **Ark of the Covenant** as symbol generating power in the American sacred notion of spirituality, religiosity, honor and solemnity.

"We're going to keep the focus on making sure that we present the truth to the American people as it relates to the stunning abuse of power, as it relates to the Trump Ukraine scandal. That's what before us right now." **Hakeem Jeffries**

WHEN IS A "GANGSTER GOVERNMENT"? A "GANGSTER GOVERNMENT?"

"People will remember the denigrating of Congressman Dingell and his wife." **Maggie Haberman**

44. WISHY-WASHY OR ZIG-ZAG SENATOR LINDSEY GRAHAM BY DR. FRED MONDERSON

Republican Senator Lindsey Graham represents South Carolina, the state that held the greatest number of Africans in bondage during which time "Cotton was King" and the institution of slavery made many persons wealthy. South Carolina had a troubled past upholding slavery and was a significant issue in the 1832 South Carolina Nullification Act, pursued by Mr. Calhoun. This egregious act forced President Andrew Jackson to dispatch federal troops to the state, that ultimately became a member of the secessionist movement of the Civil War from 1860-1865. In more recent times, the iconic activist Jesse Jackson indicted South Carolina for having 36 state prisons and 1 state college. Arguably, a large percent of the prison population is comprised of African Americans and this unquestionably is part of a disfranchisement *modus operandi*. Notwithstanding, however, a significant proportion of Democratic voters in the state are African-American, despite Republican behavior in recent years that consistently sought to purge these voters using a number of strategies including Gerrymandering, shenanigans with and at voting places, and most significant denial of voting rights of persons who were incarcerated even though they paid their debt to society. Nevertheless, the Senator seems oblivious to all of this which makes one wonder why a credible challenge has not been mounted to remove this gentleman from office. Fortunately, in the 2020 election such a challenge has materialized.

Malcolm X, in commentary on Black voting strength has made it clear, African-Americans "can determine who go to the White House and who go to the Dog House." Equally, the reality demonstrates, Black voting strength is assessed and enhanced through coalition building and this must materialize in serious compromise to remove Senator Graham. The Senator was tremendously vocal in opposition against President Obama as did the Republican "Party of No." Yet, when President Obama proposed a measure to declare war in Syria, Mr. Graham was the first to declare, "I will vote for it." Otherwise, he was opposed to everything Obama did and accomplished.

In the era of former President Bill Clinton's Impeachment, Graham laid down a Constitutionally mandated remedy. Now, in comparison with Mr. Trump's behavior, particularly in its totality for much of which Mr. Graham has remained silent, he objects to the basic guidelines and rules he himself established. No wonder he has earned the moniker "Mr. Zig Zag" whose behavior is "Wishy-Washy."

WHEN IS A "GANGSTER GOVERNMENT"?
A "GANGSTER GOVERNMENT?"

"President Trump risked our national security, jeopardized the fairness and honesty of our next election, and worked to conceal the truth from Congress in violation of his responsibility to the American people. Today is a sad and somber day for the nation. Yet we must meet the challenge posed by a president who puts himself before the country, whose actions post a direct threat to the integrity of our elections, and to the separation of powers that safeguard our liberty." **Jerry Nadler**

When is a "Gangster Government" a "Gangster Government" Photo? One of the Union Station entrances.

"It is laughable that Mr. Trump wants to preserve the integrity of the White House!" **Kirstin Powers**

FREDERICK MONDERSON

"Trump learned his lesson after firing Jim Comey. He will not fire Christopher Wray after his pushback against Trump's claim about the **FBI**."

45.   DECEMBER 7, 2019 –
Dorian Miller Day!
BY
DR. FRED MONDERSON

December 7, 1041, "A day," as President Franklin Delano Roosevelt determined, "will live in infamy," is a solemn but equally a joyous one for those who served in the military fighting against aggression and in defense of the Constitutional tenets that support this nation's democratic system. Many in the African-American community consider it "Dorian Miller Day," in honor of a Black man serving as a cook in a segregated army and called to action amidst a devastating and deadly attack on US forces by the Japanese Navy. Given Mr. Miller's second-class citizenship status at that time, particularly in front-line combat action makes his heroism extraordinary.

In the tradition of Crispus Attucks, America's first authentic hero, who stood against the might of a well-organized army, on December 7, 1941 Dorian Miller put duty and country before citizenship and fear as the Japanese attack on Pearl Harbor unfolded. Emerging from the "Mess hall confinement," as naval service determined, and realizing members of a nearby machine gun position had been wiped out, our

WHEN IS A "GANGSTER GOVERNMENT"?
A "GANGSTER GOVERNMENT?"

hero took their place and began laying down targeted and effective rapid fire. So much so, several Japanese planes were struck and plunged to the sea. On that day, December 7, 1941, our hero stood tall as did Salem Po and his guys in the foundation war; the Marine buried in the Brooklyn Navy Yard in 1801; Samuel Carson in the Mexican War; Harriet Tubman and the Black Regiments in the Civil War; the Rough Riders watching Teddy Roosevelt's back in the "Charge Up San Juan Hill;" despite racism and discriminatory behavior in "Don't Shake A Nigger's hand" mentality in a Southern Fort, those brave Black recruits who went abroad "To save the world for Democracy" and of whom W.E.B. DuBois reminded America – "We went abroad fighting and we return fighting;" the Tuskegee Airmen, again, despite segregation put country ahead of citizenship by being "So damn good," even white bomber crews refused to deliver their payloads unless accompanied by Tuskegee Airmen fighter escorts; Dr. Roscoe Brown, former President of Hostos Community College was himself a distinguished Tuskegee Airman from Harlem. To this we may add the Harlem Hell-fighters who equally served with distinction in World War II.

While Sonny Carson himself served in the Korea Conflict, he often told of his uncle who was among American troops who liberated one of the German Concentration Camps as the war in Europe came to an end. Whether it was Vietnam, Grenada, Afghanistan or Iraq, Black soldiers served with pride and distinction. Who could forget that iconic photo

FREDERICK MONDERSON

of President Obama visiting troops in Afghanistan? In panoramic view of soldiers in the big tent, two Black soldiers on the top row looked down proudly at the Black Commander-in-Chief, as if a caption expressed, "We have served 43 White Commanders-In-Chief, how proud it is to serve a Black Commander."

Nevertheless, in regards military service, so much needs clarification to help the narrative. We were often told the most decorated World War II soldier was Audie Murphy, who became a famous actor. In fact, the singer Harry Belafonte tells, this is not actually the case. The most decorated soldier in World War II was a Black man. Returning from the war and dressed in his military outfit with his medals in public display, he chose to sit in the front of a segregated bus in the South. The driver called cops and he was dragged from the bus. Saying "I'm just back from fighting the war in Europe, why are you treating me this way?" He was told, "This is the South, not Europe." In that encounter, the soldier in uniform was beaten to death right there in public view. Harry Belafonte insisted, this merciless action caused him to become an activist and dedicate his life to pursuing justice.

WHEN IS A "GANGSTER GOVERNMENT"? A "GANGSTER GOVERNMENT?"

When is a "Gangster Government" a "Gangster Government" Photo? General Grant keeping an eye on the Washington Monument, representing part of the founding ideals.

When is a "Gangster Government" a "Gangster Government" Photo? The lawn giving view to the Marble Terrace rear entrance of the Capitol Building.

"None of the players in the Senate trial has the same interest at heart." **Elliot Williams**

FREDERICK MONDERSON

"Donald Trump betrayed his oath of office. He obstructed Congress and is guilty of abuse of power." "Sadly, but with confidence and humility, with allegiance to our Founders and a heart full of love for America, today I am asking our chairman to proceed with Articles of Impeachment. The President's actions have seriously violated the Constitution. Our democracy is at stake. The President leaves us no choice but to act because he is trying to corrupt once again the election for his own benefit. The President has engaged in abuse of power, undermining our national security and jeopardizing the integrity of our elections. His actions are in defiance of the vision of our Founders and the oath of office he takes to preserve, protect and defend the Constitution of the United States." **Nancy Pelosi**.

46. EMPEROR, MONARCH AND KING BY DR. FRED MONDERSON

Keen observers of human behavior who see signs of arrogance, insensitivity and unethical acts, though seemingly guarded, can predict the outcome and final dismissal of any individual under study. The generally dictatorial behaviors of Emperor, Monarch and King as essentially generated the opposition that led to the American Revolution and creation of the United States Constitution; was designed to guide the nation and equally prevent abuse of power under a

WHEN IS A "GANGSTER GOVERNMENT"?
A "GANGSTER GOVERNMENT?"

system crafted with a two-house legislature and a three-tiered system of checks and balance.

In his ongoing hallucinating experience, the current President consistently and equally focuses on former President Barack Obama every time he looks in the mirror. It may be, his conscience, alas, if he has one; is so pricked by his flailing of Mr. Obama in his rise and sustaining at the pinnacle of American politics, Mr. Trump is troubled by the "cool ruler's" presence and accomplishments, every rock he turns over, nightmarishly, he sees Obama. This hallucinating brings out, seemingly, malice and hatred he holds for the man he succeeded to the Presidency of the United States.

In the James Bond Movie starring Roger Moore, "the Saint," a United Nation's diplomat was running drugs out of Harlem, New York. In one episode, the villain's man took Mr. Bond out and stranded him on a little island at the perpetrator's drug farm. To get back, he had to hop and skip on the backs of alligators and as events have transpired, a somewhat similar form of danger seems to characterize Mr. Trump's three years in office. In fact, his disturbing behavior garnered public view and scrutiny during the Republican primary campaign wherein he pummeled his opponents with name calling and other disgusting forms of behavior. However, while Jeb Bush exclaimed, "Donald Trump is insulting his way to the Presidency;" folks in red outfits loved his performance, and as one writer put it, they all "jockeyed to kiss his foot or some other part of his

FREDERICK MONDERSON

anatomy." Even "Men of the Cloth," and their congregations, so as not to be bypassed, galloped into the circus arena Mr. Trump as ringmaster was presiding over with insults, threats and other nefarious behaviors.

In comparison, while Mr. Trump rampaged in his "birther" bandwagon falsity, the "Tea Party" came out of their closet and grew legs. Sarah Palin, Jim DeMint, Chuck Grassley along with Joe Wilson, and so many others became principal actors. To this collection of circus performers, we could add some 20-Republican heads of NGOs who all pilloried Mr. Obama. When they took on Michelle, the "cool ruler" stepped out to warn, "If you're listening, stay off my wife" and they got the message! Even more sophisticatedly significant, without losing stride, he let it be known, "I know politics is a contact sport!" And so, he continued, achieving on behalf of the people; while you know who bought himself an apparatus to blow away the stench he crafted, as he kept generating more rather than "draining the swamp," as "Swamp thing" in charge.

Now, intoxicated by the perfumed reception of the people in red, Mr. Trump began trampling upon the Constitution, his ego grew so large, he once dared to exclaim, "The Constitution is wrong!"

The minions he had been cultivating in and out of government now forgot past insults and instantly lined up to kiss Mr. Trump's ring. In the movie, **The Distinguished Gentleman** starring **Eddie**

WHEN IS A "GANGSTER GOVERNMENT"?
A "GANGSTER GOVERNMENT?"

Murphy, it was said of the **Energy Secretary**, "lobbyists had to line up to get a ticket to throw money at him." Now "Moscow" Mitch, who prefers the moniker "Grim Reaper," Zig Zag Lindsey Graham, and John Kennedy, not from Massachusetts but from Texas, have been so domesticated by "the man who would be king," they are demonstrating the most unreasonable, unthinkable behaviors in blocking interference on Mr. Trump's behalf. Some think such unreasonable assessments are simplistic because these individuals are afraid of the usurper to the throne. Against the narrative of the White House and cowardly Republicans, it is not that the Democrats hate the President or that they want to overturn the wishes of the American people and results of the 2016 election.

Mr. Trump took the oath of office to defend the constitution, unite the nation, administer good government, drain the swamp, hire the "Best people," not appear spiteful and punitive, act presidential, maintain harmonious relations with the nation's allies, not profit from his office, etc., to which among other promises he made was to release his tax returns, not golf as much as his predecessors, not seek foreign interference in American elections as his request to "Russia if you are looking…" and much more. The "phone call" which John Kasich former Republican governor of Ohio said was "inappropriate" was simply the tip of the "iceberg." These are "long train of abuses" and unchecked who knows where he will take this nation; he was not willing to serve its military to defend, the privileges he now enjoys with the power to send others to fight wars abroad.

Men of such stature should have known of Edmund Burke, who, during the backlash of the French Revolution wrote, "The only thing necessary for evil to triumph is for good men to say and do nothing." However, if they did not hear of the above, they may know the French people led the king to the guillotine. Recently, in a case involving Mr. Trump's taxes, a federal judge reminded Mr. Trump's attorneys, "No man is above the law," and because this is a Republic, Mr. Trump needs to know he is president and not king. More significant, there are limitations to his power in a system with three co-equal branches of government. Knowingly or unknowingly, Mr. Trump seems to have compromised the integrity of the judges he and Mitch McConnell have appointed to the Supreme Court. Regarding that judge's declaration, Trump's White House retorted instantly, "We will appear this ruling to the highest court." This could possibly be argued for other judges' positions both Trump and Senator McConnell tout. Perhaps, in fact, they wanted to flaunt a perceived compromised status of the nation's Supreme Court with the appointment of "Mr. Trump's Judges, Gorsuch and Kavanaugh."

In the heyday while Rudy Giuliani was strutting his stuff as Mayor, one writer penned a memoir entitled, "Emperor of the City" and this probably got to Mr. Giuliani's head. However, responding at the dedication of the rehabilitated Franklin Avenue

WHEN IS A "GANGSTER GOVERNMENT"? A "GANGSTER GOVERNMENT?"

Shuttle, former New York City Councilmember Mary Pinkett expressed, "Tell the Monarch at City Hall," this is indeed a democracy.

When is a "Gangster Government" a "Gangster Government" Photo? James Madison, the man so often spoken of as a "Founding Father," residing in the Library of Congress, Madison Building, named in his honor.

"(1) President Trump – acting directly and through his agents within and outside the United States Government corruptly solicited the Government of

FREDERICK MONDERSON

Ukraine to publicly announce investigations into – (A) a political opponent, former Vice-President Joseph R. Biden, Jr.; and (B) a discredited theory promoted by Russia alleging that Ukraine – rather than Russia – interfered in the 2016 United States Presidential election.

(2) With the same corrupt motives, President Trump – acting both directly and through his agents within and outside the United States Government – conditioned two official acts on the public announcements that he had requested - (A) the release of $391 million of United States taxpayer funds that Congress had appropriated on a bipartisan basis for the purpose of providing vital military and security assistance to Ukraine to oppose Russian aggression and which President Trump had ordered suspended; and (B) a head of state meeting at the White House, which the President of Ukraine sought to demonstrate continued United States support for the Government of Ukraine in the face of Russian aggression. (3) Faced with the public revelation of his actions, President Trump ultimately released the military and security assistance to the Government of Ukraine, but has persisted in openly and corrupt urging and soliciting Ukraine to undertake investigations for his personal political benefit

Article One – Abuse of Power!

**WHEN IS A "GANGSTER GOVERNMENT"?
A "GANGSTER GOVERNMENT?"**

"All roads lead to Putin!" **Nancy Pelosi**

47. SONNY AND RUDY BY DR. FRED MONDERSON

To compare Sonny Carson with Rudy Giuliani, seem a difficult proposition, but if there is only one kernel of similarity, the significance is telling. More important, however, such comparisons attest how the low has risen and the high have fallen. However, while Sonny has passed on to African-American ancestor glory, Rudy is alive and seemingly will face the wrath of an American people who frown on betrayal by persons they once put great faith in.

Sonny Carson was a Brooklyn "bad boy" who graduated from the "school of hard knocks." Wearing this designation as a badge of honor, Sonny's social consciousness evolved as he traveled a lane parallel to the legal sanction. In such travels, his reputation not only preceded him but also brought a recognized notoriety by folks on both sides of the law. Yet, he constantly found himself straddling both lanes. So much so, Sonny and some associates were accused of kidnapping. This arrest and charge action, however, was not inconsistent with the thrust of law enforcement behavior in the reality of Black urban youth in the 1950s and 1960s, in an era contemporary with the emerging Civil Rights Movement.

FREDERICK MONDERSON

Nevertheless, regarding the issue of kidnapping, whether it was Sonny Carson's reputation or the police's lack of credible evidence, their strategy evolved as such. Sonny Carson received a phone call from New York City law enforcement to the effect, "Mr. Carson, we intend to charge you with kidnapping. When will you come to turn yourself in?" Not we are coming to arrest you, but when will you turn yourself in? Yet, suffice to say, he would later beat the charge, they generally call such, "trumped up."

Notwithstanding, after turning himself in, perhaps in or another run in with the law, Sonny was moved to a prison upstate. As he defiantly stood in the lobby downstairs waiting to be processed, word began circulating in the prison, "Sonny Carson is downstairs!" Thereupon, the prisoners rioted! Giving credence to such a thing as a "good riot;'" this riot was a sort of congratulatory welcome attesting to Sonny's stature as a "Good bad boy!" Of course, he would go on to do many wonderful things, most important of which was the Repatriation of the "Bones of Samuel Carson" to Ghana, West Africa, and the burial, an act which was principal in the **Inauguration of the First African Emancipation Festival** on August 1, 1998.

In this momentous act, Sonny Carson returned his ancestor, Samuel Carson, an enslaved African who ran away from South Carolina, joined the United States Navy, fought and died in 1844 in the war with Mexico. Subsequently, he was buried in the Brooklyn

WHEN IS A "GANGSTER GOVERNMENT"?
A "GANGSTER GOVERNMENT?"

Navy Yard, a Black and segregated cemetery at the time. There were Black servicemen, army, navy, marine, from as early as 1801, if not before, until 1926 when many were reinterred in the National Cemetery at Cyprus Hill. In 1996, the navy discovered the bones of Samuel Carson and turned them over to his grandnephew, Sonny Carson. Thereupon, Sonny formed "The Bones Committee," of which this writer became Chairman. It met regularly for nearly two years strategizing among other issues, about what to do with it. Some thought he should be buried in Arlington Military Cemetery while the Committee settled on Ghana, West Africa. Samuel Carson, along with Crystal, an ex-slave female from Jamaica, West Indies, were interred beside the river at Assin Manso, in Ghana. This river, is where Africans were given their last bath before being ushered through the "Door of No Return."

In this act, Sonny Carson opened "The Door of Return" and created a place of Pilgrimage and point of departure for African-Americans seeking their "Roots" in Africa. As such, then, one can see the utility of the congratulatory prison welcome, that not simply emboldened Sonny Carson, but ultimately reinforced his stature as a "Good Bad Boy!"

Adding more to his evolution as a well-regarded ancestor in the African-American Afterlife Pantheon, Sonny Carson advocated on manty fronts, even going to court in support of tenants victimized by unscrupulous landlords; he challenged the Sony Corporation then encouraging creation of "Gangsta

FREDERICK MONDERSON

Rap" designed to demean Black women. He insisted, however, that young artists continue to produce creative lyrics but "tone down the negativity." In similar challenge, at the funeral of James Brown, the "Godfather of Soul," Rev. Al Sharpton asked the provocative question, "How did we get from 'Say it loud, I'm Black and proud,' to 'Bitches and hos?'" Equally, in constructive protest, Dick Gregory, in his book *Callous on My Soul*, unequivocally stated, "Gangsta Rap was created by white folds to demean the Black woman." Sonny Carson went on to further advocate so that Medgar Evers College would become a four-year institution and the establishment of Restoration Corporation, under Mayor Lindsey, would become an economic engine for the revitalization of the Bed-Stuy Community in Central Brooklyn. He founded organizations to challenge Crack as a scourge in the Black Community and created the Committee to Honor Black Heroes in a climate where "great Blacks" were cast aside.

Through this vehicle Sonny Carson championed and orchestrated changing street names as Malcolm X and Marcus Garvey Boulevards and Harriet Tubman Avenue. He was equally instrumental in creating the Malcolm X school and naming a school for Toussaint L'Ouverture, the Haitian revolutionary. This much and more Sonny helped bring about and as a principal activist he was heavily demeaned and maligned for his role in the Ocean-Hill/Brownsville protest that opened the heavily populated New York City Board of Education with next to nothing teachers and administrators. This effort also led to the creation of

WHEN IS A "GANGSTER GOVERNMENT"? A "GANGSTER GOVERNMENT?"

School Boards in the New York city Education system.

Thus, and in retrospect, it's now apparent why the prisoners welcomed the arrival of Sonny Carson to begin his sentence. His subsequent behavior seems to justify his sentence. As such then, historical forces can make or break, elevate the law and discard the high.

On the other hand, and within the last few months, Rudy Giuliani has been basking in TV limelight, making points as President Trump's private lawyer, seeking to explain, rationalize and defend every facet of his client's behavior. So much so, some commentators openly thought Rudy Giuliani lost credibility falling from his once fable perch. Fact is, Rudy was a federal prosecutor heading the New York City Attorney General's office. Well, with this fame to his credit, he ran for Mayor in 1993 and in a thuggish manner ousted the city's first Black Mayor, David Dinkins, seeking reelection. While Mr. Giuliani posted signs in the Black Community as, "Rudy G. fights racism," he turned out to become a polarizing figure, the most racist of all the City's previous mayors. Particularly disturbing, Rudy removed Mayor Dinkins' portrait from its rightful place in Gracie Mansion, the mayor's residence. In wake of the **Million Man March** phenomenon, Sonny Carson launched a **Million Voter Drive** to unseat Rudy in the upcoming New York City election of 1997.

FREDERICK MONDERSON

Unfortunately, yet fortunate for the mayor, he won reelection. However, by the year 2000 Rudy's popularity had plummeted. Equally significant and more, 9/11/2001 happened and America rallied to the wounded city with Rudy at its head. Between September 2001 and January 2002, with America backing him, Rudy performed admirably. Rev. Sharpton pointed out, given the generated favorable conditions, any mayor would have performed in similar fashion. Nevertheless, and so much so, rather than relinquish his role as mayor in January 2002, as "Term limits" dictated, the Mayor wanted to remain beyond his tenure. This however was not to be, even though he was dubbed "America's mayor!" Thereafter, Rudy ran for president twice and was rejected by the same Americans who had lauded him. Perhaps, *writ large*, they say the inner man. Given the many investigations pending against Mr. Giuliani today, as some have indicated, he may end up in prison and so the Mob he pursued in his rise, will probably we waiting to give him the type of warm reception accorded Sonny Carson in his day. Sonny always insisted, "Be careful of the toes you mash on the way up, for they will be attached to the ass, you have to kiss on the way down!"

WHEN IS A "GANGSTER GOVERNMENT"?
A "GANGSTER GOVERNMENT?"

When is a "Gangster Government" a "Gangster Government" Photo? The iconic Ionic capital column.

"President Trump abused the powers of his high office through the following means – (1) Directing the White House to defy a lawful subpoena by withholding the production of documents sought therein by the Committees. (2) Directing other Executive Branch agencies and offices to defy lawful subpoenas and withhold the production of documents and records from the Committee – in response to which the Department of State, Office of Management and Budget, Department of Energy, and Department of Defense refused to produce a single document or record. (3) Directing current and former Executive Branch officials not to cooperate with the Committees – in response to which nine Administration officials defied subpoenas for testimony, namely John Michael 'Mick' Mulvaney, Robert B. Blair, John A. Eisenberg, Michael Ellis, Preston Wells Griffith, Russell T. Vought, Michael

FREDERICK MONDERSON

Duffey, Brian McCormack, and T. Ulrich Brechbuhl. These actions were consistent with President Trump's previous efforts to undermine United States Government investigations into foreign interference in United States elections."

"What I'm trying to do because, quite frankly, I didn't sit in front of the TV set the entire time the last two or three months, I've been trying to read this. I'm trying to see if the dots get connected. If that is the case, then I think it's a serious matter. I think it's an impeachable matter," Jones said. "But if those dots aren't connected and there are other explanations that I think are consistent with innocence, I will go that way too." **Senator Jones** (D. Ala.)

When is a "Gangster Government" a "Gangster Government" Photo? Miniature of the US Capitol.

"I think Nancy Pelosi is just putting a spotlight on McConnell." Quoting Robert Frost, who stated, "The only way out is through," thus, **David Brinkley** applies a historic vision of the Presidency.

WHEN IS A "GANGSTER GOVERNMENT"? A "GANGSTER GOVERNMENT?"

"While the President can exert Executive Privilege on specific things, certain things, certain conversations, he cannot exert Executive Privilege over the entire testimony of John Bolton. Equally, the President also cannot restrain Bolton from testifying." **Carrie Cordero**

48. THE CRUX OF THE PROBLEM BY DR. FRED MONDERSON

President Trump has finally relented, saying he would love if Secretary Mnuchin, Secretary Mulvaney, Secretary Pompeo, former White House Chief of Staff Bolton, all would testify to the Intelligence Committee's **Impeachment** hearings. First, for anyone who travels abroad, it is sad, even psychologically and emotionally debilitating for anyone to say, "your president is a liar!" Nevertheless, and despite some 15,000 lies, Mr. Trump has said many things but chose not to deliver.

All can remember his being under audit and will release his tax returns. Fact is, if Mr. Trump wanted these persons to testify, he could insist they hurry across town and have them testify. Even more, extreme, Mr. Trump could walk into Pennsylvania Avenue, hail a cab, pack these folks into it and instruct the driver to drop them off at the Capital

FREDERICK MONDERSON

Building. However, as many should recognize, "talk is cheap!"

During the Muller Inquiry, Mr. Trump did everything he could to prevent credible individuals from testifying. Naturally, he himself refused to testify under oath and the written testimony he submitted, sanitized by his lawyers, has been reported containing false statements. Those Americans who were courageous enough to testify under oath and whose testimony did not favor Mr. Trump, he attacked in the most vituperative manner using such disgusting terms as "rat," "traitor," "low life," and "scum!" Those individuals such as Paul Manafort who chose not to speak against Mr. Trump he congratulated; some argued, "he dangled a pardon!"

When is a "Gangster Government" a "Gangster Government" Photo? "When going to visit a Lady, be sure to take flowers!"

"I'm sorry Debbie Dingell had to put up with this. It's a shameful disgrace." **Douglas Brinkley**

WHEN IS A "GANGSTER GOVERNMENT"? A "GANGSTER GOVERNMENT?"

"We have to ensure the Senate will come to the table with fairness. He is trying to bring this office down to him rather than lift it up. He's trying to make the Presidency about himself rather than the country."
James Clyburn

49. THE MAN WHO WOULD BE PRESIDENT BY DR. FRED MONDERSON

The idea of becoming President of the United States is to serve the nation in a manner reminiscent of a father to a family, for good or bad, but more so for the former and not the latter. To be President seems a calling from an early period in a sort of work-your-way-up approach. In business it can sometimes be equated with beginning in the mailroom and ultimately rising to managerial status. In the "Old country," a childhood colleague began as a police recruit and ultimately became Commissioner?

In the military one begins as a recruit and all things being equal, promoted in the evolving experience in the ongoing desire to serve. There one can develop an acumen for politics and so for high office and finally being elected to the position sought after. After a period of committed and constructive service people elevates the individual to even higher service and so, ultimately the aspiration to be President becomes more real. Consistent with the arduous challenge to beat back competitors, one can reach the top.

Thus, only in America can a "Poor boy" rise from the humblest beginnings to become the most powerful man in the world. As such, the position comes with a number of privileges and responsibilities of a practical, moral even ethical standard. Interesting, however, and having reached a particular destination, whether economic, political, educational, even religious, a trail is implanted in the path one travels that reflects character, moral, philosophical, humanistic, even courageous, on part of the individual making the journey. Thus, the finished product is indicative of the glorious, bruising or challenging path the individual has tred.

Strange, but this character sketch is designed to assess and create some understanding of the man holding the office of President of the United States, who today is Donald J. Trump.

One of the reasons some prominent persons choose not to run for an office such as President of the United States is because of the invasive nature that accompanies the quest. Friend and foe want to know more. The press exposes everything in order to sell more news stories, whatever it be the Media mode they employ. Some years ago, many thought General Colin Powell would run for President but he chose not to. Some believed the nation was not ready for a Black President then; he could be in harm's way, even that, despite their disguised chatter, Republicans

WHEN IS A "GANGSTER GOVERNMENT"? A "GANGSTER GOVERNMENT?"

would not have chosen him as the party's standard bearer. Suffice to say, Secretary of State Powell may have decided because of the invasive nature of the process.

"Everything falls to the advantage of Putin!" **Carl Bernstein**

Washington Post report on how Donald Trump "knew" Ukraine meddled in the election, "Putin told me so!" Strange, but over a dozen meetings with Russians; that is, Putin, the Foreign Minister, the former UN Representative, and there is no transcript of any and all details of these meetings. What's going on with Donald Trump and Russia, particularly when the American ally, Ukraine is under invasion from Russia?

A question asked of **John Kerry**, "Why does President Donald Trump invoke the name of former President Obama so often?" to which he replied, "I don't know!"

A.B. Stoddard argued, "Bolton offers something new to the House hearings. We must remember Bolton told Fiona Hill to go to the lawyers because he did not want to be in a 'Drug deal.'"

"Executive Privilege does not protect in committing a crime and not everything said is privileged." **Gene Rossi**

FREDERICK MONDERSON

50. CONCLUSIONS: MORE OBAMA AND TRUMP
"What Goes Around Comes Around!"

As the men in red outfit triumphantly hoist their hero Donald Trump, accompanied by thunderously deafening celebratory rejoicing, observes must conclude these people are certainly confident in their beliefs the Donald is it! This leader, Donald J. Trump invokes Barack Obama's name more often than "Carter's got liver pills." As such, and as former President Barack Obama inveighed during the 2016 presidential election, "What if we are wrong?" As such, we can propose the same question relative to today's events and so ask, "Are these men in red outfits right or wrong?"

As a New Yorker, President Trump must be familiar with the old aphorism - "What goes around comes around!" Today, despite his projected bravado, Mr. Trump seems to have ended up sitting in an ants' nest. Meanwhile, his nemesis, Barack Obama is probably sunning himself somewhere on a beach in Hawaii and perhaps drinking Pina Coladas, virgin or otherwise `1and seemingly without a care though concerned all his efforts on behalf of the American people are systematically being dismantled by Donald Trump. Thinking individuals, however, see a rope not a line

WHEN IS A "GANGSTER GOVERNMENT"?
A "GANGSTER GOVERNMENT?"

connecting Mr. Trump's "birther conspiracy falsity" with the systematic dismantling in a clearly vexations manner seemingly fueled by racial animosity. The sad thing is, unmindful of the Edmund Burke admonished "The only thing necessary for evil to triumph is for Good men to say nothing," the whole "kith and kaboom" of Republicans are silent in ongoing vilification fueled by envy or simply vindictiveness which is not primarily an American trait.

More important, however, in comparing the two men, ne is methodological and systematic while the other is impulsive and fraught in faulty judgment. While one builds the other tears down. While one is concerned with the entire American population, the other is concerned about himself primarily and a segment, called his "base" secondarily. While one is considered a gentleman and international statesman, the other is considered a bully and thug, somewhat synonymous with the pariah and barracuda species. While true Christian saints continue to pray for one, the other's Christian followers remain blind-folded to his gross indiscretions and while the world community praises and extols the one, across the globe curses are heaped simply at the mention of the other's name.

Mr. Trump's road to political success was paved with the most vile, vituperative and seemingly vindictive pejoratives leveled in a scatter-shot manner across the human landscape from the Constitution to the Pope. As such, Mr. Trump earned the designation "Equal opportunity abuser," a badge he wears on his puffed-up chest! Philosophically speaking, without being facetious, when one looks at an individual seemingly "messed-up," it forces the query, "What did he do to deserve this retribution resulting in all manner of scenarios. The same conception can be applied to Donald Trump as he basks at the top of the "Pile" he created. The only problem, we see Mr. Trump on the current page towards his book's ending though, the early chapters, while there is, not available for many to see. That is, when he set out, particularly making the rounds in New York especially trying to be hip!

1. Obama brought elegance of mind and nobility of spirit as opposed to Trump's bluster, brinksmanship, insults and mob talk.

2. Obama brought jet age constructive thinking to solve problems while Trump brought a crass, archaic mentality and pedestrian views in praise of wealth favoring the one percent who continue to get richer by the day.

3. While Trump sees "Race" and demeans women, Mexicans, the disabled and even gays, Mr. Obama sees equality and proposes efforts to level the playing field of acceptance, welcome and adoration as opposed to disfavor and condemnation.

4. Though on a Divine Mission, Obama did not flaunt his heavenly connection while Trump and his lackeys Giuliani, Rendell and Perry falsely tout

WHEN IS A "GANGSTER GOVERNMENT"? A "GANGSTER GOVERNMENT?"

Trump's supposed "The Chosen One" self-proclaimed mission. While all look to the heavens for confirmation, it is really being fearful a thunderbolt may descend from above for such blasphemy.

5.   Beatitudes Jesus admonished in Matthew 5: 3-20

Blessed are the poor in spirit, for theirs is the kingdom of heaven.

Blessed are the meek for they shall inherit the earth.

Blessed are those who hunger and thirst for righteousness, for they will be filled

Blessed are the merciful for they will be shown mercy.

Blessed are the pure in heart for they will see God.

Blessed are those who are persecuted because of righteousness, for theirs is the kingdom of heaven.

We could also add, blessed are those who benefitted from Barack Obama's Affordable Care Act that Donald Trump is relentlessly trying to overturn

6.   Compare the richness of Obama's diction in his quotations to the poverty of Trump's sayings or speeches. Mr. Trump's behavior is so funny, he

probably laughs as he replays his own statements and even "high-fives" himself.

7. Obama gave hope in a vision of the future, while Donald Trump rather than "drain the swamp" helped enlarge it!

8. The richness of Obama's discussions contrasts remarkably well with the poverty of Trump's invectives.

9. In the philosophic mantra of "Yes, we can," Mr. Obama inclusively offered justice, equality, opportunity and prosperity; while Donald Trump offered "The largest tax cut" principally benefitting the wealthy and his lies to all remain unquestioned by a "Gullible base," Evangelicals and all.

10. While Obama's Supreme Court and other Judicial appointments sought to balance the scales of justice, Donald Trump chose to stack and weigh the Court in conservative favor which raises the question whether his judges are "compromised" in their Constitutional responsibilities of being fair and impartial.

11. Obama uses precedent, custom and constitutional prerogatives in reasoned and intellectual decision making while Trump subscribes to an "Only I can" philosophy to wily-nilly make important government decisions.

WHEN IS A "GANGSTER GOVERNMENT"? A "GANGSTER GOVERNMENT?"

12. Mr. Obama builds coalitions to confront major issues, domestic or global, while Mr. Trump only appeals to his base and insults and threatens the nation's staunchest allies even declaring global organizations such as NATP obsolete, yet must seek their assistance when his vision falls short.

13. Obama abides by his Constitutional responsibilities as Trump believes he is above the law and "The Constitution is wrong."

14. Obama appears "frightenly prepared" on the issues in his unbelievably focused work ethic, while Donald Trump takes a hands-off approach to presidential responsibility, visits Mar-O-Lago, governs by Twitter, flays golfs, and employs "Executive Time" watching TV particularly Fox News to get his ideas and messages out.

15. Obama praises and tries to uplift people, Trump consistently demeans, degrades and demonizes.

16. Obama constantly praises the American people and puts their interest first and foremost while Donald Trump puts his personal and private interest before the nation's interest.

17. Obama attends church and follows Christian tenets of love thy neighbor but Trump does not attend church but follows only his rules.

FREDERICK MONDERSON

18. When Hurricane Sandy struck the Eastern Seaboard, particularly devastating New Jersey during the 2012 election cycle, politics aside, President Obama instantly responded despite the state's Governor Christie was Republican. In praising President Obama for his magnanimous response to alleviate suffering and hardship caused by the Hurricane, the Governor was resoundingly criticized by the likes of Rudy Giuliani and his ilks. The governor, however, saw the humanitarian not the political side of Obama.

19. Obama's legacy is one of leveling the American landscape through love, justice, equality and the audacity of hope; while Donald Trump still evolving legacy is one of arrogance, disrespect, hate, racism, lies and equally misogynistic and vindictive behaviors.

Two days ago, a second earthquake struck Puerto Rico and yet President Trump in his indecent puffed up cloak of bravado has yet to mention the tragedy or offer a hand of assistance or words of comfort and empathy to these American citizens. Fortunately, along with the "tin can" around his ankle, this shortcoming will be remembered.

18. Obama opposed Putin but Trump embraced him. Why?

20. While historians down through the ages will praise Barack Obama for his timely intervention to rescue America on a near-fail-state precipice; the

WHEN IS A "GANGSTER GOVERNMENT"? A "GANGSTER GOVERNMENT?"

same will focus on Donald Trump's **Impeachment** and his behavior beneath the dignity of the Office of the United states' Presidency.

21. The image of Barack Obama's **Situation Room** looked tremendously different from the picture of Donald Trump's **Situation Room** as his team contemplated the Iran response right after the brewing controversy.

22. Obama opposed Putin but Trump embraced him. Why?

Voters, think Hard – to the **Editor** of *The New York Times* - "If American democracy is to survive, it is imperative that voters who stayed home or who couldn't abide Hillary Clinton – even for the singular purpose of opposing Donald Trump – rethink the wisdom of their decision.

While it's still unknown who the Democratic nominee in 2020 will be, there isn't the slightest question that Donald Trump will stop at nothing to remain in office.

It is collective responsibility to prevent that from happening. Choosing the lesser of two evils may feel depressing. Would an indefinite future in a totalitarian state feel better?" **Cathy N. Goldstein**, New York

FREDERICK MONDERSON

John Kerry, former Secretary of State in the Obama Administration was recently reminded on a CNN news-show, "Donald Trump invokes Barack Obama's name so often as at a recent Rally he claimed Obama gave Iran some $150 Billion dollars. Iran used this money to sponsor terrorism all over and to purchase all manner of destructive armaments."

Secretary Kerry responded: "First of all this was no-way-near the amount we paid; it was money we held up; the American government was paying interest on these funds; Iran owed enormous amounts to various sources and much of this was used to fulfill this obligation." He continued, "What resulted from the strenuously negotiated **Nuclear Deal**, to which we had global partners, was a halt put to Iran's nuclear ambitions of some ten years and any number of developments could take place over that period. They were abiding by the terms of the agreement. Then there's the negotiations as to the actions of Hamas, Hezbollah, Syria and all across the Middle East. With withdrawal from the Iran Nuclear Deal now means there is no negotiations, their desire to acquire a bomb becomes unrestricted as evidenced in their now revamping up the process which makes the whole region less safe."

If Donald Trump wants to return to the negotiating table, he will have to give up much of what was achieved and still settle for less. This is not what he tells his "base" who are fed lies and refuse to question anything he says while the world sees different. Let us remember, he has been **Fact-Checked** at

WHEN IS A "GANGSTER GOVERNMENT"? A "GANGSTER GOVERNMENT?"

nearly 15,000 lies and mis-statements over a 3-year period and his "base," even Evangelicals have never questioned this figure and associated behavior. What manner of man is this? The "Chosen One?" For heaven sake, the "Divine Council" sitting above must be considering what type of unethical, destructive and unrepentant conundrum now unleashed on this earth in their name.

When is a "Gangster Government" a "Gangster Government" Photo? View of the fountain and lawn fronting the rear of the Capitol Building with its Marble Terrace that looks out across the Great Lawn towards the Washington Monument and the Lincoln Memorial further on beyond the Reflecting Pool.

"When the History books are written this Senate trial with McConnell presiding will be debated as the biggest sham, the biggest con, ever imposed on the American people." **Gene Rossi**

www.ingramcontent.com/pod-product-compliance
Lightning Source LLC
Chambersburg PA
CBHW071448250426
43671CB00042B/1863